BROTHERHOOD
OF THE
DIVINE

Other Books by Terry Fritts

BIO-TERROR SERIES

TAKA
KONA SNOW
KAPU 'AINA*(Forbidden land)*

The Kevin Bridges Spiritual Warfare Series

CONSUMING FIRE
SEVEN OF THE CROSS

BROTHERHOOD
OF
THE
DIVINE

A KEVIN BRIDGES SPIRITUAL WARFARE NOVEL

BY

TERRY FRITTS

THRILLOGY
PRESS

The **Kevin Bridges Spiritual Warfare Series** came as a surprise. I had just returned from Russia with an idea of writing a spiritual warfare novel about archangels and End Times. As I began writing, I had several bizarre vivid dreams. I remembered them all in detail which guided the direction of the first book ***Brotherhood of the Divine***. The book took on a life of its own with characters and historical events arriving at the right time. Kevin Bridges became a wonderful character that needed to be explored so I wrote a prequel, ***Seven of the Cross***. It deals with fallen angels and it too spurred some characters I hope to explore in later books. It also inspired me to write another prequel featuring Keven Bridges titled ***Consuming Fire***. ***Consuming Fire*** is a very intense look at evil and the power of prayer. In this new Thrillogy Press edition of the series, all three books have been edited and modified from the originals to allow continuity of character and story.

This book is a work of fiction. Any similarity between characters in the book and real people is coincidental, except, of course, the historical figures that did exist and did play a part in a particular era or event. However, some of the actions attributed to those historical figures are part of the fiction story that is woven into the actual historical events. The Book of Revelation, written by Apostle John, as told to him by Jesus, is the supporting structure for the novel. There are many eschatological opinions about the End Times. This novel presents one possibility.

ISBN 978-1-950376-00-1
Published by Thrillogy Press in 2019
EPUB Edition ISBN 978-1-950376-01-8
ThrillogyPress.com
First published in hardback edition 2008
ISBN-13: 978-0-9791514-4-6
Published by ECHO PARK PRESS LLC 2009

Trade Paper First Publication 2008 ISBN-13: 978-0-9791514-9-1
Library of Congress Control Number: 2009933704

Cover art is from the Sistine Chapel and depicts Satan falling off the cliff. It is from the top right corner of Sandro Botticelli's painting: Scenes from the Life of Christ, The Temptations of Christ. This art work plays an important part in the story.

Printed in the United States of America

ACKNOWLEDGEMENTS

Brotherhood of the Divine is quite a change from the type of novels I have been writing. I want to thank Pastor Larry Kapchinsky whose sermons guided me in the right direction as the story developed. I also want to thank Mike Corwin who always knew the right question to ask me or had the answer to my questions, especially about the Bible. I want to thank Joshua Kapchinsky for allowing me to share and elaborate on one of his life experiences as part of my story. I need to thank Fred Ilyan for showing me Russia and Berch Papikyan for answering my Russian questions. Roger Hull helped out with the Japanese translations. I want to thank all my editors, Jennifer, Brandon, Pauline, and Gary. And, of course, I want to thank my wife and family for their continued support of my writing.

BROTHERHOOD
OF
THE
DIVINE

BROTHERHOOD OF THE DIVINE

I warn everyone who hears the words of the prophecy of this book: if anyone adds anything to them, God will add to him the plagues described in this book. And if anyone takes words away from this book of prophecy, God will take away from him his share in the tree of life and in the holy city, which are described in this book.

Revelation 22:18-19

CHAPTER ONE

And when the seven thunders spoke, I was about to write; but I heard a voice from heaven say, "Seal up what the seven thunders have said and do not write it down."

Revelation 10:4

Achmed had prepared his entire life for this moment. Year upon year he perfected his craft. His hands twisted with debilitating cramps as though he suffered some cruel affliction. And the burning! At times his hands would ache so badly it was as if they had been dipped in the pools of hell. But now, it was his time, his time of prostration for his chosen God, his time to prove his devotion.

Achmed was a literate craftsman trained in making tight calligraphy with very controlled and deliberate copying. Unlike the other two scribes who sat next to him in the small dimly lit room in the monastery, Achmed was a devout Christian who knew well the text they were hired to copy. This canon, like most copies Achmed had seen, consisted of several scrolls of continuous Greek capital letters with no spaces separating them. Writing the Scriptures in such a way could lead to misinterpretation of God's word because it depended on where the reader placed his emphasis and pauses. Achmed knew where the text needed divisions to make it easier for other Christians to read and understand, so he added them. He hoped his divisions in the text would help clarify God's meaning. The Word as it was meant to be. The Word Achmed had been taught from his teachers. It took Achmed longer to copy it with the divisions added and, like all scribes, he was paid by the letter and not by the scroll. Being Christian he did not mind spending the extra time serving his God, nor did the monks seem to notice or care that he used more papyrus than the other two scribes.

All three of the scribes thought it peculiar that they had to perform their craft at this new place called a monastery rather than at the Scriptorium. There were no windows inside the small room where the scribes worked. If there had been, it would have made their task more pleasant and easier. A worn cloth hung over the entrance to the room. A monk sat outside the doorway keeping disturbances to a minimum and the task inside as secret as possible. The scribes copied by the light of several candles. A smoky haze hung heavily in the air. Still, the room remained quite cool even as the sun blazed outside baking man and animal alike. It was also unusual that all three scribes were assigned the same task of copying the canon in its entirety. They had been at the task for several months and Achmed was approaching completion of his copy. One of Achmed's fellow scribes had completed his copy of the canon and had headed home to Alexandria. Of course, that scribe's copy was nowhere near the quality of Achmed's version. This other scribe was prone to errors due to haste as well as to having a tendency to prune, edit, and paraphrase as he copied.

"You will suffer God's fury for having altered the written word," Achmed raged at his fellow scribes. "Did you not read and even copy what John had to say in Revelation about those who took away from or added to what is written? God has said anyone who takes away his words of the holy prophecy will lose their share of the tree of life in the holy city."

As much as Achmed preached to the other scribes, they were not Christian and did not abide by the teachings of the canon, nor did they concern themselves with

Achmed's warning. To them it was a task they had been assigned to perform. And if they sometimes made their job a little simpler by altering the text they were copying, to whom would it really matter? Achmed, however, believed these words to the soul of his existence and would never presume to alter the word of God. His fellow scribes would but nod as Achmed continued to berate them, struggling to keep from laughing out loud in Achmed's face. But they knew to do so might anger the anchorites, or monks, and neither chose to jeopardize such a lucrative assignment.

Suddenly, a puzzled look came over Achmed's face and his hand froze. "What is this?" Achmed screamed at the monk whose task was to replace burned-down candles and distribute the blank papyrus rolls. "This is not right. This is not the canon as God intended it to be. I have never read or heard these words before. They do not belong here. I have heard Irenaeus preach. He learned from the elders of the church, from Polycarp himself who was a direct disciple of the apostles. I have heard him recite these Scriptures and this is not part of the Revelation by John. How could anyone presume to make such an addition to the Gospel of God?" A fury engulfed Achmed as he demanded an answer.

The monk remained calm as Achmed leaped from his chair and snatched the tainted canon from the table waiving it in defiant anger. The monk looked at Achmed and smiled. "Brother, you are indeed a true believer. We had hoped to find a scribe who knew and believed the power of God's prophecy." The monk turned to the other scribe. "You may go. We no longer are in need of your services."

"But I am not finished," the scribe responded. "I was hired to copy the entire canon. I need to complete it so I can be paid in full."

"Please, that won't be necessary. We will pay you the full sum. Now that the manuscript you copy from has been questioned, we must stop and discover if in fact it is the true word of God." He escorted the scribe from the room leaving Achmed alone and confused. Achmed fell to his knees and began to pray.

The monk returned with the abbot accompanying him. In the abbot's hand was a small papyrus scroll. Before he spoke the abbot asked the monk to leave. When the monk left, he began speaking softly and reverently, almost as if apologizing to Achmed.

"I would like you to read this epistle written by the Apostle John when he was in exile in Patmos. It was given to Bishop Pothinus by John himself, who in turn passed it to Irenaeus for safe keeping. Irenaeus passed it to me to keep and pray over until God revealed his plan. It has never been copied or read by anyone but myself, its creator and the two men who possessed it before passing it into my safekeeping. My prayers were answered as God told me in a vision how I should proceed. He told me I would find a Christian scribe who was a true believer and would understand the task. He wants you to make two copies of this epistle and finish the canon as it is written. You must also finish the other scribe's copy of the canon. I know it is not the true word of Christ as described by John, but when you read the words that Christ spoke to John, you too will understand." The abbot handed the papyrus to Achmed and left. He knew Achmed would respond just as God had said. Although feeling relief that the prophecy was being fulfilled, the abbot knew there was a grisly task to be completed before his vision from God was realized. It was a non-Christian-like task to be sure, but one his most trusted monk must perform. For this too was written, or at least soon would be.

Achmed slowly read the epistle written by the Apostle John. Just holding such a sacred document as this made him feel closer to God. As he read, he began to weep at the power of the prose drawing him ever so closer to God. Strong Christian beliefs had led Achmed to study the scriptures, including the Book of Revelation. Achmed had often written the Revelation as practice for refining his calligraphy. What he was now being asked to do by the abbot was inconceivable. That was what he thought until he read the epistle of John. What a burden it must have been for the abbot to keep in trust for so many years. What he was being asked was far beyond a mere mortal's ability to comprehend. It required faith, an unshakable faith in God. A faith strong enough to allow a man to follow a direct command from God, as given to his disciple John, that seemed to contradict Christ's own scriptures as written. Yet that was what the epistle was asking him to do. The same apostle who wrote the Revelation was now asking Achmed to alter them. Add to them. How could this be? As he read, Achmed felt comforting warmth engulf his body. He began to relax and felt at peace with the task requested of him. It was as if God himself was already welcoming Achmed into the promises that awaited him in heaven.

Achmed finished reading the secret letter John had written. He closed his eyes and listened to God explain what needed to be done. A serene smile spread across Achmed's face. He began copying the epistle. He made two copies. The difficult tasks now lie ahead. Achmed must now rewrite Revelation. He knew that is what God and Apostle John desired. Still, Achmed felt by doing this, he was condemning himself in the eyes of the Lord as the prophecy of Revelation foretold.

He had been halfway through a scroll when he had come upon the addition that had caused him the initial anger. He had written the first verse before he realized it didn't belong. Now he began where he had so suddenly stopped. Instinctively, the letters seemed to fly onto the papyrus with tight precision. When he reached the end of the added verses, he placed a space signifying a division in thought. He finished the canon as he knew it had been written by John. He picked up the scroll which the other scribe had been copying. This scribe's work was very good, but not nearly the quality of Achmed's calligraphy.

Achmed completed this version in the same manner. He did not include the divisions in the canon as he had done with his own copy.

Achmed sighed as he finished the second copy of the canon. The monk entered, carrying the first scribe's copy finished earlier. He collected both of the new copies of the completed canon, the two copies of the epistle by John, and the original copy of the Apostle John's epistle. "The abbot will be in directly, my brother. What you have done is a greater deed than you can ever imagine. Though I know not the details of the task you had to perform, I am aware of its importance to Christians for generations to come."

"What will you do with the three altered copies of the canon and the original altered one?" Achmed asked.

"That would not be for me to say, brother. I know not the answer to your question. But I am sure in His wisdom, God has told the elders what is to be done."

"I pray that is so," Achmed replied. The abbot entered the room and took possession of the original epistle and the two copies. The three copies of the canon were placed in clay jars that another monk had brought into the room. They were sealed with wax and then taken away. The abbot carefully rolled up the two copies of the epistle Achmed had made and placed them in clay jars that resembled tubes. He placed them in a small satchel that hung securely from his shoulder. The original letter he placed in a separate clay tube and handed it to one of the monks waiting just outside the door.

The abbot reached into his satchel and removed Achmed's payment for the work. "No sum is sufficient for what you have done, my son. You must speak of this service to no one. The agents of Satan are everywhere and would stop at nothing to learn the information you have written. I will send one of my most trusted monks with you on your journey back to Alexandria. He will keep you safe."

"God will keep me safe," Achmed replied, "but I will welcome his company on my journey. I would like to leave immediately."

"And so, you shall," replied the abbot, "but first we must pray."

The abbot, Achmed, and several monks all prayed together in the dim, smoky room. A sliver of sunlight tried to pierce the cloth curtain and cut the thick haze still hanging inside. As Achmed prayed, the plagues described in Revelation whirled in his mind, as did the verse admonishing that anyone who added to these words would unquestionably suffer the plagues described within. Surely God didn't include Achmed in that warning. "Was that truly an epistle from the Apostle John that the abbot had asked me to copy? Why would the abbot lie to me?" These and other thoughts began to fill Achmed's mind. "No! No!" Achmed shouted, shattering the reverent silence and startling the abbot and monks rapt in pious prayer.

"Satan is a strong adversary," the abbot said to

Achmed, knowing of the demons Achmed was fighting in his mind. "I know you are questioning if what you did was really God's will. I too questioned and fought the same battle. God showed me the way, as I am sure he has shown you. Do not be afraid." The abbot held Achmed's trembling hand. "Remember the words of Jesus our Lord. 'I am the resurrection and the life, He who believes in me will live'." The abbot left the room leaving Achmed alone with the monk who would accompany him on his journey home.

"But he didn't finish the verse," Achmed said to the monk, who either didn't hear or pretended not to have heard.

"We must go," the monk said. "It will be dark soon and we will need to find safe lodging before it becomes too late."

The monastery was situated less than fifteen miles from Alexandria. It was an easy day's journey for most men, but a very dangerous journey if tried after dark. Irenaeus had started the monastery at this location and had placed the current abbot in charge, after receiving a vision from God foretelling what was to be done with John's epistle and the canon. The monks serving this monastery received a divine charge to perform a specific task that had now begun and would continue until the second coming of Jesus. A task explained in John's epistle that was essential for realizing the prophecies as Jesus told them in Revelation.

Darkness fell on the two companions. Few words were spoken. Achmed thought about the abbot's final words. The abbot had not finished the verse and Achmed could not recall how it ended. The monk seemed distracted as he continually glanced behind them. He was sure he had seen a stranger watching them from a distance. It was as if he sensed evil growing ever nearer behind them.

"Let us rest for a moment," the monk said to Achmed.

"We are almost at tonight's lodging. We can rest when we arrive."

"No," the monk said. "Now is the time to rest." Achmed was bewildered, but followed as the monk walked off the road to an outcropping of several large rocks.

"Even though he dies," the monk said quietly.

"What did you say?" Achmed asked the monk who continued towards the rocks with his back turned. Achmed moved closer to where the monk had suddenly stopped.

"Even though he dies," the monk repeated as he turned towards Achmed.

"That's it," Achmed said. "That's how the verse ends. I am the resurrection and the life, He who believes in me will live, even though he dies."

Suddenly, Achmed understood. In the monk's hand was a falcate. It was an older style Greek sword of about eighteen inches with a slight curve in the blade. Just like those Achmed had seen in the hands of warriors. The monk's hand was inside the protective guard as he slowly raised it above his head. He was in no hurry for he knew Achmed would not run.

Achmed dropped to his hands and knees and began to repeat the verse that had been in his head since leaving the monastery. "I am the resurrection and the life. He who believes in me..."

The monk slashed down on Achmed's exposed neck severing the head from the torso. The head dropped to the ground as Achmed's body remained in place. Then miraculously Achmed's head with its eyes still ablaze spoke, "even though he dies." Slowly the eyes closed. The headless torso collapsed to the ground.

The monk used Achmed's robe to clean the blood from the falcate. He turned the torso and removed the pouch holding Achmed's money. The abbot had instructed the monk to make it appear like Achmed had been robbed.

Achmed was destined to die. He could not fall into the hands of Satan, or the Stranger, as he was often called. Killing was not a task the monk found pleasurable, but it was one the abbot told him he must perform for God. He knew this to be true, for God had spoken to him. That was why he had joined Irenaeus' monastery, The Brotherhood of the Divine. He wanted to weep as he started his journey home, but knew evil lurked nearby and he must be on his guard. As the darkness deepened, the monk silently slipped away distancing himself from the road he had traveled.

CHAPTER TWO

When the day of Pentecost came, they were all together in one place. Suddenly a sound like the blowing of a violent wind came from heaven and filled the whole house where they were sitting. They saw what seemed to be tongues of fire that separated and came to rest on each of them. All of them were filled with the Holy Spirit and began to speak in other tongues as the Spirit enabled them.

Acts 2:1-4

Gabe awoke suddenly as the doors to the train noisily slammed together. He was dazed from having fallen asleep and he wasn't sure if he was on his way to work or on his way home from work. As if it really mattered. The days and nights seemed to blend together. He got as much sleep on the train as he did at home. It had been months since he had had a decent night's sleep. Through glazed eyes Gabe looked out the train window. The sky had that dingy look that all too often engulfed the L.A. basin in its foulness. It could be dusk, it could be dawn. There was a moon--at least Gabe thought he saw the moon when he got on the train. If he did see it, then he must be on his way to work. That being the case, it appeared he had just missed his stop.

"Oh man, not today," Gabe said.

Gabe had been making this commute by train to Los Angeles for nine years. Everyday it became more difficult and more wearing on his soul. Life had become pretty mundane.

Gabe staggered out of his seat heading for the exit door. He felt he was in a fog, unable to clear his vision or his mind. The scenery whizzing past the window panel in the door was unfamiliar. He tried to focus his eyes on the buildings as they rushed by, but the blurred scenery kept him confused.

"God, I must have really slept past my stop. None of this looks familiar. Where in hell am I?" Gabe said to himself.

"Precisely," a voice said from behind.

"Pardon me?" Gabe said as he turned to see who had invaded his private conversation.

"You asked where in hell you are and, I answered, you are precisely here," the stranger said as he pointed to a spot on the route map.

Gabe didn't look at the map. He stared at the stranger. The man was tall and thin, maybe six feet two inches. His black hair was slicked back. He had a scraggly beard that did a poor job hiding his scarred pock-marked face. Gabe could not see his eyes, for the stranger wore dark black wrap around sunglasses. He had on black slacks with freshly polished black shoes. He wore a black long-sleeved sweater with a dark gray diamond pattern woven across the vest.

"I said you are precisely here," the stranger repeated pleasantly as he continued to point.

"Oh, oh I'm sorry," Gabe responded as he snapped out of his dumbfounded stare. "Thank you very much." Gabe smiled at the stranger and turned to look at the map. "I guess I slept past my stop."

"You've been asleep for some time. I noticed you when I got on the train. You didn't look like one of the regular riders. You've been out for several stops." The stranger smiled, waiting for a response.

"Man, I must have been out for a while. Nothing looks familiar to me. I was supposed to get off at the State University stop. My ride is probably still waiting. I gotta call him." Gabe reached for his cell phone, but it wasn't there. "I must have been really tired this morning," Gabe said. "I guess I forgot my cell phone. Oh well, it's not the first time for that either. My ride will be pissed, but he won't wait long. I'll just be late for school."

The stranger smiled a crooked grin and just nodded his head as Gabe turned back towards the door.

"I've got to stop drinking so much from the fruit of the vine every night," Gabe said to himself.

The stranger overheard his comment, smiled and replied, "That depends on from what cup you drink."

"What did you say?" Gabe said as he turned back to the stranger.

"I said, that depends on from what kind you drink. I hear red wine is better for you than white wine and there is less chance of a hangover with better wines." Gabe was sure that was not what he had heard. Twice now the stranger had interrupted Gabe's private thoughts, but Gabe was in no mood to challenge the stranger. He had to figure out how he was going to get to work.

"Where are you trying to get to?" the stranger asked. "Did you say you were trying to get to a school? You do look like a teacher. Maybe I can help. What school are you trying to get to?"

Gabe's mind went blank. He had just recently changed schools and couldn't remember the name of his new school. The stranger sensed Gabe's confusion and made a suggestion.

"Is it Petra Elementary on 60th Street?"

That name jarred Gabe's memory. He didn't work at Petra, but he thought it sounded like one of the feeder schools that sent students to the high school where he did work.

"No, no, not Petra," Gabe responded. "It's that new high school just three blocks northeast of there. I just can't think of the name. Actually, I don't think it has been named yet. No wonder I can't remember the name, it doesn't have one."

"Oh, that's no matter," the stranger responded. "I can tell you how to get to Petra, and from there you should have no problem getting to your school."

"Great," Gabe replied, "I would appreciate that."

"As a matter of fact, I get off at that stop and can

point you in the right direction, if that is the way you want to go. It is coming up next," the stranger offered.

Gabe didn't care for the stranger. He knew the man had not been exactly truthful with him up to this point. He did need to get to work and the stranger inferred he could assist Gabe. Whether it was last night's wine or the dazed stupor of an interrupted sleep, Gabe for sure wasn't thinking straight.

"Several of us get off at the next stop," the stranger continued, "just follow us to the elevator. It will take us down to the corridor that will lead you in the right direction. When you get to the street, turn right and just follow the road up the hill. When you get to the top, turn right again and in a couple of blocks you will be at Petra. Oh, that's right. You are not going to Petra. Just near there. Doesn't really matter. From there you will know where you need to go."

A crowd gathered around the exit door as the train began to slow. Gabe looked about the large group of passengers, but failed to recognize any faces. As the doors opened the throng of people exited from all of the train's cars pushing their way through the crowd waiting to board. The mass of people headed to a bank of elevators opposite the platform. Gabe entered an elevator with the stranger and several others. No one on the elevator spoke. Only the stranger was heard whistling a soft tune under his breath. Gabe waited patiently for the elevator. It seemed to take an inordinate amount of time to reach its destination. The doors opened and the stranger guided Gabe into a lobby area with several exits.

"This is the path you should follow," the stranger advised as he pointed to one of the exits. "I would enjoy leading you down that path, but it is a journey you should make on your own. I wish you well and assure you someday we will meet again."

"Thanks," Gabe said to the stranger a little hesitantly. This man was too strange for Gabe to deal with right now. He just needed to get to work as quickly as possible.

As Gabe started down the corridor towards the street, the stranger yelled after him. "It's okay to embrace the fullness of joy from the second cup of wine, for who am I to pass judgment?"

Gabe turned to respond, but the man had disappeared. "What a freak," Gabe said softly, "but I guess he's no weirder than some of those other whackos I've been unfortunate enough to sit next to on the train."

The corridor was much shorter than Gabe expected and within seconds he was standing on a crowded sidewalk next to a busy thoroughfare. It was still dark outside. The sun had either not yet risen or the dingy overcast was keeping the sunlight from reaching the ground. Gabe looked to the right and could just make out a hill about two blocks away. To the left he could see about a block before visibility was lost to the murky fog. Immediately to the right were two sets of tracks. They were not wide enough to be train tracks and did not have the overhead wiring to be light rail. Gabe turned to the right and began to jog down the sidewalk crossing these peculiar tracks. He was wearing his sandals and snagged one of the ankle straps on a rail. That in turn forced an edge of a metal buckle into his foot, gashing the flesh. It was a sharp initial pain but a minor wound and did not slow Gabe's hurried pace. The blood from the cut ran down onto his sandal and created a sloshing sound with each step. As he entered the second block, the number of pedestrians diminished. By the time he reached the base of the hill he seemed to be alone. Cars were speeding by hurtling up the hill. Just as many cars seemed to be rushing down. "Where are all these people going in such a hurry?" Gabe said. He looked up ahead. There was no sidewalk on either side of the street. Gabe saw there was also no guard rail on the edge of the road. He noticed several rather large potholes towards the right edge of the road and even the road itself looked precariously close to sliding off into a haze shrouded abyss. Gabe thought about crossing over and going up on the other side of the street. He knew it would be a lot smarter to walk facing the oncoming traffic, but noticed the oncoming cars left no room for a pedestrian to walk. Also, it would mean having to try to cross the street without getting run down by one of these maniacs. On the right side the potholes discouraged the cars from getting too close to the edge leaving plenty of room for him to walk.

"Either I walk up the hill or I head home," Gabe again was talking to himself. "Well, I've already come this far." He headed up the hill praying all of those drivers were awake and had their eyes wide open. He kept looking back at the oncoming charge of traffic and listening as every car approached, hoping they would avoid the potholes and him. He was halfway up the hill when everything suddenly went dark.

* * *

It was pitch black. Gabe was on his hands and knees crawling over rough terrain. He couldn't see more than a few inches in front of his face. He wasn't sure if he had slipped and fallen off the road or if a car had run him off the road. He must have been knocked out for he couldn't remember what happened. At this point it didn't really matter. He was alive and needed to safely get back on the road. As he groped along the ground his left hand grabbed what felt like the curb of the street. He pulled his body over the smooth curb and saw a dim blue glow. It wasn't much, but it was enough for Gabe to see that it wasn't the road he had found, but a sandy pathway cut into the side of the cliff. He clamored over the edge and dropped down onto the path. Up ahead the path turned to the right and he could see the glow grow brighter. Down the path the glow faded into darkness. Gabe headed up the path towards the blue glow. The pathway took a sharp turn to the right and Gabe could see where the glow was coming from. Immediately after the sharp right turn, the path turned left onto seven steps and entered a room that appeared to be carved out of the cliff. The glow came from several very dim fluorescent light fixtures shining through a glass door and windows that looked to be of post-modern 1950's design. They were cleverly hidden in the face of the cliff and not visible until you were right upon them. Gabe walked up the steps and entered the unlocked door. There was no sound except for an irritating electrical buzz coming from the failing transformers of the light fixtures. To the left was an open metal staircase that seemed to go up and down with no apparent end. To the right was another door carved into the stone wall. Gabe turned to the right and walked through the stone threshold.

He entered into a room that appeared to be some sort of control center. There was a large console with numerous microphones and banks of flashing lights. Several chairs seemed to be pushed up against the consoles waiting for their occupants. The console itself was against a wall of glass that overlooked a desert. Outside the window, carved into the pale reddish sandstone cliff, was a facade of ornate pillars supporting a portico surmounted by a central urn with two flanking blocks. To the right and left were several other facades that looked like ornate entrances to tombs carved into the great cliff. "Oh man, I must be dead," Gabe said to himself.

That was when he heard the voices. It sounded like children but he couldn't understand anything they were saying. As a matter of fact, it sounded like they were speaking several different languages at once. He turned but saw no one. Then the chairs sitting at the console began to turn around. In each chair was a small childlike person. They looked to be female. Their bodies appeared to be normal but their faces were grossly distorted. They looked like bad caricatures of Jay Leno, each with an inordinately long chin with a large dimple that looked like a handle to a pan rather than a chin. Their eyes were slightly slanted and their hair was reminiscent of the way a geisha would wear her hair up and back. They each looked to have fought and lost a rather severe bout with acne. By far what stood out the most were the vivid colors of their skin. Each of the creatures was a different bright color. One was a bright scarlet, another a shocking green, a third a deep blue and the fourth a burning orange. Each of the creatures was talking at once, but Gabe understood nothing they were saying. He heard footsteps behind him and turned to see a bright yellow being, similar to the others, coming into the room. The others all continued talking at once, but now focused their attention on the yellow creature that had walked up in front of Gabe. After what seemed like an eternity, but was actually only a few seconds, the yellow creature turned to face Gabe and began to speak. This time he could understand what it was saying.

"You don't belong here. You must leave at once before it is too late," the creature seemed to be pleading with Gabe.

Before Gabe could answer, the red creature started talking in a lilting manner and now Gabe could understand what it was saying as well. "Go down The Siq, back the way you came, down The Siq."

"I'm just trying to get to work. The stranger told me this was the path to take," Gabe told the nervous creatures.

"The Stranger?" they all shrieked in unison.

The blue and the green creatures started running in circles and crying. "The Stranger will punish us, the Stranger will punish us, the ..."

The yellow creature made a noise that seemed to scold the two running in circles and they stopped. It turned back to Gabe and spoke, "You must leave. You should not have come this way. You need to go back and take the elevator to the Hermitage."

"The Stranger sent him, the Stranger sent him," the red creature sang. "He must leave before he learns too much of the Stranger's plan."

"It is too late for that," answered the yellow creature, "he already has the power to understand."

"He must leave now," the orange creature insisted. "This is a place of temptation, not a place of deliverance."

"The Stranger will punish us, the Stranger will punish us," repeated the green and blue creatures who were running in circles again.

"BRZZ, BRZZ, BRZZ," an alarm had started to scream. The little creatures all covered their ears and started to screech in a shrill earsplitting ululation as they ran towards the door.

* * *

"BRZZ, BRZZ, BRZZ," the alarm continued to blare.

"Are you going to turn off that alarm or what?" Gabe's wife said, roused from a sound sleep.

It was very unusual for Gabe's alarm to even go off. Usually he was awake a good twenty minutes before it was due to sound. "I must be really tired if it took the alarm to wake me," Gabe said to his dozing wife. He laid there for just a moment then rolled out of bed. His clothes for the day were all ready to go in the living room. He did not want to have to disturb his wife again after his shower by coming back into the bedroom to get dressed. It was not a big deal and he had made it part of his daily routine.

"Don't forget to take an apple," Gabe's wife called to him as he started to close the bedroom door. Every morning this was part of his wife's routine to try to help him get healthier.

Gabe paused…for some reason today it sounded kind of funny when she said it. "I won't forget."

Through bleary eyes Gabe headed for his bathroom. He left the lights off. He wasn't ready for that shock quite yet. After using the toilet, he got up to wash his hands. "What in the world?" Gabe said. He reached over and turned on the light switch. He had blood on both of his palms. "How in the world did that happen?" He then noticed the cut and the blood on his foot. "She has got to trim her toenails." Gabe said out loud. He washed the blood from his hands and turned on the shower.

Gabe's morning shower was the crux that dictated how his day would go. Age and weight had put a lot of stress on Gabe's body, especially his back. His poor sleeping habits kept him from ever awakening fresh and free of pain. It was the hot shower running ceaselessly on his aching back for at least five minutes that eased his soreness enough to allow him the energy to face yet another day. For some reason, today his back did not ache. The stiffness he had grown so accustomed to seemed to be missing.

Gabe went into the living room and dressed as he normally did. He entered the kitchen, made his lunch, then fed the dogs and put them out. Once his morning home routine was complete, he headed out the door for his twenty-minute walk to the train station. This daily walk to the train was Gabe's opportunity to do a lot of thinking, planning, and reflecting. It was also the one time he could sing without anyone telling him to be quiet. Often the day's song came to Gabe when he was in the shower, but today it came when he began his walk. It was the chorus to one of the worship band songs from last Sunday's church service. Gabe couldn't remember the verse, but the chorus was blaring in his head.

"Yes Lord, yes Lord, yes, yes Lord."
"Yes Lord, yes Lord, yes, yes Lord."
"Yes Lord, yes Lord, yes, yes Lord."
"Precisely!"

Gabe suddenly stopped. "That's not right," he said out loud. "It's Amen, not precisely. What in hell possessed me to say precisely?"

Gabe felt he wasn't alone in his walk to the train. He turned quickly, but saw no one. He grew nervous and started to hurry along on his way forgetting about his mistake in the song's lyrics. The stranger from his dream came to mind. Gabe usually didn't remember his dreams, but the one he had that morning was very similar to one he had dreamed several times in the past year. It always involved him trying to get to work and having to travel a precarious path or road to try to get there. Today's dream had been a lot more vivid and detailed than his past dreams, but he couldn't remember too many of the details. He did, however, remember the stranger and that memory made Gabe even more uneasy.

Every since he and his wife got involved in that so-called terrorist attack in Madrid the previous year, Gabe's life began to change. Some of the news stories talked about it being some big religious insurrection against the Catholic Church by some group called the Seven of the Cross. When it happened, Gabe got treated like a hero for a couple of days and they gave him and his wife first-class tickets home. Made him feel pretty good, but then the dreams started. Disturbing dreams. Teaching just wasn't the passion it had aleays been. He started going regularly to church but wasn't sure church was the answer he was looking for either. The dreams kept coming.

He had barely gone ten steps when a severe stomach cramp folded him over. He stepped off the sidewalk and onto some grass separating the sidewalk from the street. Gabe's stomach went into spasms. He was heaving violently, but nothing was coming out. Suddenly he convulsed sharply and a vile visceral looking yuk exploded from his mouth and into the gutter of the street. Gabe felt instantly relieved and refreshed. As a matter of fact, he hadn't felt so good in years. As he stood on the curb marveling at how well he felt and pondering what in the world had caused him to throw up so violently, four pairs of pink eyes appeared in the storm drain on the opposite side of the street. Gabe watched as four black opossums skittered out of the sewer opening and quickly crossed the street to where he had just vomited. The aggression of the opossums startled Gabe and he moved back across the grass and onto the sidewalk. In a matter of seconds, the opossums had digested all the grossness he had left in the gutter. As quickly as they had come, they just as quickly disappeared back into the storm drain.

"That was bizarre," Gabe said to himself. He had often seen opossums and raccoons on his morning walk to the train, but never had any of these animals approached like that before. It was as if they were waiting for him to throw up so they could come take it away. A little shiver vibrated up and down Gabe's whole body.

Gabe thought about going back home and climbing back into bed, but only for a moment. He was already up, dressed, and almost to the train station. Even if he went back home he probably wouldn't be able to go back asleep. He would just sit and worry about a substitute teacher taking over his class and him not leaving any lesson plans. And besides, although he was a little freaked out by all that had happened so far that morning, Gabe was feeling better than he had in years.

* * *

Exactly fifty-three miles from where Gabe stood throwing up, sat Jose Flores. Jose was sitting at a No-Bust Blackjack table at the Bicycle Casino in Bell Gardens with sweat dripping off of his face. Jose had been drinking and snorting methamphetamines for the past thirty-eight hours. He was losing. He was losing big. The more he lost, the angrier and more aggressive he became. He had just about lost all of his final paycheck money that was to go to his wife to pay the bills. That is, the part he hadn't spent on the baggie of speed he had been snorting. That too was almost gone.

"Bring another damn drink," Jose shouted.

The dealer nervously glanced at the pit boss who in turn motioned to the security guard who had been alerted earlier regarding the belligerent man.

"Sir, we think you have had enough to drink. We also feel it is time for you to leave for the day," the pit boss said.

"Go to hell you *pendejo*," Jose screamed at the pit boss. "You take my damn money and won't even let me have a drink." Jose threw his empty glass to the floor where in shattered into hundreds of shards. The security guard approached quickly and Jose lifted his arms up as if to surrender.

"Don't touch me, don't you dare freak'n touch me or I'll sue," Jose yelled at the security guard. "I'll leave, but don't you dare touch me."

The pit boss waved off the security guard as a second guard arrived to lend a hand with the drunken patron.

"Escort this man off the premises," the pit boss instructed, "and don't touch him unless he forces you to."

Jose was already headed for the door with the two guards hot on his heels. Jose was swearing loudly as he left the casino. The two guards followed him to his car and withstood a barrage of racial slurs as they made sure Jose would cause no more trouble. One guard waited at the end of the aisle of cars while the other followed Jose down to his car. Jose started his car, revved the engine loudly, and slipped the car into reverse causing the car to lurch suddenly backwards almost hitting the guard and other cars. The guard yelled at Jose to slow down and struck the right rear passenger quarter of the car with his baton to make sure Jose got the message. This infuriated Jose and he started to get out of the car. The second guard saw the potential confrontation and started running down the aisle to assist. Jose jumped back in the car and slammed his foot on the gas pedal. Jose's sudden change of plan caught the second guard unaware and he had no chance to get out of the way of the speeding car. Jose ran him down, killing him instantly. The first guard grabbed his radio and called for immediate help from the local police as Jose sped out of the casino parking lot.

Jose knew the guard was dead and the other guard had read his car's license plate. It wouldn't take long for the local police to track him down. If he ditched his car and stole another, he might be able to make it across the border, but that would mean leaving his wife and baby son. He didn't really care about leaving his wife. She had already left him and had taken his son with her to live with her parents. That was what had set off his latest alcohol and drug binge. It was his son he didn't want to lose, but first things first. Jose needed to score some more crank and he knew where to go. He also knew there was no way

Rudy was going to front it to him. It was cash or don't bother to come by. Rudy was a member of the Wilcox Street gang. He was in his twenties and had been affiliated with the gang since he was ten, but was by no means an 'OG". He was put in charge of the local drug trade while most of the Original Gangsters spent time in prison. If and when they got out, Rudy's status would improve tremendously with his Home Boys. He kept all the drugs at his house and sent his runners out to deliver. Rudy did not like it when people just dropped by his house, but Jose had no choice. He was desperate. He needed to score so he could keep the edge going. Keeping his high going was his only chance of getting his boy, stealing a car, and disappearing into Mexico. He couldn't wait for Rudy's runners. There was no time. Besides, he had no money. The runners wouldn't even talk to him unless they saw the cash up front. He needed help and was sure Rudy would be able to give him that help, one way or another.

"Bam, bam, bam!" Jose pounded on the front door, paced and waited impatiently.

"Bam, bam, bam!" He knocked louder this time.

"Who the hell is it? What do you want?" A voice called out.

"It's me, Jose. Open the door Rudy. I need your help," Jose said nervously.

"Get out of here before I blow you away," Rudy called out the door as he opened it up slightly with the chain still secured. "The only help you are looking for is the kind you can put up your nose. I told you never to come by here to score. Now get out of here."

Jose could see the shotgun in Rudy's hand. Rudy stood just inside the doorway wearing only boxer shorts.

"No man, I'm in big trouble, I need your help."

"Then that's even more reason for you to get the hell out of here. I don't need anybody bringing trouble to my house. You understand?"

Jose grew desperate. He had to make Rudy understand. "I really need you to..."

Rudy interrupted, "I don't want to hear any crap from you. I told you to get the hell out of here." Rudy emphasized his demand by sticking the shotgun through the crack in the door.

Jose grabbed the barrel of the shotgun as he threw his full weight against the door. The chain snapped like a piece of string and Rudy tumbled backwards onto the floor. Jose had kept a grip on the barrel of the shotgun. Rudy lost his grip on the gun when Jose crashed through the door. Jose slowly turned the gun towards the startled Rudy now sprawled on the floor. Rudy began to rise and speak when Jose pulled the trigger blowing most of Rudy's vital organs out his back, splattering them on the living room wall.

"Don't ever interrupt me again when I am trying to tell you something," Jose said to the lifeless body. Jose stepped over the body and headed into the bedroom where Rudy kept his drugs. He had never been in the room before and was surprised to see just a small quantity of speed on a digital scale, a couple of dime bags of grass, and less than a hundred dollars on the table. He knew there had to be more somewhere in the room, a lot more. He threw open the closet and saw the huge locked safe.

"Damn," Jose said. "I shouldn't have killed him till he opened the safe." Then he heard the siren in the distance and realized a shotgun blast at that time in the morning would warrant several calls to 911. He grabbed the little bit of money and drugs sitting on the table along with a box of shotgun shells. He saw Rudy's pants lying on the floor in the bedroom. He grabbed the wallet from the pants and found several hundred more dollars. He also found the keys to Rudy's Cadillac Escalade.

* * *

Gabe had no more adventures on the remaining portion of his walk to the train station. He punched his ticket and sat on his usual bench to await the inbound train. Gabe could see the three headlights of the stopped train as it picked up passengers at a station a couple of miles east of him on the tracks.

The 5:30 a.m. train was fairly crowded by the time it reached Gabe's stop. The train consisted of five passenger cars and an engine that pushed the train from behind. The train was driven by the engineer in the front passenger car, also known as a cab car. On the outward trips the engine pulled the train instead of pushing and the engineer would drive the train from the engine as one would expect. The disadvantage to driving the train from the cab car was, if debris was encountered on the tracks, the cab car was unable to push the debris aside without suffering damage. Gabe preferred to sit in the third car. He felt it was the safest car on the train. It was also the most convenient car to the elevator and stairs when he arrived at his station. So many people had started riding the train and sitting in the third car that Gabe had been forced to change to the second car. The car located right behind the cab car. Not quite as safe of a car location, but still convenient to the elevator and stairs. It was not nearly as crowded as the third car when it arrived at Gabe's station for the morning commute. Another advantage was that this car was quiet compared to the third. It had become quite unpleasant if you wanted to rest or try to think or read on the commute. The second car seemed to attract mostly readers. Gabe had noticed an increasing number of the readers chose the Bible instead of the most recent mindless thriller or "Oprah" recommendation. The second car also seemed to host a much wider variety of ethnicities. One could hear quite a mix of languages, Korean, Filipino, Serbo-Croatian, a couple of different Chinese dialects, and most definitely Spanish.

More people than usual were drifting towards Gabe on the platform that morning. They all seemed to want to strike up a conversation. He remained polite, but all his replies were curt in hopes of discouraging further conversation. Fortunately, the train arrived quickly and Gabe boarded. There were several empty seats on the train. There were even a couple of groups of four seats still available. Quite unusual. Gabe selected a seat in an empty foursome facing the direction the train was heading. Immediately the other three seats in the foursome were filled by commuters, two by Korean ladies who had entered at Gabe's stop and one by a man in a painter's uniform who moved from across the aisle. Gabe thought this a bit strange, but then thought he too had moved for no apparent reason on several occasions. The man sat across from Gabe. Besides his painter's outfit he was wearing a badge which identified him as a painter for the University Medical Center. The name on the badge was Zymko Branesic.

"That sounds Croatian to me," Gabe said. The man seemed suddenly surprised.

"It is," Zymko replied. "Where did you learn to speak Croatian?"

"Oh, I don't speak Croatian," Gabe replied. Gabe's reply seemed to both confuse and irritate the man. Zymko stared for a moment, then just nodded his head and turned to read. Gabe decided the man must not understand English very well and gave it no further thought. It was then Gabe noticed all three passengers in his foursome of seats were carrying and reading Bibles. He also noticed the two women staring at him in bewilderment.

Finally, one of the women spoke. "Your Korean is excellent, but I can see how it must have been very confusing for the gentleman sitting across from you. You told him in Korean that you don't speak Croatian."

"I told him what in Korean?"

Zymko closed his Bible in a huff and looked rather perturbed. "You are doing it again and it is rather rude of you to pretend you don't know what you are saying."

Gabe wanted to say "doing what again?", but instead he just mumbled "sorry", and closed his eyes pretending to try to sleep.

Even the two Korean women seemed to be a little put out with Gabe, but within a minute all three of Gabe's companions were smiling and reading from their Bibles.

* * *

So far, his luck was holding. He had been driving for twenty minutes and was almost to El Monte with still no sign of the police. Jose was starting to believe he would make it across the border and into Mexico. But first things first, he needed to get his son back from that *bruja* who had stolen him away. He pulled off the freeway onto Valley Boulevard. He turned west towards Maria's parent's house. He knew Maria's *madre* would have already left for work. She had to catch an early bus to Pasadena to go clean rich white people's houses. Her *padre*, Carlos, would be sitting on his butt drinking coffee on the back porch watching his chickens like he did every morning. Jose's son, Jesus, would be up eating breakfast and getting ready for school and that witch Maria would still be lying in bed recovering from her partying the night before. Jose pulled the Escalade into the driveway behind Carlos' old beat-up green pickup truck.

Carlos heard the Escalade as it pulled into his driveway and left the porch to see who was stopping by the house so early in the morning. He was happy to see his daughter's husband as Jose climbed out of the Cadillac.

"I hope you came to get your wife and son," Carlos yelled. "They are costing me a fortune to feed everyday." He did not see the shotgun as he walked to greet Jose. He liked Jose and thought Jose put up with too much nonsense from his daughter Maria. That girl needed to learn her place in a marriage. A few slaps had worked with his own wife and he couldn't understand why Jose didn't do the same with Maria.

"You keep the witch. I just came to get my son."

"She may be a ..." Carlos started to answer, but stopped when he saw the shotgun in Jose' hand. "Put the shotgun away Jose. We want no trouble."

"Let me take my son and there will be no trouble for you, Carlos. Just go back to your porch and your chickens. Maria is the one who must pay for the grief she has caused me."

As much as Carlos agreed with Jose, Maria was still his daughter and he wouldn't let anyone try to harm her. He grabbed a shovel from the back of his pickup and swung it at Jose. Jose raised the shotgun and fired at the onrushing Carlos. The spade of the shovel crashed against the barrel of the shotgun just as Jose squeezed the trigger. Carlos was very fortunate. The shotgun pellets ripped through his left thigh rather than his neck and face, saving his life. He screamed and fell to the ground, moaning in anguish. Jose turned and continued towards the front door. His son Jesus had heard the confrontation and had rushed to the door just in time to see his grandfather shot by his dad. Jesus began to sob and scream.

"Jesus, get in the car, we're leaving." Jose was very calm. The calmness in his father's voice scared Jesus even more. "Jesus, I said get in the car now." By that time Jose was at the front door and Jesus was too scared not to obey his father. "You wait in the car while I tell your mother you are going away with me."

Jesus nodded and ran to the back door of the Escalade and climbed in. He leaned over so he could see his grandfather squirming on the ground in pain. Jesus knew in a moment he would probably hear another blast from the shotgun. His father was not just going to talk to his mother.

Maria had also heard the blast from the shotgun. As hung over as she was, she sprang from her bed and confronted her husband in the living room.

"Just what the hell do you think you are doing?"

"I came to take my son away from the lying two-timing *puta* he calls 'mother'."

"You worthless piece of scum. You're not a man. You are nothing. Jesus isn't even your son."

Jose had suspected as much, and now his pent-up rage exploded as he swung the shotgun at Maria's head. The blow shattered her jaw knocking her unconscious and back through the bedroom door and onto the tattered carpet. Jose lifted the shotgun, aimed it at her head, and slowly squeezed the trigger. It didn't fire. He tried to pump in a new shell, but the pump action jammed. Between the shovel smashing the barrel and Jose smashing Maria's jaw, the shotgun had become useless. Jose looked out the door and saw neighbors starting to gather on the street. He threw the shotgun on Maria's limp body and bolted past the cursing Carlos and into the Escalade. Screeching the tires, he tore down the street away from what he hoped was only a bad nightmare.

* * *

It didn't take long for Gabe to doze off. He had mastered the ability to catch a few minutes of sleep before the train reached his stop. Only twice had he failed to wake in time. The conductor's announcements of pending stops usually caused him to stir. Gabe would force his eyes open and look around just to assure himself that he had not passed up his stop and that familiar faces were still on the train.

The two Korean women had continued to converse softly regarding their Bible readings, but were quiet enough not to disturb Gabe's dozing. Sitting across from Gabe, Zymko had stopped reading and seemed to have fallen asleep. As Gabe looked around the car, he noticed several familiar commuters who normally did not sit in his present passenger car. What made it even more peculiar was that most of them were holding a Bible in their hands. "Indeed, it had been a rather curious morning all the way around," Gabe thought as he closed his eyes to try to catch a few more minutes of sleep. This time when Gabe dozed off it was not a restful sleep.

Gabe dreamed again of the stranger. He dreamed the stranger was sitting across from him on the train, but he couldn't open his eyes to see him. He wanted to open them, but couldn't. It was as if they were glued shut. The stranger was trying to tell Gabe something, but he couldn't understand what the stranger was saying. Suddenly a lion appeared and the stranger was gone. A pure white lion with eyes that burned like fire and a face that blazed brilliantly. In its mouth it held a double-edged sword. It was a menacing vision, yet Gabe was not afraid. He felt at peace as the lion placed its paw on his shoulder. The lion was trying to tell him something and even though the lion's mouth did not move, Gabe could hear its voice.

* * *

The first police car was coming down the street towards the house as the Escalade tore out of the driveway and raced past. The officer radioed for assistance informing the other police cars as to the Escalade's direction. Jose had pulled back onto Valley Boulevard headed east towards the 605 freeway. Immediately there was a police car right behind the speeding Escalade. As Jose approached the freeway, he could see the entrance was already blocked by two more police cars. He raced past the onramp and made a quick turn onto East Temple Avenue in hopes of getting to the 10 freeway. He didn't see the railroad crossing was down and a freight train was lumbering steadily across the tracks until he was upon it. Jose slammed on the brakes as the Escalade burst through the flashing crossing gate snapping them like pretzels. The Cadillac skidded to a stop just inches from the freight train. Two police cars pulled behind him, remaining at a safe distance from the tracks, yet blocking any possible escape for the Escalade. What the police and Jose failed to notice was there were three sets of tracks at that particular crossing on East Temple and the Escalade had come to rest on one of those sets of tracks. Jesus was the first to notice the three headlights of the oncoming commuter train.

It takes a train traveling at normal speed almost a half of a mile to come to a stop. When the Escalade pulled onto the tracks, less than a hundred yards separated it from the engineer inside the tiny engineer's room aboard the cab car. The train smashed into the Escalade with a sickening crunching thud, killing the engineer and the first three rows of passengers instantly. The weight of the Escalade caused the train to derail and smash into the freight train traveling on the adjacent tracks. The freight train was carrying crude oil and one of the oil carrier cars ruptured and burst into flames engulfing the first car of the commuter train. Jose was killed instantly as the impact jettisoned what remained of the Escalade several hundred feet down the tracks. Jesus was thrown from the Escalade and landed in a pile of discarded trash next to the tracks. Then the real carnage began.

* * *

"Do not be afraid. I am the First and the Last. I am the living one; I was dead, and behold I am alive for ever and ever. And I hold the keys to death and Hades," the lion said to Gabe in his dream.

Suddenly there was a horrible screeching. The sound of a violent wind filled the entire train car where the panic-stricken passengers were all sitting.

"What the Hell?" Gabe said as he was startled awake.

"Precisely!" said a familiar voice. Gabe jerked his head up to see the Stranger grinning. The Stranger turned and hurried towards the front of the train car. People were beginning to scream as the train began to shake violently. The passenger car began to sway and jackknife as the exit doors next to the Stranger flew open. The Stranger turned and smiled once again at Gabe, then leaped out the door as if sucked out by a tremendous vacuum. There was a huge burst of flames and what then appeared to be tongues of fire shot through the open doors. These flaring tongues seemed to separate as if they would engulf each individual passenger. Gabe began to pray. He had never prayed before and he wasn't sure where the words were coming from, but the words seemed to just flow out of his mouth. Gabe suddenly realized that his prayer had the exact same words the lion had spoken in his dream. The screaming of the passengers instantly ceased as they all heard Gabe's prayer in their own native languages and joined in. Then occurred what would come to be known as the first new miracle of many.

CHAPTER THREE

Hail to the princes and the armies who fight for Christendom against the infidel hosts. Glory to the princes and to the army. Amen

XV APODOSIS
Lay of Igor's Raid

His mere presence was intimidating. Astride his horse his looks alone could lay a man to defeat. Sviatoslav of Kiev, the Varangian Warrior Prince, son of a Scandinavian mercenary invited to Novgorod to bring order to the warring Slav tribes. One side of his head was shaven clean while the other side was covered in long matted brown locks soaked in sweat, blood, sand, and grime from his many battles. Upon his ear was a large golden earring taken along with the ear of a Bulgarian of the Danube monarch whom Sviatoslav had conquered. It had been a truly great battle with a decisive victory for Sviatoslav and his druzhina, as well as for his ally the Byzantine Empire.

Sviatoslav was a pagan. He worshipped the gods the Varangians brought with them to Novgorod. His mother had converted to Christianity even before Methodius and Cyril were sent from Byzantium to convert the pagans to the new Christianity that was sweeping northward into the Baltic and eastward towards Asia. It was an awkward alliance between the pagan prince and the Byzantine Emperor John. An alliance that could not last for long.

* * *

When Achmed had completed the copies of the canon, the abbot took the clay jars that held them and commanded several of his monks to take them to Irenaeus in Lyons. The jars were to be protected from bandits at all costs. The journey took several weeks with storms at sea almost ending their journey before they were halfway to the opposite coastline. Upon their arrival at the church of St. Johns, they were met by Irenaeus. He wept when he received the epistle of John. Apostle John the Divine, John the Evangelist, the Revelator, Saint John. Such a great Apostle that any devout religious man was moved to tears by The Divine's words. That was how the Brothers of the Divine in time became known as the Weepers. Irenaeus and the three Brothers of the Divine spent the next two days in prayer seeking guidance for the tasks that lay ahead.

Irenaeus kept the original canon and one of the copies of John's original epistle. He ordered one of the monks to take Achmed's copy of the canon along with John's original Epistle to Rome. "Keep these safe and deliver them to the Church only when you are sure they will be safe and well-protected. Even if it takes several generations, that shall be your task. Soon there shall be a great church in Rome. They cannot forever deny God's Christianity. You are to recruit and train fellow monks to carry on the assigned task of the Brotherhood of the Divine. Do not let your focus waiver. Our task must be completed. So sayeth the Lord." The monk understood what he must do and left immediately in the company of two monks whom Irenaeus had assigned to join him. They too would eventually join the Brotherhood when the time was right.

A second copy of the epistle and canon were sent to Smyrna in Galatia. That was where Irenaeus spent his childhood, as had Polycarp his teacher and mentor. Irenaeus advised the monk to place the jars containing the copy of the canon in the grave where the ashes of the martyr Bishop Polycarp were buried inside the city walls. That monk was then to stay in Smyrna to watch over the grave until God revealed what was to be done. As had been told to the other monk, he too was instructed to recruit members into the Brotherhood for generations to come if necessary and await God's plan. With two more monks from the monastery accompanying him, he also set out on his journey.

The third copy of the canon was to be sent to Greece. Saint Paul had been driven from Thessaloniki by the Jews in the first century to Veroia. With his missionary companion Sosispater, he had established a sect of true believers in Veroia. The third monk was charged with the task of finding these followers of Paul and to find a safe place to hide the final copy of the canon which contained the additional Revelation. He was not to tell them the significance of the canon, but was to dedicate his life to protecting it. Irenaeus did not offer to send any additional monks on this journey. As it turned out, this copy of the canon remained safer than any of the others. The monk had hidden it in a Jewish Synagogue in the southern portion of the city. It was protected by the great defensive walls constructed to safeguard the city from invading tribes from the north. There it remained constantly until the 9th century when Methodius became a member of the Brotherhood of the Divine during his theological studies. Just two days before Cyril and Methodius had returned from their previous mission, the two Brothers of the Divine who had been watching over the canon in Veroia had been brutally tortured and murdered. One had both his eyes speared by a burning stick and his torso ripped open by what looked to be a giant claw of some huge beast, leaving organs strewn all around. The second monk had been flayed, the bloody pulp of his body massed on the floor in a heap, and tacked to the wall was his skin as if the empty shell was being crucified. No man could have withstood such torture without telling whatever was demanded of him. A stranger had been seen several times at the synagogue after the murders, but had been run off. An armed guard was posted to keep the worshipers safe. All of Veroia lived in fear. When he and his brother Cyril went to propagate Christianity to the Slavs in 862, Methodius decided to take the copy of the canon with him and find a safer place for it.

The original copy of the canon, along with the copy of John's Epistle, was buried with Irenaeus beneath St. John's Church in Lyons. This copy, along with the remains of Irenaeus, was destroyed in the Calvinist Wars of 1562.

* * *

Sviatoslav of Kiev continued his battles throughout Byzantium and the Slavic regions. On his return from a humiliating defeat in the Byzantine campaign, Sviatoslav was ambushed and killed by the Pechenegs who also had a secret alliance with Emperor John of Byzantine. Sviatoslav's head was severed from his body and the skull turned into a chalice. His death led to a bloody battle between his sons to see who would ascend as the new Prince of Kiev. After several years, his youngest son, Vladimir, took command and ruled the Novgorod. For years he remained a pagan, taking more than two hundred concubines. He knew a continued successful reign relied on him uniting his people in religion. He examined several and chose Christianity. Being the Prince, he could claim a supernatural sanction that the religion demanded of its believers. As was common, to strengthen your control as a ruler required a marriage to take place between two powerful ruling dynasties. Vladimir negotiated a marriage with the Greek Princess Anna, sister to Emperor Basil II. But for such a princess to marry a pagan was preposterous. Vladimir called for Princess Anna to bring her priests so he could be baptized. When she arrived in the city of Kherson with her entourage, Princess Anna learned Vladimir was in great distress having lost his vision to a disease of the eyes. The Princess said her Christian God could cure Vladimir and restore his vision if he were to be baptized immediately. When the Bishop of the conquered city of Kherson laid his hand upon Vladimir during the baptismal ceremony, Vladimir's sight was at once restored.

"I have now perceived the one true God," Vladimir exclaimed, after experiencing the miraculous cure. Having seen the power of this Christian God, all of his followers were also baptized. Upon his return to Kiev he destroyed all the pagan shrines ordering them to be cut into pieces and burned. Thousands of his people were converted to Christianity. He had numerous churches and monasteries erected throughout the region. It was at one of these monasteries that the canon from Veroia found a safe home.

CHAPTER FOUR

I call on you, O God, for you will answer me;
give ear to me and hear my prayer.

Show the wonder of your great love,
you who save by your right hand
those who take refuge in you from their foes.

Psalm 17:6-7

There was an eerie silence among the passengers sitting in the same car with Gabe when the train hit the SUV parked on the tracks, a silence that seemed to scream. Gabe's car now sat upright and relatively undamaged more than thirty yards from the mangled burning pile of wreckage that had been three other passenger cars of the commuter train. The screaming silence instantly turned into the screams of the injured and dying who were trapped in the badly shattered and disfigured cars. The engine and two of the six cars were jackknifed across the tracks, severely damaged, but not part of the debris that continued to burn. The freight train had contributed several derailed cars to the massive pile of carnage. Fireman worked frantically to keep the remaining tanker cars from fueling the fire with their loaded tanks of crude oil. It was a chaotic scene. The burning oil crept slowly towards the jackknifed cars as the police, who had been chasing the SUV, now rushed to the aid of the passengers trapped.

"Please," a severely injured man pleaded, "I don't want to burn. I'm dying, but I don't want to burn." Two passengers were able to free the man and carry him safely away from the flames. They laid him in a parking lot next to a strip club where several others of the injured were brought or had wandered to. Within moments he died from his injuries, but thankful his body wasn't consumed by the fire and thankful his family could look upon his face when they mourned his death.

Several of the passengers in Gabe's car started praising God for sparing them from this horrific tragedy, while Gabe and several others quickly exited the train to lend assistance in evacuating the injured passengers from the other cars. Gabe continued to assist in the rescue operations until finally ordered out of the area by the rescue crews on the scene.

"Thank you, thank you so much for saving us." It was one of the two Korean women who had been sitting by Gabe.

"I didn't save you."

"Your prayer saved all of us," one of them replied, as several more passengers who had been seated near Gabe came over to join the two Korean women.

"God worked his miracle through you," another passenger interrupted. "God has filled you with the Holy Spirit and given you the power to speak in all tongues."

Gabe seemed confused by what the crowd was telling him.

"As you prayed, we all heard your prayer in our native languages."

"It is like the Day of the Pentecost," someone yelled from the crowd.

Another passenger had opened his Bible to Acts 2 and began reading. Several people dropped to their knees in prayer as he read. Gabe was feeling uncomfortable at the attention. He turned and ran from the crowd, hoping they all would forget he was a part of what had just happened. As he ran, he saw a little boy lying in a pile of trash near the wreckage. The boy wasn't moving and Gabe prayed that the boy wasn't another victim of the horrific wreck. When he approached, the boy stood to look at Gabe.

"My name is Jesus," the boy began, "have you seen my father?" Gabe wasn't quite sure how to answer.

"Are you hurt?"

"No, but my father hurt my *abuelo*."

Gabe took Jesus' hand and they walked to where a group of policemen had gathered by what remained of the SUV.

"These men will be able to help you," Gabe told the boy.

Standing next to one of the policemen was Maria. Her face was badly swollen from her broken jaw and from crying. She had refused to let the paramedics take her to the hospital until she found Jesus. One of the policemen had brought her to the accident scene and, with his help, she had been combing through the triage areas searching for any sign of her son. The bruises on her face were covered with tears as she stared at the wrecked shell of the Escalade.

"We found only one man's body," a fireman who had searched the wreckage explained. "There was no sign of a child in this mess."

"Mama!" Jesus cried when he recognized his mother.

"Jesus!" his mother cried, wincing in pain. Jesus ran to her open arms.

Gabe turned to walk away when Maria ran up to him and grabbed his hand. "I must thank the man who returned Jesus back to my life." Suddenly her knees weakened as a flush of heat swept through her body. She collapsed into Gabe's outstretched arms.

"Are you, all right?" Gabe asked. The policeman who had brought her to the scene ran to assist when he saw her swoon. He held her arm to support her. Her chin had dropped to her chest. When she raised her head to respond to Gabe's question, the swelling of her jaw was noticeably smaller, and only some slight bruising could be seen where the shotgun had hit her face, breaking her jaw.

"My face," Maria now spoke with a clear voice. "My face doesn't hurt anymore and I can talk. You have healed me." She made the sign of the cross.

Gabe started to back away as several of the policeman came over to see what had happened.

"It's a miracle!" Maria yelled. "God has performed a miracle. He has healed my broken jaw through this man." She turned to point at Gabe, but he was quickly moving towards the road.

"Hey get back here," One of the policemen yelled but Gabe just walked faster.

"He wouldn't dare shoot me for not stopping," Gabe said, trying to convince himself to keep going. "He can't shoot me just because I performed a miracle." Gabe almost did stop at what he had just said. "I performed a miracle. What am I saying? That's impossible." Then again, the entire morning had been impossible.

Gabe walked for a couple of more blocks, watching while dozens of emergency vehicles rushed to the area. He called his wife to tell her he was okay and not to worry. He told her the commuter service was making arrangements for everyone to return home safely, but it may be quite some time until he would be home. Several helicopters were overhead and the first local news vans were beginning to arrive for what would be the headline story for several days to come.

Gabe did his best to avoid the media frenzy. Newscasters from several competing stations grabbed anyone in the area to see if they had first-hand information or even a good story regarding the accident.

The coverage from the air showed just how horrific the train crash had been, the hollow shells of three badly mangled train cars still smoldering in a twisted pile of broken rails and buckled aluminum. Rescue workers were still retrieving the shattered bodies of the victims. But beyond explanation, even beyond reasonable belief, seemingly so out of place in this surreal picture of preeminent disaster, was the remaining passenger car. It had been the second car of the six as the train headed west. It sat undamaged at least thirty yards from the track. Rescue workers marveled at how it escaped this holocaust while the car preceding it, and the two following it, provided the majority of the catastrophic damage and most of the fatalities.

Gabe stood beside one of the news vans so he could watch the bank of televisions inside. Most news trucks didn't have the capabilities to monitor the competitor's programming, but for such a big story the satellite truck was sent by one of the local stations so they could broadcast live nationwide. This truck had access to all the other programming being broadcast at the wreck site. Several people being interviewed kept using the word miracle to describe what had happened to the second car. Even the news reporters were referring to it as a miracle. On one of the broadcasts, Gabe could see Maria holding Jesus along with the policemen who had helped her. Gabe was unable to hear what was being said, but Maria was pointing at something in the distance. There was little doubt what the topic of conversation was when the camera turned and zoomed in on a figure standing near a news truck. Fortunately, the zoom on the camera was not powerful enough to get a closeup of Gabe. Gabe quickly turned his back to the camera when he realized what was happening. The camera turned back to Maria as she continued to talk and point at her face. It was time for Gabe to disappear and to do it quickly before he was swamped by news reporters. He slipped behind the truck, just as the producer handling the broadcast from inside the truck rushed out to find him. The producer no doubt had been monitoring the broadcast and recognized the man standing outside his truck as the one people were saying was responsible for several miracles. "This story has Pulitzer Prize written all over it," the producer said as he hurried to scoop the other local and network news. Gabe was already gone and all the producer, or anyone else, had on this fast-breaking story was a grainy long-distance camera shot of this miracle worker and the descriptions and testimonials of dozens of people.

CHAPTER FIVE

My soul faints with longing for your salvation, but I have put my hope in your word.

Psalm 119:81

Dr. Lucy Ilves was alone. She was on her knees praying in the Sistine Chapel like she had done so many times in the past. Since she was a little girl she had come to the Vatican and explored the hallways, chapels, and meeting rooms, but she always ended up in the Sistine Chapel after the tourists had gone for the day and the Swiss Guard had completed their search for stragglers. Praying alone in the Sistine Chapel surrounded by priceless artwork was impossible for anyone to do. One would surmise that to be especially true for such an outspoken non-Catholic Christian like Lucy. And in fact, it was impossible, even for the nuns cloistered at Vatican City who spent their days in pious reverence. Impossible for anyone, unless of course, you were Dr. Lucy Ilves. Even then it would still have been impossible, had her father not been the famed philanthropist Astan Ilves.

As Lucy prayed, she could feel herself growing closer to God. She imagined it was her hand, not Moses', reaching out to receive the enlightenment God was offering. As her hand grew closer, her thoughts seemed empowered. She envisioned solutions to problems that had been weighing greatly on her mind. Often, when Lucy had been troubled, she had come here to pray for guidance. More often than not, guidance came to her. Many of those solutions revealed to her were what had brought Lucy her own world fame and fortune.

Lucy knew the paintings in the chapel well. Extremely well. She had learned much more than an appreciation of art from her father. Astan had spent much of his life on a quest to authenticate and discover long-thought missing works of art. That was his passion, at least his passion for the last twenty years. At one time building his media empire and making money had been his focus. He had created the world's largest media conglomerate. He had turned the running of his business empire over to his hand-picked associates, many of whom Lucy could barely tolerate. Ever since Lucy was a young girl she had only known her father in his role as a philanthropist and art collector. That was what brought her so often to Vatican City. She was at her father's side as he spent countless hours filling his insatiable appetite for the religious artwork that filled the walls and ceilings throughout the vast maze of structures that made up The Holy See. However, even Astan Ilves would never have been granted such access had it not been for the fact that he had used his own personal assets and banking connections to save the Vatican from financial ruin on more than one occasion.

As Lucy prayed, her thoughts wandered from painting to painting. Today she kept being drawn to a panel painting by Sandro Botticelli entitled “Scenes from the Life of Christ”. It was located on the side wall of the chapel. She kept thinking about the upper right-hand panel showing Satan being cast off the cliff by Christ, as three Archangels observed from behind a table. Two of the angels Lucy recognized from several others of Botticelli’s works and knew them as being his vision of Gabriel and Michael. Since she was at Vatican City it would make sense that the third angel was Raphael. Lucy only considered Raphael to be a great painter, not an Archangel. Botticelli had several other paintings with Raphael in them and this angel looked nothing like the other Raphael angels he had painted. In fact, Lucy thought this angel looked much more feminine than any of the others she had seen in his work. She knew young men were painted with a feminine look by Renaissance artists, but she wasn’t sure if the same could be said for young angels. Lucy decided that was something she would have to research. Her father had even joked with her years ago, calling the third angel in the painting his “Little Lucy”. Lucy mouthed the words as she thought of her father’s teasing.

“Precisely!” A clear soft voice whispered.

Lucy turned to see who dared to interrupt the sanctity of her private prayer. At the back of the room, just stepping out of the shadows, was a man dressed in the robes reserved for a cardinal.

"Were you speaking to me?" Lucy said rather harshly, too harshly for someone of his stature in the Church.

The cardinal smiled broadly, disarming and calming Lucy's angry demeanor just the way her father had so many times in the past when Lucy was upset.

"I'm sorry if I startled you. I thought you knew I had entered the chapel. I also thought you were speaking to me when you called Botticelli's angel little Lucy. That's what your father calls that angel as well, is it not?"

"Do I know you? How do you know that's what my father calls me? And I don't recall having said anything out loud just now."

"Forgive me. Perhaps you don't recall when we were first introduced by your father. It was here in this very chapel before that very painting several years ago. We were both much younger, though I must say you haven't changed much. You are still indeed a beautiful woman both spiritually and physically. Truly an angel."

Lucy was taken aback. What an odd thing for a cardinal of the church to say. Lucy stared at the cardinal as she tried in vain to remember their initial meeting. His face did look vaguely familiar, but Lucy couldn't place him, which was highly unusual. Lucy prided herself in her adeptness at remembering important people and faces. A cardinal of the Catholic Church did indeed qualify as an important person. The cardinal waited politely. It was the cardinal's smile that convinced Lucy to lower her defensive wall.

"Please forgive my brusqueness. I'm usually excellent at remembering people whom I've met, but for some reason I just can't place your face. Though I have the feeling I do know you from somewhere," Lucy confided.

"When we first met I wasn't a cardinal," he responded, "just a priest on an extended visit to Vatican City. Not someone important enough that would require someone of your stature to recall."

Lucy was still a little wary. Before she could reply the cardinal spoke again.

"It is curious Botticelli painted three Archangels standing behind the alter watching as Christ cast the fourth and greatest angel off of the cliff." He walked towards Lucy.

Lucy was again taken aback by the cardinal's reference to Satan as being the greatest angel. She felt uneasy as the cardinal approached. Lucy backed away from the wall towards the center of the chapel. As she began to respond, her ears were filled with a high-pitched ringing and she was unable to speak.

"It truly is an amazing scene," the cardinal said, moving towards Lucy, "but it's the scene above your head that will always be with you."

Lucy did not want to take her eyes off the approaching cardinal, but as she stared at him the ringing in her ears grew louder. Suddenly the cardinal's disarming smile turned to a freakish twisted grin and he began to laugh. Lucy covered her ears with her hands trying to stop the deafening ringing. Lucy lost her balance as the room started to swirl at a dizzying pace. The ringing and laughter turned into a cacophony of voices praying, yelling, and screaming. What Lucy had thought at first to be the room swirling about violently was actually the scenes in the paintings all coming to life. The images were closing in on Lucy and she cried out. Lucy reached her hand towards Michelangelo's painting of God's hand in the ceiling's center panel and she screamed. The hand of God reached down to Lucy as she reached in vain with her outstretched arm, seeking relief from the horrible nightmare. Lucy dropped to the floor, covered her ears and closed her eyes, trying to block out the confusion. A pinpoint white glow started to emanate from God's outstretched finger. A burst of light engulfed Lucy in its bright glare as she fell unconscious.

* * *

Astan Ilves could cast himself as a foreboding and ominous man or as a tremendously charming and suave individual, which-ever personality best suited his needs in a particular situation. In either persona he would always get what he desired. That was why he had accumulated such tremendous wealth and power. It was extremely difficult for anyone to say no to Astan Ilves. Those who did always seemed to regret having made that decision. Much of Astan's time was spent researching artworks and historical writings in the various archives hidden around Vatican City or, possibly, one of the hundreds of storage vaults located in, under and around the Hermitage in St. Petersburg. Both places held a wealth of artwork and writings that had never or rarely been in the public view. Most of the documents and writings that interested Astan were those canons that had purposely been excluded as part of the canonical source of knowledge called the Bible. Not just those writings that the Christians discarded from their Codex Synaiticus and that the Catholics chose to include in their Alexandrian manuscript, but also those writings that were so contradictory or outrageous the church tried to deny there vary existence. Preservation of the integrity of the Bible that Christians had come to know and understand was the church's concern.

One of the most notable of these writings was the Book of Enoch. Portions of the book were included in the Dead Sea Scrolls and for a hundred years the book was part of the standard canon. Then late in the second century it was deemed as heresy and all copies of the book were ordered removed from the canon and destroyed. It seemed all copies were lost until portions of the Book of Enoch were discovered in late seventeen hundred by James Bruce in Ethiopia. Three separate copies were found in a church, all of them incomplete. The book told of fallen angels and how they took human form. There were inferences that many angels who had not fallen also had the power to take a human form. This was of great interest to Astan and he spent much time pursuing these writings. That was what had brought him once again to Vatican City. Although he had searched and researched the galleries, libraries, and storage vaults for several years, he still had not accessed all the art and documents the Vatican kept hidden away. Even someone of his stature met with resistance from the ever-changing hierarchy of the Catholic Church. In time, Astan knew he would receive access to those vaults.

He was also curious about the new Vatican miracle investigator, Kevin Bridges. There was much talk about Mr. Bridges' personal experience with some of these fallen angels in Madrid, as well as the rumors of Mr. Bridges' own performed miracles in a serial murder case in New Orleans. It was this New Orleans incident that brought Kevin Bridges to the Vatican, but Astan was well aware of that story.

Astan Ilves' power and prestige often drew comparisons to Lorenzo de Medici's influence at the Vatican during the Renaissance. They both had tremendous wealth, both had a deep love for the arts, and both had at one time been the financial banker for the Vatican. Astan had not actually been the banker, but had arranged and provided loans for them when they ran into some serious financial difficulties. Of course, this was never made public but it was well known to those in the top echelon of the world financial community. He also had an uncanny ability to make law suits seem to just disappear. When it became the trend to sue the Catholic Church for long past sexual indiscretions perpetrated by some of the church clergy, Astan supplied a team of attorneys that handled many of these cases at no cost to the church. The Vatican was indeed indebted to Astan Ilves. Like Leonardo de Medici, Astan was a master of backroom politics. This allowed him much influence as to the direction of the Church as well as to who would be guiding it. Some in the Church felt it was Astan and not the College of Cardinals who elected the last Pope, but no one would ever speak of such allegations publicly. For that matter, few would speak of it in private. No one knew for sure just who might be listening or if their friend and confidant just might be on Astan's payroll. It was funny how over the years certain members of the church were misfortunate enough to meet with untimely accidents when they crossed paths with Astan. Still others, like the Bishop of the Doctrinal Office, seemed to flourish under Astan's tutelage.

Like her father, Lucy could exude a presence that could match any situation. She was never intimidated by any man, except possibly her father, and would indulge pretentious behavior only when she knew she could turn it to her advantage. A master of manipulation, which of course she had learned from one of the best. It was apparent at a young age, that Lucy was an exceptional child. She advanced quickly through Roedean in Brighton, England's premier women's preparatory academy founded in the late 19th century. She entered Oxford at the age of fourteen. By the time she was twenty-four she was a licensed physician and held PhDs in Endocrinology and Neuroscience. She spent her first two years after graduation traveling the world with her father as he researched art. She would volunteer her skills as a doctor to those in need in places like Rome, St. Petersburg, and Paris. Lucy was dedicated and worked very hard, though she did manage to spend a considerable amount of time with her father learning the finer aspects of art and aestheticism. Now she ran a humanitarian research institute dedicated to finding cures for the diseases and conditions the major drug companies deemed unprofitable to invest their time, money, or manpower into trying to cure.

One of Lucy's first breakthroughs was finding an injection and electronic stimulation therapy that would allow the brain to work up to a thousand times faster in repairing itself. It really doesn't repair itself, but it allows the brain to search different routes for the electrical signals to follow, in order to bypass the injured portion and repair or more accurately, reboot itself. In essence, a way to bring people out of comatose and vegetative states. Initially, it worked on the less severe comatose patients, but she had experienced recent success with reversing vegetative states. A remarkable breakthrough, earning Lucy the title "miracle worker".

Several of Lucy's assistants continued to work on that project, while Lucy had moved on to others that required her inspirational insight as well as her serendipitous good fortune. She was a brilliant innovator and seemed to be a step ahead of the next pandemic. She had surpassed her father in fame and was recognized as one of the most influential people in the world. That was how Astan preferred it. He knew he was still the money and the power behind the scene. It was he who allowed Lucy the freedom to use her talents to the fullest. He knew she still had a lot more to offer that even she was aware of.

* * *

Lucy awoke in a strange bed in a small sparsely decorated room. On the wall was a portrait of the new Pope. Hanging just to the left of the room's one door was a simple wooden cross. The room smelled like it had been recently painted. There was a window in the room, or at least there was a heavy curtain covering an area where one would expect a window, but no light penetrated the curtain. Lucy thought the sun must have set. The only light in the room came from outside the door, which stood three-quarters of the way open. It wasn't natural light and seemed to come from an overhead fixture. She could make out voices and footsteps that were growing louder. As she lay in the bed, she tried to remember what had happened. She remembered being in the Sistine Chapel and hearing a loud ringing in her ears. "I must have fainted," she said out loud, "but why?" Lucy was in excellent health. There had to be a physical reason that caused her to pass out. She shuffled through her medical knowledge and dismissed every possible diagnosis. "It just doesn't make sense."

"What doesn't make sense?" Lucy looked up as a handsome man about her age, with a neatly trimmed beard, short cropped hair, and wearing an expensive tailored suit entered the room.

"What doesn't make sense is what I'm doing in this room being questioned by a total stranger," Lucy replied.

"Please forgive me. I'm sorry if I offended you, Ms. Ilves. My name is Kevin, Kevin Bridges. I work for the investigation branch of security here at Vatican City."

"I find it strange that we have never met before now, Mr. Bridges. I have spent a good amount of time here at Vatican City since my childhood and have met just about everyone who works here."

"I am relatively new here and my normal assignment usually takes me away from Vatican City the majority of the time. It just so happens that I was filling in for an associate who needed some time off to attend his daughter's wedding back in United States. That's why I was called by the two guards who found you. Can you tell me what happened?"

"I was hoping you could tell me. The last thing I remember was standing in the Sistine Chapel looking at the art, the Sandro Botticelli to be exact. Everything began to swirl around me and my ears started to ring. I must have fainted."

"Were you alone in the chapel?"

"Of course, I was alone, why do you ask?"

"Both the guards reported hearing two voices in the chapel, a woman's and a man's."

"No, I was alone."

"Of course," replied Kevin politely. He paused to take a moment to think and to let Lucy try to remember. "Forgive me for pursuing this, but if you had fainted and no one else was present, why did you not injure yourself when you collapsed to the floor?"

"I must have felt dizziness coming on and lay on the ground."

"That would explain why you were unhurt. But I'm curious as to where the cardinal's vestment supporting your head came from and how you were able to fold it so neatly to serve as a pillow, if you were becoming faint?"

"I have no idea what you're talking about. I don't remember any cardinal's vestments being in the room."

"And you are sure you were alone?"

"I'm absolutely su..." Lucy stopped in mid-sentence. "Little Lucy! He called the angel Little Lucy."

"Now I'm a little confused," Kevin said. "Who called the angel 'Little Lucy' and what does it have to do with what we're talking about?"

"That doesn't matter as long as my Lucy is safe," a loud voice bellowed, as Astan Ilves entered the room. "I understand you fainted. Let me get you back to the house so the doctor can take a look at you. I've already called him." Astan walked over and took Lucy's hand in his own and smiled at her. She still was daddy's little girl.

"I had a few more questions that..."

"And I'm sure Lucy will be happy to answer them after she sees her doctor," Astan said interrupting.

"Dad please, I'm fine. I can answer Mr. Bridges' questions now."

"Kevin Bridges? The Vatican miracle investigator?" Astan asked.

"Actually, I'm acting security chief right now." Kevin replied.

"Whatever," Astan huffed. "You and I need to talk later." He exclaimed. "But right now, if Mr. Bridges has more questions for you Lucy, he can come by the house tomorrow morning."

"I have a better idea," Lucy spoke. "Why doesn't Mr. Bridges join us tonight for dinner? That way I can answer his questions and he can answer a few of mine. Would that be all right with you, Mr. Bridges?" There was something in Lucy's tone that made it obvious she had more interest in Kevin than just having questions answered.

"Lucy," Astan started to say, "I'm sure Mr. Bridges has..."

It was Kevin's turn to interrupt. "I would be honored to join the two of you for dinner."

"I'm so sorry Lucy. I forgot to tell you; I have a previous engagement tonight which I must attend. Maybe Mr. Bridges could join us tomorrow evening."

"Then I guess it will be just you and I for dinner tonight, Mr. Bridges," Lucy said smiling at her father. After all, she was almost thirty and was tired of her father always trying to control her social life.

"I insist you first let the doctor check you out," Astan said.

"Daddy, I am a doctor, and I know I'm fine, but I'll agree to let him look at me."

"Well," Astan paused, "then I hope you two have a pleasant dinner. Lucy, we need to go now."

"I'll expect you at ten o'clock. That will give the doctor plenty of time to check me over."

"I look forward to it. I'll bring some wine."

"That would be lovely," Lucy responded, as Astan hurried her out the door.

CHAPTER SIX

My soul is weary with sorrow; strengthen me according to your word.

Psalm 119:28

Basil was a Brother of the Divine. He lived as one of the twelve followers of Reverend Anthony at the Varangian caves. They had built cells and a temple in the caves and lived there receiving pilgrims and the faithful seeking Reverend Anthony's word about the One and only God. As Christianity grew, more people came to visit Reverend Anthony including princes and emperors. These visitors all brought money and soon, above the caves, a huge overground monastery was constructed. The caves became nothing more than a burial place for members of the Brotherhood for the next seven hundred years. It was here the canon from Veroia was hidden away. The monastery continued to grow and soon was the largest in all of Russia. It attracted enumerable visitors from throughout the world. One of those visitors was a tall Grecian monk from Smyrna. Soon after his arrival, the first of what would turn into several monks was found horrifically mutilated in the caves below the monastery. Most of the murdered monks showed signs of torture no man could possibly bear. There were a dozen Brothers of the Divine living as monks at the Monastery of the Caves. It would not be long before one of them became the next victim of this macabre murderer.

As the number of murders increased, Basil knew something would have to be done to protect the canon. He knew that was what was behind these gruesome murders. The Brothers of the Divine met one evening in a secluded cave temple.

"Brothers, the enemy is upon us, searching for the canon as he did in Veroia two hundred years ago. It is no longer safe here, nor are we safe. Several brothers, though not members of our sect, have been killed. They suffered unspeakable torture before they joined our Lord. Had it been one of us, we surely would have revealed the hiding place of the canon."

"We must move the canon before the enemy discovers it," said one of the brothers, igniting a spirited debate.

"Brothers, quiet please, quiet," Basil said, trying to restore order. "I have worked out a plan that will keep the canon safe. I have already retrieved the canon from its hiding place and placed it in one of these twelve clay jars you see before you. The others contain worthless scrolls of birch bark paper. Each one of us will select a jar and leave immediately in twelve different directions. A note is attached to the top of the jar informing you where you are to go. When you arrive at your destination, you are to open your jar. If you have the canon, hide it and guard the secrets until God reveals his perfect plan. Remember to always look for fellow Brothers of the Divine on your journey. Our brotherhood must always carry on. Do not speak of the Brotherhood to any others, unless you're sure they can be trusted to devote their life to protecting the canon and the epistle of John. Among ourselves we will be known as the Weepers, but still do not speak of our Brotherhood until you're sure it is a true brother who greets you. Tell no one where you're headed. Make sure you're not followed and leave immediately. Let us pray."

For the next thirty minutes the twelve monks prayed for strength to accomplish the task facing them. Then each, without speaking, picked up one of the clay jars, collected their simple belongings, and quietly slipped away from the Monastery of the Caves.

Basil eyed the last clay jar. He was the only one who knew the truth. The only one with the knowledge that could put his brothers in harm's way. The only one that stood between Satan and the secret canon.

Basil had spent the last three days in his cell praying for the guidance and the strength necessary to perform the task that lie ahead. He took his jar and smashed it against the floor of the cell. He kicked at the pile of scrolled paper and crushed the jar into smaller pieces. He reached to a shelf along the side of the cell and swept his arm across a pile of bones that lay stacked on the shelf. They crashed noisily to the floor, covering the shards of the clay jar and the few scraps of paper. No one would notice. Piles of bones were everywhere. Basil turned and slowly shuffled out of the temple cell. He entered the sanctuary where he collected his few possessions and left the monastery without a word. But not unnoticed.

A tall stranger followed as Basil walked the path towards the footbridge by the Dnieper River. The same river Vladimir had tossed the pagan idols into when Christianity came to Kiev. The same river where thousands were baptized on their journey with the Lord. The same river that would take Basil on his final journey and walk with the Lord, for God had answered his prayers. Basil knew what must be done. The Stranger followed along the path and began to gain on Basil. He knew Basil was one of the elder monks at the monastery. He also had learned from some of the monks so horrifically tortured that a small contingent of monks within the monastery seemed to hold allegiance to Basil. The Stranger knew these monks must be part of the Brotherhood of the Divine that he had spent so much time over the centuries trying to track down. The Stranger knew they were protecting a secret, but what that secret was he had no idea. Basil had reached the river and started across the bridge. He was only half way across when a loud screech filled the night as if a large animal was mortally wounded. In the moonlight he saw what he thought to be a man. But the man seemed to turn into a wolf with giant wings like a bird. Basil knew Satan had come. God had told him he would. Without hesitation

Basil leaped into the middle of the Dnieper's swift current. As he hit the water, he heard the sound of the creature's leathery wings beating as it soared downward towards Basil. The river was swift and the waterfall came quickly. Basil dropped twenty feet before he hit the first rocks, then bounced and continued to plummet another seventy feet, his body tumbling on the rocks as he fell. The beast tried to grab Basil in its massive talons as the river rushed Basil over the waterfalls, but Basil's body was gone before the beast could reach the falling monk.

* * *

A week before his death, Basil had given the Veroia canon to Nestor the Chronicler, a trusted Brother of the Divine. That very day Nestor left on his journey to the Archangel Michael Monastery on the river Dvina near the White Sea. It was a perfect place to hide the canon. It was far from any major city or town and not on any of the trade routes. Nestor left the canon with a Brother of the Divine who had traveled with him and would stay at the monastery to oversee the safety of the canon. Basil had designed a plan to send all of his fellow monks that belonged to the Brothers of the Divine in twelve separate directions, all with a destination far from the location of the Veroia canon. Basil was confident he had outwitted the Stranger who was now in their midst. What Basil hadn't counted on was the monk Nestor leaving the canon to one who did not understand its significance. This uninformed brother set about the task of translating the canon into the new Cyrillic language being taught to all the Slavs in the region. For more than a year he painstakingly copied the Greek letters on the Papyrus onto birch bark paper using the new language taught to him by Cyril during their long mission journeys. As the canon was copied, the scrolls were ripped and damaged, then carelessly stuffed back into the clay jar and thrown into a pile of bones in a vault below the monastery.

The monk doing the copying knew the canon well and recognized several books and scriptures that seemed not to belong. He thought it best to precisely copy this canon onto his birch bark copy. The abbot could decide what should be removed. The monk had kept his work secret in order to surprise the abbot with the first Cyrillic copy of the canon. Each night as he completed his work, he would hide the birch bark papers behind a false wall he had constructed at one end of his small cell. It was a wonderful gift he had created for the Archangel Michael Monastery and would have been a splendid surprise had the monk not suddenly died of tuberculosis just as he completed the translation. His cell was sealed so no others would become ill from the mysterious disease. The canon of Veroia was soon forgotten, if in fact it was ever known to the monks of Archangel Michael's Monastery.

CHAPTER SEVEN

And there was war in heaven. Michael and his angels fought against the dragon, and the dragon and his angels fought back.

Revelation 12:7

A burst of machine-gun fire from the Israeli Uzi submachine gun was unmistakable. Bullets ripped the wall just inches from Mika'il's head, sending clouds of plaster and razor-sharp splinters of cement into the air. He could feel the intense heat of the bullets as they whizzed less than a foot from his scalp, searing the skin and singing his hair.

"Mika'il, Mika'il!" Ahmed yelled, "Mika'il, are you safe?"

"I am safe my friend, the bullets have missed me once again."

"Allah has surely blessed you, Mika'il. I pray you remain safe." Ahmed paused to catch his breath, the fear still caught in his throat. "But how are we to escape from this Zionist trap? They must have known of our plans. Who knew we would be here tonight preparing the bombs?"

"It was I who allowed the soldiers to discover this address. I told one of our men whom I believed was the informer. I had to be sure it was he who was telling the soldiers of our movements. Now I will make him pay for his disloyalty. It is all part of my plan."

"But we are trapped, Mika'il. We cannot escape."

The situation did indeed look grim for Ahmed and Mika'il. Three armored personnel carriers had disgorged their contingent of Israeli soldiers. A tank could be heard in the distance moving into position on a knoll overlooking the small village. The village was not far from the border of Israel. Just off Road 465 near the settlement of Rantis in the southern portion of the West Bank.

Static erupted from a small walkie-talkie in Mika'il's hand. It was a cheap inexpensive walkie-talkie, not much more than a child's toy, but with a range sufficient for Mika'il's needs.

"The tank is in position on the knoll just as you said it would be, Mika'il, and the cowardly Zionist soldiers have taken the positions as predicted," a voice squawked.

Mika'il knew these Israeli soldiers were anything but cowards. They were some of the best trained military soldiers in the world. He would never underestimate their abilities like so many of his comrades seem determined to do. That was why so many Palestinians were killed. They failed to understand their enemy. "Wait for my signal. Are our men in position?"

"Our brave comrades are ready to martyr themselves in the name of Allah. We will fight to the death," the soldier on the walkie-talkie replied.

This was the second fault in the thinking of his soldiers. They would make insane decisions in the heat of battle thinking Allah would protect and guard over them. If they were to die, it was the will of Allah and they would be martyred. Allah was great, but men were foolish.

* * *

Mika'il Azazy had been born on the fifth of June, 1967. The same day Israel attacked Egypt, Jordan, and Syria simultaneously. There were some complications with his birth that required him and his mother to remain in the hospital in Nablus a few extra days. When he and his mother returned home, the West Bank was occupied by Israeli soldiers. His father, Esa Azazy, was unable to be at his birth. He had joined with several of his PLO neighbors to fight the invading Israeli forces. However, their defeat was rapid and decisive. The Israeli military was one of the best trained and deadliest in the world. They also enjoyed massive economic and military assistance from one of the greatest superpowers in the world. Esa was lucky to escape the massacre and make it home to see his newborn son, Mika'il. Esa had insisted his son be named Mika'il, for the Islam Archangel Mika'il, the angel charged with bringing thunder and lightning onto the Earth. His father prayed to Allah that his son Mika'il would someday bring that thunder and lightening to the Zionists who stole their land.

Esa formed a guerrilla group with several members of the PLO in his home city of Nablus. For years he and his brothers in Allah attacked Israeli military targets in an effort to redeem Palestine. Many of his brothers were killed, but there always seemed to be fresh recruits to replace those who were martyred in the name of Allah. In 1982, when Mika'il turned fifteen, he became one of those recruits. Mika'il's mother was not pleased with his decision. She had dedicated her life to making sure he received the best education possible. The family did not want for money, so Mika'il studied with some of the best scholars available in the war-torn region, several of whom had been University professors and had studied abroad. Mika'il astounded his teachers with his ability to grasp concepts and engage them in serious debate over the political issues not only facing the Palestinians, but how the Palestinian conflict affected world politics and economics.

Mika'il joined his father's guerrilla fighters in Beirut, Lebanon. Israel had occupied several areas in Lebanon, but was under constant attack from PLO guerrilla insurgents. The majority of these groups used Beirut as their base camp. In the summer of 1982, Israel started an offensive aimed at wiping out these guerrilla groups. By mid-August, after several intense battles, the PLO agreed to withdraw their guerrillas from Beirut. Israel now occupied much of southern Lebanon.

Mika'il quickly learned the tactics of the guerrilla fighters and was schooled in the art of war at a terrorist training facility in Pakistan. Soon Mika'il led his own band of guerrilla fighters. He proved to be a fierce and smart leader. His fame and power grew quickly as news of his success reached the Palestinian Authority. By 1987 Mika'il was one of the leaders of the intifada, coordinating and staging a series of uprisings in the occupied territories.

Mika'il believed that a Palestinian State would eventually become reality, but it would require years of diplomacy and negotiations. He believed the acts committed by his team of guerrillas helped to strengthen the Palestinian bargaining position. At least that was what he had believed up until a few weeks ago. That was when he started hearing the voices, and the weeping.

The voices. The constant voices. Weeping, calling to him. At first Mika'il was confused, scared. Then he began to listen. He had no choice. Mika'il knew whom the voices and the weeping belonged to. The dead, the martyred, the victims of the suicide bombings, the Israeli soldiers, his Palestinian brothers, and all those who had died over the past two thousand years in the name of religion. Jews, Christians, Muslims, they all seemed to be calling out to Mika'il. They all seemed to be weeping. "Why me?" Mika'il would ask himself as the voices grew louder and more incessant. "Why do you call to me?"

"We are here for you. You are the one. Lead us. Free us. Save us." Then there were the anguished cries and the weeping continued. The ceaseless weeping, the perpetual, unremitting weeping, too great a burden to ask of any man. It was beginning to drive Mika'il mad.

Mika'il sought help through his prayers at a local mosque in a village where he and his guerrillas had taken refuge. He faithfully went for his daily prayers seeking guidance and protection for his men.

"Allah, you are great. Protect my men as we go into tomorrow's battle. Protect them as you have always protected me," Mika'il hesitated for a moment. "You must surely guide me as to what you ask. These voices I hear. These voices must be a message from you who are so great..."

"Precisely!" A cleric stood behind Mika'il.

"What did you say?" Mika'il said.

"I said nothing," the cleric responded. "Perhaps it was Allah who has spoken to you."

Mika'il continued to stare at the cleric. Mika'il had never seen this man before, but yet he looked so familiar. The cleric was tall. Much taller than the average Palestinian and very thin. His eyes seemed to sink inside of his head, casting foreboding shadows as if the cleric had no eyes. But they were there. They forced you to stare into his face. The cleric's vacant look captured your attention and seemed to draw your very soul into his own.

"Precisely what was it you were asking of Allah?" the cleric continued.

There was that word again. It had to be the cleric who had whispered to him. Mika'il continued to stare without responding as he tried to make sense of what was happening.

"Allah has spoken to me as well. He said to watch for a man who will come to pray. A stranger," the cleric said. "He told me of this great and powerful man who would come and unite his people. A man who understood the pain these religious wars have caused throughout the centuries, a man who would perform miracles. I believe you are that man."

"No, Allah did not speak of these things to me, it was you who whispered in my ear. I am no great and powerful man. I am but a soldier in the war against the Zionists."

"Perhaps that is true, but what about the voices?"

Mika'il was stunned. How could this cleric know about the voices? Surely what the cleric described must be true. Allah had spoken to the cleric.

Suddenly there was a loud buzzing. Mika'il turned to look as a swarm of thousands of locusts poured through the doors of the mosque. No one else seemed to notice this plague that had overtaken the mosque as all inside continued in their prayers.

"These are the voices you hear. These are the souls of the dead and fallen who now call to you. These are the minions you shall lead," the cleric said.

The locusts attacked those still in prayer, yet no one seemed to notice. Mika'il could see these were no typical locusts. These had mouths with sharp needle-like teeth made for ripping flesh and a stinger like that of a scorpion. They began ripping the flesh from the exposed arms and necks of the praying men. The large stingers found their marks, flesh blackened and fell away as if rotting. Still, no one seemed to notice as their bodies were decimated by the deadly swarm. Muscle and bone began to show through the pouring blood. Mika'il tried to run to his friends and swat these aberrations away, but found he was unable to move his feet. More of the mutant locusts descended on the mosque and soon the swarm had grown so large that the room looked like a black carpet whipping in the wind. And the sound. The buzzing grew to be unbearable. Then came the sound of crackling bones as the flying beasts began to tear apart the skeletons. Mika'il felt his head begin to swim as he grew dizzy.

"Bzzzz, bzzzz, bzzzz!" the buzzing and crackling became deafening to Mika'il.

* * *

"Bzzzz, bzzzz, bzzzzz, Mika'il, Mika'il, the tank is preparing to fire." It was the walkie-talkie buzzing and crackling as one of Mika'il's scouts tried to reach him.

Mika'il was dazed. What had just happened? "Mika'il, it is time, we must do it now."

Mika'il suddenly remembered where he was and why he was there. For the first time he felt anguish as he thought of what he was about to do. He used to relish the thought of killing the murderous Israeli soldiers. Now, it troubled him dearly. He was beginning to question his own ability to lead his men. Had he lost his desire for Palestine to once again be its own country? He knew that was not true, but he questioned why others must die to realize his dream. A free and safe Palestine. But wasn't that what the Israelis had also desired, freedom and safety? These new thoughts confused Mika'il. Just whose land is this anyway? How can any one group claim it to be their own? Why must we fight over land and shrines we both could share? Mika'il felt as if a shroud had been pulled over his head. Again, the crackling static of the walkie-talkie jarred him from his confused state. That's when Mika'il heard the voice begin to speak in his head. "I am the thunder and the lightening. I am the thunder and lightening." The voice grew louder as it continued to repeat until it became an unbearable chant throbbing inside his head. Mika'il wanted to scream. He had to scream. He picked up his walkie-talkie and pushed the talk button.

"Detonate the bombs, detonate the bombs." There was a series of deafening explosions in and around the village. The chanting in his head stopped and he heard only the ringing in his ears.

* * *

For several nights, Mika'il and his most trusted companions had worked for hours carefully hiding American Claymore mines in the walls of several of the buildings surrounding the house he was now in. They had cut holes in the plaster of the walls and placed the mines inside these holes. They covered them and the wires that led to the detonator with plaster and paint to hide them from the enemy. Beneath the knoll where Mika'il was sure the tank would stop; his men had placed several pounds of plastic explosive supplied by their Iranian friends. These too were hardwired to a triggering device hidden in a spider hole, or disguised bunker, several hundred yards from the village.

* * *

As the explosion echoed off the surrounding hills, Mika'il waited to hear the machine gun fire from his men as they swooped in from their hidden positions. He heard none. Only the screams of the Israeli soldiers, who were unfortunate enough to have not died instantly, echoed from the streets. Mika'il left the room and walked fearlessly out the front door confident his enemies were destroyed. Ahmed raced out behind him, gun in hand. Ahmed was Mika'il's bodyguard and had swore to Allah to let no harm come to Mika'il. The rest of Mika'il's soldiers were still on the outskirts of the village looking for Israeli soldiers who might have survived the explosive ambush. As soon as Ahmed joined Mika'il in front of the small house, two Israeli commandos who were not injured in the blast opened fire with their Uzi's on fully automatic. Both commandos pulled their respective triggers simultaneously and held them for less than three seconds unleashing a barrage of more than forty of the 9-mm projectiles straight at the two Palestinians. Several of Mika'il's men arrived just as the Israeli's fired, but were too late to stop the intended carnage. They were able to fire at the Israelis, but they knew it was too late to save Mika'il. Suddenly, there were sparkles and flashes of bright blue and purple light. A flaming sword appeared in front of Mika'il and Ahmed slashing the air and casting a shadow of a giant winged angel. The same flashes and shadows instantly appeared before the two Israeli soldiers. The bullets from the Israeli's guns, as did the bullets from Mika'il's men's guns, stopped in mid-air and dropped straight to the ground. It was as though they had hit a solid wall, yet they showed no signs of having smashed into anything. Mika'il's men, as did the two Israeli soldiers, dropped to the ground as if having been stung by a giant wasp. They were unable to speak, but still able to witness the miracle taking place before them. Only Mika'il and Ahmed remained standing, seemingly not afflicted by what had stricken the others. As soon as the bullets hit the ground, the apparition was gone and the men were able to move. The Israeli commandos, as did Mika'il's men, all grabbed their rifles and pulled their respective triggers trying to kill before they were killed, but nothing happened. No bullets fired.

"Lay down your weapons for they are useless," Mika'il said to all present. "You have witnessed a miracle. Be it a miracle of Allah, or a miracle of your God, it was divine intervention, and you were witness to it. You Israelis return to your superiors and tell them of the miracle you have seen here today. Tell them of the Archangel Michael who came to protect the Palestinians and the Israeli soldiers. Tell them I am sorry for the deaths of all your comrades, but now we have seen that Allah and your God want the killings to stop."

In the distance was the thumping of helicopter blades. "We must leave at once," Ahmed pleaded with Mika'il, "I must keep you safe."

"My safety is no longer your responsibility, my friend."

Reassuringly, he touched Ahmed on the shoulder. It was as though the weight of the world was released from Ahmed's heart with Mika'il's touch. With a hand signal from Mika'il, his men moved swiftly away from the area and out of sight, leaving all of their weapons behind.

"Tell them this will be a new beginning," Mika'il yelled at the two Israeli soldiers. "Peace is at hand." He and Ahmed quickly disappeared down an alley.

CHAPTER EIGHT

The first angel sounded his trumpet, and there came hail and fire mixed with blood, and it was hurled down upon the earth. A third of the earth was burned up, a third of the trees were burned up, and all the green grass was burned.

Revelation 8:7

Katia Miduq was a slight woman, but extremely hearty for a forty-three-year-old mother of three. Living in a small village along the Northern Hudson Bay would require any person to be hearty. Conditions were harsh. Life was harsh. Katia was walking her eight-year-old daughter to school as she did everyday. She was a few paces in front of her daughter when she turned and saw the polar bear stalking her daughter and preparing to attack. She charged the bear to save her daughter's life, striking the 700-pound bear in its chest with her fists. It was enough to distract the bear, which slapped her twice to the ground with its large paw, ripping open her parka and her skin with its long claws. A hunter who was driving by stopped and shot the bear, but not before it had taken Katia's life. It was becoming all too common in a place where the habitat and climate were so rapidly changing. The ice pack that supplied the polar bears for centuries with a safe feeding ground had all but disappeared, driving the creatures to fend for food in the populated villages along the bay. Within fifty years the entire polar ice cap would vanish and, somewhere during that time, the polar bear would cease to exist.

* * *

"Get the horses in the trailer, now," Jim shouted at Bobbi Sue. The smoke was getting thicker, making it difficult to breathe and impossible to see. Bobbi Sue had come home for the weekend from Texas A & M to see if she could help out. Like everyone else in Texas, she was keeping a close watch on the wildfire that had ripped through tens of thousands of acres, destroying everything in its path. Now the farm that had been in her family for one hundred twenty years was dead in the sights of the firestorm.

"Dad, we've got to go now, forget about the horses." There was panic in Bobbi Sue's voice.

Her dad looked towards the field of cotton, or at least where the field of cotton should be. All he could see was smoke. "You're right," he finally replied. "I'll get your mom out of the house. We need to get the hell out of here fast. You take the truck. Go now! Your mom and I will follow in the car. Hurry!"

Bobbi Sue jumped into the truck, waved at her dad and tore down the driveway. She wasn't sure which way to turn, but to the left the smoke wasn't quite as thick. Her parents never made it out of the house. When her dad went in to get his wife, he found her barely conscious on the floor. The smoke had caused a severe asthma attack and she was gasping, trying desperately to catch her breath. Bobbi Sue's dad grabbed his wife off the floor and headed for the door. He never made it. The high cholesterol that had built up in his arteries over the past fifty-three years finally caught up to him. He collapsed in the hallway just six feet from the front door, dropping his wife who had already slipped into unconsciousness. Seconds later, the farm house he had been born in, the farmhouse his father had been born in, the farmhouse where he raised his daughter, the farmhouse that had served five generations of his family, exploded in flames like dried kindling in a fireplace. There would be similar tragedies throughout Texas, in Alaska, in Indonesia, Australia, Canada, Europe, and in Africa where timberlands and grasslands parched by draught brought on by global warming would feed the wildfires that were burning up Earth at an alarming rate.

* * *

The United States was still reeling from the effects of the Katrina disaster as the next hurricane season quickly approached. Bodies were being found weekly in New Orleans. Cleanup had barely begun. The government failure to react in time was still being debated in Washington and there were increasingly more calls for the

President to deal with the global warming crisis, which was theorized to be the reason for the severity of hurricanes the past few years. Even the skeptics were conceding global warming was more than a theory and mankind was indeed bringing disaster to Earth. Yet even with all the facts and figures supplied by science, the United States failed to act. In fact, the government exacerbated the problem with their continued lax pollution standards and America's addiction to fossil fuels. Earth was collapsing at an exponentially quickening pace while several governments stood by and watched it happen. The balance of nature was no longer balanced and the world was destroying itself, but with a lot of help from mankind.

CHAPTER NINE

Each one should use whatever gift he has received to serve others, faithfully administering God's grace in its various forms.

1 Peter 4:10

Gabe hurried down Valley Boulevard, putting as much distance between him and the accident scene as possible. He walked for about twenty minutes until he found the El Monte bus terminal. He caught the next bus home and spent the rest of the day watching the news about the train wreck. To his dismay, the focus was shifting from the horror of the accident to the miracles performed by this mystery commuter. Several passengers came on the broadcasts telling of what had happened in the second car. Even more compelling was the testimonial by Maria about her broken jaw. Fortunately, the only picture of Gabe was the one taken from a distance and even his best friend would be hard pressed to identify Gabe from the picture.

For the rest of the week, and the following week, Gabe drove his car to work each day. It was out of necessity that first week while the train tracks were being repaired. Gabe drove the second week to avoid being seen by the other commuters. He wasn't prepared to have to answer questions and did not need the stress. Gabe wasn't dealing well with what had happened to him. He didn't understand just what was going on with his body and mind. He had not felt so physically well in years and his mind seemed to be sharper than ever. He tried to explain these changes and the miracles to his wife, but only managed to frighten her. She suggested he go see the pastor at their church. That was a suggestion Gabe did not feel the least bit comfortable with. He attended church regularly, yet hadn't been able to cross that line and declare Jesus his one and only savior.

When Gabe did return to the train station for his commute to work, he decided to take the earlier scheduled train in hopes of avoiding any awkward situations with his fellow passengers. He wanted to blend in and go unnoticed as he always seemed able to do prior to the horrendous accident. No such luck. A news van had been parked at the train station since the line had reopened. Several passengers were able to confirm this was the station where the mysterious miracle worker boarded the train, but no one actually knew his name. A catering truck was parked next to the station serving breakfast and coffee and several people seemed to just be milling around, waiting. The entire area looked like an encampment as dozens of people all waited for someone or something to appear.

"This is not good," Gabe said under his breath as he approached the station. "Not good at all." Gabe turned and headed the opposite direction.

Two men in a dark sedan watched as Gabe approached the station. They had a clear view of the happenings at the station and of anyone who approached the station down the main street. They watched intently as Gabe passed them by, stopped, and then headed back in the opposite direction towards where they were parked. The driver stared down at the picture that lay on the seat between them. It was an artist's rendition of the alleged miracle worker that had been compiled from the numerous eye witnesses and passengers.

"That's him, no doubt about it." The two men exited the car as Gabe approached. They both had on jogging suits and aroused no suspicions in Gabe.

"Mojhete skazat' gde nahoditsya 'Starbucks'," one of the men asked Gabe in Russian.

"Sure," Gabe replied pleasantly. "It's just one block back up this street and two blocks to the West. It should be open by now."

"Kono hen de ni asp goha wo taberavevu tokoro ga arimasuka," the other man asked in Japanese.

"There are a couple of good places in the Village. We have Walters and the Village Grill. The Grill opens at six and I think Walters opens at eight. The Grill would probably be your best bet."

The men pulled out what looked like FBI badges. "Can we see some identification?"

"Why, what did I do?" Gabe replied, reaching for his wallet as his mouth suddenly went dry.

"You either just hypnotized both of us or you just performed a miracle," one of the men said. "You answered our questions in two different languages at the same time. I asked you a question in Russian and I heard you answer in Russian."

"I heard you answer it in Japanese," the other agent said. "Then I asked you in Japanese about a place to eat breakfast and you answered in Japanese."

"But I heard you answer in Russian," the other agent said. "I didn't believe it when they assigned me to find you. I thought it was the biggest wild goose chase of all time. Boy was I wrong."

"You guys must be crazy," Gabe responded, but still handed them his license. "What's going to happen now?"

"We were told just to find you, which we've done. Some people from our office will no doubt be in touch with you very soon. You're not planning on leaving the country anytime soon, are you?" the agent asked jokingly, as he continued to write down Gabe's information.

"I hadn't thought about it, at least not until now."

"I wouldn't if I were you. As a matter of fact, if I were you, I probably wouldn't leave my house for a while. Look at that mob at the station. It has been getting larger every day. In a couple of hours, there'll be over two hundred people hoping to find you there. Half of them will be in wheelchairs looking for you to perform a miracle. Can we give you a lift back to your house?"

"No thanks, I can walk."

"You might as well let us drive you. We're going to be parked across the street for the next few weeks and, anyway, we're going to be following you home."

Reluctantly Gabe climbed into the back of the car. "Like I really have a choice?"

As the car pulled away, two other cars started their engines and began to follow. One car belonged to a reporter with the *L.A. Times*, the other to a private detective who worked for Astan Ilves. Within minutes, Astan would know that Gabe Brown was one of the three he had been searching for. And within hours the world would know the name, Gabe Brown, thanks to the *Los Angeles Times.*

CHAPTER TEN

'and while praying he falleth into a trance three days before his apprehension; and he saw his pillow burning with fire. And he turned and said unto those that be with him, 'it must needs be that I shall be burned alive'."

Letter from the Church of Smyrna to the Church of Philomelium describing the martyrdom of Polycarp

Polycarp had fled Smyrna and hid in a farmhouse outside the city. When his pursuers neared, he fled to another farmhouse. Two slaves were tortured until one betrayed Polycarp's place of retreat. He refused to run any more and met with those that were seeking to capture him.

"Denounce your Savior and you shall live, curse your Christ and your life will be spared," the proconsul pleaded with Polycarp.

"Fourscore and six years have I served him and he has done me no harm. How can I curse my King who saved me?" Polycarp responded, sealing his fate.

The arena was closed, so it was too late to throw Polycarp to the beasts. It was decided he would be burned alive. The fire was lit but, instead of consuming the body, it formed a wall around Polycarp as if protecting him, keeping him unharmed. The executioner was ordered to stab Polycarp and, when he did, blood rushed forth and quenched the flames. Then miraculously from the large gashing wound the executioner had delivered to Polycarp's torso, a pure white dove seemed to spring from inside the body and rose skyward. The body was removed from the stake, laid on a pyre and burned. The ashes and bones were collected and hidden in a suitable place of rest.

* * *

Smyrna was arguably one of the finest cities in all of Asia Minor. It had one of the earliest Christian churches and was a center of trade. That is until Emperor Constantine took power and built Constantinople in the image of Rome. The importance of Smyrna quickly declined. Polycarp had long since been martyred and the sub-Apostolic age had come to its end.

When the three Brothers of the Divine from St. Johns arrived in Smyrna, they found the persecution of the Christians had waned, although danger still persisted. From fellow monks they found the burial tomb of Polycarp and hid the canon and epistle within. For the next several hundred years the Brotherhood maintained their vigil disguising and protecting the canon and the tomb. Over the centuries a continual lineage of monks swore their allegiance to protecting the secrets of Apostle John and joined the ranks of the Weepers. During those centuries Smyrna was ravaged several times by invading Turks, pirates, and Mongols. Through each invasion, the Brotherhood of the Divine remained true to its purpose and no harm came to the canon, although the city was left in ruins.

In 1222 Emperor John Ducas Vatatzes rebuilt the city and covered over the hidden grave of Polycarp that also held the canon. The monks of the Brotherhood of the Divine remained unconcerned until 1330 when Smyrna was conquered by Aidin, who made it the port of the Aidin emirate. Soon he appointed his son Amur as the governor of Smyrna and the city was no longer a safe place to hide the canon. The number of Weepers watching over the canon in Smyrna had declined to three. The Brothers realized they would have to seek outside assistance to recover it from its hiding place. Two of the Brotherhood members journeyed to Rhodes where they met with Grand Master Fulkes de Villaret of the Knights Hospitaller or, as they were also called, the Order of Saint John of Jerusalem. This was a religious order created by the Pope to serve as the military arm of the Christian Church. They had joined together over two hundred years before with the Knights Templar, who now had dissolved surrendering their property to the Knights Hospitaller. The two members of the Brotherhood were forced to reveal their secret to de Villaret to secure his help in trying to retrieve the canon and epistle. In 1332 the Knights Hospitaller attacked Smyrna, but were unable to conquer the main citadel in the city. They were able to advance far enough into the city to recover the canon and epistle. Though they believed they had accomplished their mission in secrecy, the enemy had spies even within the ranks of the Knights Hospitaller. Word of the three monks exhuming the grave of Polycarp and removing sealed jars reached the Stranger. This was the very type of activity the Stranger had been searching for throughout the world for the past one thousand years. His hope lifted at the thought of more such treasures entombed with the dead.

Timur, or Timur the Lame as he became known after an injury he received during one of his many battles, was a direct descendant of Genghis Khan. He was a disciplined reader of the Qur'an, but soon found his beliefs drifting to the more mysterious side of Islam. He was converted to be a Nusairi by a stranger who came to Kesh with temptations Timur couldn't resist. He was at a crossroads with his religion and his desires to become a great military leader. The Stranger offered him the latter if Timur would promise to invade certain cities at the bequest of the Stranger. It was a promise Timur was quick to make. For more than forty years Timur was constantly at war conquering new lands. One such conquest was partial repayment to the Stranger. In 1402 Timur invaded Smyrna, massacreing all inhabitants and destroying much of the city and desecrating all tombs and graves of Christians. At his side was the Stranger, always looking for something. Like most of Timur's conquests, once everyone was killed and the city laid to waste, he and his men would move on. No governing apparatus left behind to secure the city in his name, thus often forcing Timur to return to fight the battle again. The Stranger didn't find what he was seeking in Smyrna.

* * *

When the monks of the Brotherhood of the Divine retrieved the canon and epistle, they moved it to a safer location. A location far from its previous hiding place and far from the prying eyes of the Stranger's spies. For years Abyssinia was thought to be a safe haven for Jews, Christians and, above all, the most sacred of all Christian icons, including the original Ark of the Covenant. The Queen of Sheba is said to have brought it back from Jerusalem where she had gone to meet King Solomon. On her return she gave birth to Menelik I, who would become known as the founding father of the family known as the King of Kings. The Ark was placed in the main church in Axum. It was there, beside the Ark, that the Brotherhood of the Divine took the canon to once again be hidden away until God revealed his plan.

CHAPTER ELEVEN

The LORD is the strength of his people,
a fortress of salvation for his anointed one.

Save your people and bless your inheritance;
be their shepherd and carry them forever.

Psalm 28:8-9

Kevin Bridges was at the gate of the Astan Ilves estate at exactly 9:45 p.m. and it was fortunate he had arrived early. A crowd of more than one hundred people were gathered around the gate. Some were in wheelchairs, some on crutches, many being held up by friends. Some were so weak they just lay on the side of the road. All had come seeking a miracle. Two security guards were on duty outside to keep the crowds from blocking the gate and a half dozen more guards were just inside the electric gate. As Kevin's car approached, several people rushed over to see who was entering, but those were the few who had not seen Lucy enter three hours earlier.

"Mr. Bridges?" one of the guards asked Kevin as he pulled up to the gate.

"Yes, I'm Kevin Bridges." The other guard forced several people away from the vehicle. In his hand the guard held a recent photo of Kevin and compared it to the real Kevin sitting behind the wheel. "Is it always like this?"

"Only when Ms. Ilves is in town," the guard replied. "Somehow the word gets out even before she arrives in Italy and a crowd begins to form. It's amazing."

Several of the guards who had been just inside the gate now formed a barricade behind Kevin's car as the gate swung open. It was their job to make sure no uninvited guests entered the grounds. Kevin drove through the gate and into a passageway that opened up into a large private piazza. It had an intricately sculpted marble fountain comparable to the finest fountains in the larger public piazzas found throughout Rome. Lucy must have been notified of his arrival for she was waiting by the fountain when Kevin pulled his car to a stop.

"Pretty impressive, don't you think?" Lucy said as Kevin climbed out of the car.

"Yes, you are."

"I was talking about the fountain," Lucy replied, rather embarrassed.

"Oh, oh yes, it truly is a magnificent fountain," Kevin replied, with a sly smile. He had known exactly what she was referring to.

Lucy stared whimsically for a moment at Kevin. "Dinner's ready, so why don't we head inside." Lucy realized she was being teased by Kevin, something most people were too intimidated to try with Lucy, except for maybe her father. Something even he never seemed to do any more. He was always too busy researching his art icons, or on his way to some meeting on the other side of the world. Still, he managed to be around enough to mettle sufficiently in Lucy's life.

"I hope you remembered to bring the wine."

"Of course, though I'm sure it's not up to the quality you are accustomed to."

"Don't be ridiculous. Just because my father is one of the top wine connoisseurs in all of Europe, and has one of the largest wine collections in the world, is no reason to feel your wine is inadequate."

Now it was Lucy doing the teasing.

"Touché." Kevin replied, and they both laughed.

They sat at a large dining room table designed to hold twenty guests. Fortunately, someone had situated the place settings opposite from each other at one end of the large table. As soon as they were seated, the room became a beehive of activity. There was a startled look on the wine steward's face when Kevin passed him the wine he had brought, which prompted a smile from Lucy and Kevin.

"My father seems to think it wasn't a coincidence you were at Vatican City today."

"What makes him say that?"

"He says you're probably there specifically to talk to me. He says you are some kind of a detective for the Vatican. I believe he called you the 'miracle detective'."

Lucy was grinning, knowing she had put Kevin on his guard.

"Your father is a very informed man, Lucy. Not many people know that someone actually investigates miracles for the Vatican. It's the kind of thing the church doesn't like to advertise."

"So, it's true, you were there to investigate me today."

"Why? Have you been performing miracles I should know about?" Now it was Lucy who was struggling as to how to respond, but Kevin spoke before the silence became too awkward. "Actually, I was hoping to get a chance to meet and speak with you during your visit here. Judging by the crowd outside of your gate, and with what the press is writing about you, I do have some questions about these miraculous cures of yours."

"Well, I think it's all been blown out of proportion by the press. I'm just a hard-working research scientist who happened to discover some amazing cures for a few diseases and conditions the major research firms didn't find it profitable to undertake. Nothing miraculous about that."

"Tell me what happened in the chapel today. You say you were alone, but the guards swear they heard a man's voice inside and we did find those cardinal vestments you were using as a pillow."

"I really don't remember what happened. One minute I'm looking at the art work on the ceiling, I hear a loud buzzing and the next thing I know I wake up in the guard's room and you're coming through the door. The doctor says I must have fainted. He could find nothing wrong, but I already knew that. Where the vestments came from, I haven't the slightest idea. One of the cardinals must have left them in the chapel. Did you ask to see who might have left them?"

"As a matter of fact, I did ask around to see whom they belonged to."

"And?" Lucy interrupted.

"And it seems no cardinals reported any of their vestments missing."

"Well, that makes no sense."

"What makes less sense is those vestments were not contemporary cardinal vestments. The material, stitching and label indicated they were the type worn by cardinals more than three hundred years ago. Rather strange, don't you think?" Kevin asked, watching to see how Lucy would react to the news.

"They must have come from one of the public displays showing the history of the Vatican."

"I thought of that, too," Kevin said. "So far nothing has been reported missing or out of place, but we'll continue to look." Kevin wanted to press Lucy about the man's voice that was heard, but decided it could wait. Now that the subject of miracles had been breached, he would take the opportunity to find out all he could along those lines. After all, that was why he had been at Vatican City that day.

"People say it was your touch and not the treatment which brought that fireman out of the coma. His parents wanted to take him off the ventilator years ago when the doctors said there was absolutely no hope. They said there was no brain function. How do you explain what happened?"

"I can't really explain it. I saw the brain scans, I knew there was no brain wave activity, but his wife insisted we try the experimental treatment. She said we were the answer to her prayers. Maybe that's the answer. Maybe it was her prayers that brought a miracle from God."

"I've no doubt God did perform a miracle that day, but my question is, did he use you to perform it?" Lucy didn't answer. "I must be honest with you Lucy, there have been several other reports of miraculous recoveries from people you have touched and worked with and several didn't involve your new treatment."

"My father warned me you would ask me about this. I really don't know how to answer. It's true that people have experienced miracles when I've treated them. And yes, some claim my touch alone healed them. It's just very difficult for me to understand. That was why I was at the Sistine Chapel today. I went to ask God if he was using me as His servant. My father has said this is what God wants from me."

"What did God say?" Kevin asked.

"I'm not sure I even had a chance to ask Him. I really don't remember what happened today," Lucy almost cried as she answered. "My father says God is calling me to serve Him with this healing ability. I'm afraid my father wants to put me on stage in front of the world to perform these miracles. I just don't know."

"I'm sure God in all his wisdom will reveal his plan to you." Kevin sounded like a priest as he tried to reassure Lucy.

"You know there are others?"

"Others? What do you mean?"

"My father has found two others who he claims have also been performing miracles for God. I'm to meet them soon. Perhaps you should meet them as well.

"I would love to meet them, that's if your father doesn't mind. I would imagine one of them is the man from California, Gabe, I believe his name is. I had planned on visiting him very soon anyway."

"I'm sure my father won't mind. Well, maybe he will, but I'll talk him into it," Lucy replied with a sly smile. "Any more questions, Mr. Bridges?"

"I do have one more about today. You said something right before your father came in. You said he called the angel 'Little Lucy'."

"I must have been thinking about my father and the Sandro Botticelli painting in the chapel. I remember I had been looking at the painting. I guess I look at it every time I visit. Since I was a little girl and my father showed me that painting, he has teased me about one of the angels looking like me. He calls the angel his Little Lucy. When I fainted, I must have been thinking about the Botticelli and my father's teasing."

"I'll have a look at the painting to see if it could possibly be as beautiful as you."

Lucy blushed at Kevin's comment.

"What an exquisite meal," Kevin continued.

"And the wine wasn't that bad either," Lucy replied.

"It is getting late and I do have to be at work early in the morning. Thank you for a most pleasant evening." Kevin's heart wasn't in his goodbye. He found Lucy to be wonderful and would have loved to have sat and talked with her for hours. "Oh, and tell your father I'm sorry he wasn't able to join us tonight. I've heard a lot about him and would have enjoyed talking with him." Kevin had some questions he wanted to ask Astan as well, but didn't want to tell Lucy. Not everything he'd heard about her father was good.

"I'm sure he would love to have joined us as well. I know he has some questions for you about something that happened in Spain. He even mentioned you have displayed some rather miraculous powers that got you hired by the Vatican. I'm a little curious about that too. Actually, I'm rather glad he had a previous engagement." Lucy gave a sly smile to Kevin.

Now it was Kevin's turn to blush.

"I will call you as soon as my father arranges whatever it is he has in mind with his miracle workers. Excuse me if I sound facetious, but I'm a little skeptical about this whole thing. I just don't understand what he has in mind, but I promise I'll call you. Now I do need to get to bed before my father gets home and keeps me up all night asking me questions about our dinner." Lucy also found Kevin to be a very charming and witty person. It wasn't often she had the opportunity to spend a relaxed dinner with someone like Kevin. She'd actually had a truly wonderful evening.

The two parted, each one thinking about the other. Kevin planned to head straight to Vatican City. He wanted to have a look at the Sandro Botticelli painting. He also needed to see if there had been any developments in finding the source of those vestments. He was troubled about what Astan had planned for these miracle workers. He knew Lucy was one of them. Kevin had been following the reports about her for over a year. He had interviewed dozens of witnesses and several people who claimed they'd been healed by Lucy. According to the medical records, some of them actually had recovered from their death bed. Kevin had no doubt Lucy was performing miracles. He was also sure this man from California, Gabe somebody, had to be another of Astan's converts. An odd choice of words Kevin thought, "Why did I refer to him as a convert of Astan?" Something didn't sound right about the word convert. He had already started his investigation into Gabe, but Kevin needed to find out about this third miracle worker. It was going to be a long night at Vatican City, but Kevin had no idea just how long.

CHAPTER TWELVE

This is the verdict: Light has come into the world, but men loved darkness instead of light because their deeds were evil. Everyone who does evil hates the light, and will not come into the light for fear that his deeds will be exposed. But whoever lives by the truth comes into the light, so that it may be seen plainly that what he has done has been done through God.

John 3:19

Baldassare Cossa stood in the backroom of the Medici family store. The back room was where the Medici family conducted their banking business. In the front the family sold wool. Baldassare was a pirate, a murderer, and a thief. He had many business dealings with the Medicis in the past, selling them treasures he had acquired on his many voyages. On this visit he brought them a proposition. A proposition that would require a substantial investment from the Medicis and, if successful, it could pay the Medicis a return in wealth far beyond what most people could imagine. He also brought with him a stranger, The Stranger.

Florence was the perfect target for the Stranger. It was a city of godly people. The Medicis were godly people. Godly people who had forgotten the word of God and could be easily swayed by the Stranger's temptations, and the Stranger did know how to tempt. Subtle temptations, reasonable temptations, logical temptations. The Stranger made them sound like they were the right thing to do, the godly thing to do. Only they weren't according to God's word. It was not the way it was written in the Bible. It was the Stranger's way, but it made perfect sense, and many people fell victim to his temptations. Such was the case with Giovanni Bicci de Medici. He had spent years building a fortune and a vast web of loyal allies, for Giovanni valued loyalty as much as profit. He gave much thought to the offer before him. It would require a large initial investment and several followup loans if it were to be done right. The temptation for power and wealth was too great and he loaned Baldassare the money necessary to bribe and extort his way to becoming a priest, then cardinal, and finally Pope. Pope John XXIII. And, as promised, when Baldassare became Pope, the Medicis became wealthy, the wealthiest family in Florence, and quite possibly, the wealthiest in all of Europe. They were now the bankers for the Vatican and the Church. Temptation would prevail through all of Giovanni's life as gonfalero of Florence. It would be his son Cosimo who took the family business to new heights. He would rule Florence for sixty years and, during his rule, temptation grew ever stronger and bolder.

Cosimo spent a fortune searching for lost secrets from the ancient world. The past was exciting and also somewhat dangerous to Cosimo. He made great sums of money in his dealings and in his network of banks throughout Europe. He became a great patron of artists, architects, and poets who captivated his sense of aesthetics. He used his great wealth to commission hundreds of works by these master artists. It was possibly not the wisest investment, but one that would pay dividends throughout the lives of the generations of Medicis to follow. Cosimo had started the great rebirth known as the Renaissance. Unbeknownst to Cosimo, he had been the instrument that allowed the Stranger to begin to accomplish his task. The temptation had been too great.

Lorenzo the Magnificent, il Magnifico, this is how Lorenzo de Piero de' Medici was known to the people of Florence. Lorenzo the Magnificent, the most remarkable man of the time. The son of Cosimo Medici, Lorenzo, a man of God, the true Renaissance man. Actually, he followed his father's lead as a patron of this enlightened thinking and became the man most responsible for the early Italian Renaissance. Leonardo da Vinci, Donatello, Sandro Botticelli, Angelo Poliziano, and Michelangelo Buonarotti were just some of the poets and artists whom Lorenzo discovered and supported. None did he support more than Sandro Botticelli. Lorenzo was able to provide Botticelli the freedom to paint nontraditional subjects, which at times bordered on heresy. Botticelli was caught up in the lifestyle of excitement Lorenzo was able to offer. As repayment for Lorenzo's patronage, Botticelli would often include the faces of the Medici family members in many of his paintings. It was the Medici commission for the painting of the Birth of Venus that brought Botticelli so much fame, and in the end, so much grief.

Poliziano was a stranger when he came to Florence in 1464, soon after the murder of his father. He attracted the attention of Lorenzo de Medici with his progressive thinking and he became a great influence on the Italian Renaissance. He made his ideas sound so logical and tempting, no matter how strange they may have been. Always done in the name of God, but not always, according to the word of God.

The Medici household was the hub of discussion where ideas and philosophies were debated. Angelo Poliziano, the poet and mystic, usually led these curious talks as they progressively became more outlandish and paganistic. Poliziano greatly influenced Lorenzo's thinking as well as that of Botticelli. Lorenzo became convinced that the mythical legends of the ancient Greeks and Romans, like the legend of Venus rising from the sea, was a divine message representing beauty coming into the world. He commissioned Botticelli to depict this scene in a painting for one of Lorenzo's villas. Botticelli, like Lorenzo, was a very godly man. He was conflicted with these progressive ideas that Poliziano expounded. Yet it was a temptation he could not resist and his art took a wilder and more bizarre direction. Florence became the center of the Renaissance and with it came more and more temptations, obsession with beauty, materialism, complacency, arrogance, ostentation, pretension, and self-worship. The vanities. A city on the threshold of Paganism. Exactly what the Stranger had planned.

***

It was late one autumn evening in 1489 when Girolamo Savonarola and three of The Weepers arrived in Florence at the San Marco monastery. For the past four years Savonarola had traveled throughout Italy preaching his apocalyptic ideas. Savonarola had an intense passion for the salvation of those who had fallen into the enemy's evil ways. He was willing to give his all to combat wickedness and restore holiness to all of Italy. Florence became the target of his zeal as he began his mesmerizing sermons attracting great crowds to hear his interpretations of Revelation and the Apocalypse. His sermons often lashed out at the morality of the governing families of Florentine and he singled out and harshly attacked Lorenzo the Magnificent for his excessive living and his paganistic life. Savonarola's popularity grew as did his political influence in Florence and all of Italy. Still, despite his fervor, he was a Brother of the Divine and, as such, had an important task that superseded his preaching. He and his fellow Weepers had the added responsibility of guarding the original Epistle of John and the copy of the original canon Achmed had prepared. It had been passed to them, having gone through several generations of the Brotherhood. The Brotherhood had originally been charged with giving it to the Church of Rome. Of course, that was when the Church of Rome was secure and able to protect such valuable documents. The Brothers had decided a secure Church was still some time in the future and had kept it under their protection.

The Stranger knew of the Brotherhood and knew they were protecting something of extreme value. He knew copies of some important documents had been made in the third century at a small monastery near Alexandria. He had been close to capturing the scribe who had made these copies and had followed him with plans on overtaking him and the monk who walked with him after dusk. When the Stranger moved in to attack, all he found was the head of the scribe lying next to the headless body. The monk was nowhere to be found. Enraged, he had used his powers to tempt men into destroying the small monastery. No documents were found. The Stranger had reached a dead end. Still, there were many spies in the world who owed their allegiance to the Stranger. He knew someday one of these spies would again put him close to the missing documents.

The Stranger's task became even more difficult when the Church ordered several controversial books in the original canon, the apocrypha, removed and destroyed. Before he could acquire a copy of these books, the Church had achieved its goal and wiped these books out of existence. The Stranger was angered that he had been so foolish for his stubbornness in avoiding the writings of his adversary. He retained hope that somewhere he would find the information he was seeking, and was indeed slowly finding these missing alleged apocryphal books. For now, he would be content with continuing the temptations that pervaded Florence while he looked for members of the Brotherhood of the Divine.

Savonarola was greatly troubled by the depravity he found in Florence. He prayed constantly to God for guidance. It was during one of his prayers that God revealed what the Brotherhood of the Divine should do with the canon and the epistle. Savonarola gave thanks as he began to prepare for the tasks that lay ahead.

Sandro Botticelli had long completed his frescos in the Sistine Chapel and returned to Florence, where he rejoined the patronage of il Magnifico. But it was with a distressed heart. Sandro, along with throngs of other Florentines, had attended one of the fiery sermons by Savonarola in the cathedral at San Marco. Savonarola preached of the Apocalypse and condemned the immoral life so many of the Florentines had fallen into. Sandro was greatly troubled by the message Savonarola so zealously expounded and went to Savonarola to seek redemption.

"Sandro Botticelli," Savonarola boomed when Sandro walked into his cell at the monastery. "God told me you would come. You are the answer to my prayers."

Sandro dropped to his knees, "Please help God forgive me for my transgressions."

"You were forgiven for your sins when Jesus died on the cross. God has sent you to me for a purpose, a purpose only you can fulfill. God has already been working through you when you painted the frescos at the chapel in Rome. He guided your hand as you painted the faces of the angels when you depicted the scenes from the Temptation of Christ. Now He has sent you to me so I can explain the next task He requires of you."

Botticelli was overcome by emotion. "I am here to serve my God. I will do whatever He requests."

"God spoke to me and said you were his servant. He needs you to prepare two paintings. Two special paintings, depicting a chapter in the Book of Revelation. It is of a Revelation that God forbid from being written in the canon."

Sandro shrunk back in horror as he realized what he was being asked to do.

Savonarola continued, "One painting shall be titled the 'Ascension of Satan'."

Botticelli gasped at what Savonarola just proclaimed.

"The second will be titled, 'The Condemnation of Satan'."

"I don't understand," Botticelli exclaimed but, as he waited for Savonarola to explain, a bright glow began to fill the small cell and Sandro felt a calmness he had never before experienced. Savonarola dropped to his knees to pray and Sandro quickly followed. No words were spoken, but a vision came into Botticelli's mind. The vision from God showing him exactly what God wanted him to paint. Even the faces of angels were clearly defined. Sandro thought back and remembered a similar vision had come to him when he was painting the frescos at the Sistine Chapel. It was all part of God's plan leading up to this moment.

A few minutes later, or perhaps it was just a few seconds later, the glow that had engulfed the room was gone, but the calmness remained. "Tell no one of God's commission. When you have completed both works, bring them to me and I will do with them what God has requested."

Sandro understood what God and what Savonarola now asked him to do. For the first time in years he felt relieved with a clear mind and a renewed soul.

CHAPTER THIRTEEN

Wherever there is a carcass, there the vultures will gather.

Matthew 24:28

It had been several days since the lookout had reported seeing any sign of the other two ships. Snow continued to fall forming a white barrier obstructing any possible view. It blanketed the deck and ice covered the masts. It was becoming increasingly difficult to navigate the waters, for the ice flows were growing thicker as the temperature continued to plunge. The hull of the ship was constantly battered by the ice and there was a growing fear among the crew that the hull could soon be breached. The cold was becoming intolerable and many in the crew were either too ill or too scared to work. Captain Richard Chancellor knew he could no longer try to find the two other ships that became separated when they were caught in a storm off the Lofotan Islands. The three ships had sailed on the eleventh of May, 1553, from Depthford, England, to explore the northern seas. It was the first expedition for the newly founded Company of Merchant Adventurers. Sir Hugh Willoughby commanded the expedition and was in charge of the three ships, though he lacked any navigational experience. Willoughby was to captain the Bona Esperanza and the Bona Confidentia. Chancellor's ship was the

Edward Bonaventure. After becoming separated, Willoughby's two ships sailed along the Scandinavian Coast until they became trapped in ice off the mouth of the Arzina River in the Russian Lapland. The crew was unprepared for such harsh cold weather and, after a few attempts to find help, Sir Willoughby and his crew froze to death. The following year Russian fisherman found the ships still trapped in an ice flow with the corpses of the crew frozen solid.

Chancellor and the Bonaventure were fortunate to have been separated from the two other ships. They were able to reach the White Sea and found a safe harbor at the Dvina River near the Archangel Michael Monastery. Chancellor sought refuge in the monastery for him and his men while the Sea and the river froze over for the winter. Ivan IV, or Ivan the Terrible as he was often called, heard Englishmen had arrived in Russia and invited them to Moscow in the Spring when the river became passable once again. A great trade relationship was about to be born. Until then, Chancellor would spend his time at the monastery, while his men slept on the ship in the harbor; that is, once they had acquired the food and clothing suitable to withstand the Russian winter. It was at the monastery one evening when Chancellor made a most remarkable discovery.

Like many evenings, Chancellor and the abbot would spend time discussing a variety of subjects from religion to trade between their two countries. This was usually done after dinner and evening prayers in the abbot's cell, and always with several glasses of kvas. Chancellor was fascinated by the beverage made from rye bread and yeast and had grown quite fond of the taste. The fact it was mildly alcoholic made it even more pleasant. One of the monks would always prepare and light a fire to keep the two companions warm during their oftentime lengthy discussions. The monk used scraps of birch bark paper to light the fire. Birch trees were abundant in all of Russia and the monks had learned to make an excellent paper from the bark. They used the bark for making copies of the Bible as well as for writing letters. The scraps of paper that were unusable for writing were used to start the fire. For the past several evenings, the paper used to start the fire was not the scrap birch bark, but sheets of old worn discolored birch bark with writings covering it. The monk had found it in one of the old cells below the monastery.

"What are those old papers?" Chancellor asked the abbot as the monk rolled up several sheets and placed them below the logs. "They appear to have something written on them."

The abbot picked up the piece of paper on top of the stack. "These are old style Cyrillic letters. This must be a very early copy of the canon. Probably a copy of one of the originals brought to the monastery and used for the Cyrillic translation that we now use for our worship. I doubt if there is any one here who can still even read these older Cyrillic letters."

"May I have these?" Chancellor asked. "I will trade you a copy of our Bible for them."

"That won't be necessary. This is nothing more than trash to us. As you can see, we use it to light our fires, besides no one here could read your new English Bible either."

"At least allow me to have my men cut some firewood and gather some kindling to replace the paper."

"That would be very kind of you," replied the abbot, as he handed the stack of papers to Chancellor.

Chancellor knew he had stumbled on what could possibly prove to be a very valuable document. Of course, he wouldn't know until he had experts back in England look it over, but this was the very thing Sebastian Cabot, the founder of the Company of Merchant Adventurers, had advised Chancellor to keep an eye out for. Since the Renaissance, wealthy adventurers had been scouring the world for just such documents and icons. The wealthy were happy to reward the finders of such items handsomely. The next day Chancellor stored the papers safely in his cabin aboard the ship. His only concern was how many of the papers were lost when the monk used them to light the fires. Not many he hoped.

* * *

Upon Chancellor's return to England the following year he was hailed as a great adventurer for having established trade with Ivan IV of Russia. His success had been so great that the Company of Merchant Adventurers changed their name to the Muscovy Company. Political conditions had shifted greatly in England since his departure in 1553. Edward VI had died, and Mary, Bloody Mary, had ascended to the throne and set about restoring Catholicism back to England, which meant executing just about any Protestant leader or church member she could find. Chancellor had taken the documents to Sebastian Cabot. Sebastian in turn brought in a close friend, a former Protestant church leader, who was doing his best to stay hidden from Bloody Mary. Before any decision was to be made as what to do with these papers, someone was going to have to translate them from the old Cyrillic so they would know just exactly what it was Chancellor had discovered. It was a simple matter for Cabot's friend to tell them it was indeed a very early copy of the canon. However, the papers were completely out of order and there were several pages he did not recognize as being part of the Bible.

"This is very odd indeed," Cabot's friend said. "It appears this copy of the canon was done before the Church ordered several of the original books of the Bible removed and all copies burned. I have never before seen many of these stories and epistles. Quite valuable, I would think, to the right person. What I find rather curious is that it contains these apocryphal books, yet this canon is organized into chapters. That happened several hundred years after the books were ordered removed from the canon. Someone evidently made this copy from a very early canon that somehow avoided the Church's edict to remove and destroy these apocrypha."

Chancellor and Cabot's eyes lit up as they thought of the fame and money such a find would bring them. Their happiness was soon abated by the translator's next comment.

"If I were you, I would seal these papers in a container to protect them from further destruction, hide them, and then forget about them," said Cabot's friend.

"What, what are you talking about?" Cabot challenged.

"I don't understand," added Chancellor. "Of course, I understand about preserving them, but why must we hide them?"

"Apparently you have forgotten who sits on the throne. Queen Mary. Bloody Mary." he said, with emphasis. "The Catholic Church ordered these writings removed and destroyed centuries ago. If you were to try to sell them now, it would be blasphemy, and your heads would surely end up in a basket behind the tower wall as have others in these Marian Persecutions."

"How true you speak," Cabot replied, "they are worthless to us."

"I would not say that," his friend replied. "Had you brought these papers to me two years ago when Edward ruled, these would have brought a king's ransom. Edward would have knighted you for such a find and rewarded you beyond your imagination."

"But that was Edward," Chancellor replied, "and like you said, Bloody Mary is now the Queen, and the executioner has been very busy."

"Yes, but how long will she rule? That is the question we must consider. When her reign ends, who is to say the Catholics will not once again be driven from England?"

"That could be years from now," said Cabot.

"This may be true, but what choices have you?" The translator replied. "Draw up a contract between the two of you and store the papers securely where the Queen cannot get to them. In time, if not you, then your children will find themselves incredibly wealthy. Until that time, tell no one of your find and forget about having it translated."

Cabot and Chancellor realized their friend was correct so they did as he suggested, hoping someday they would realize their dreams of wealth and fame.

* * *

Chancellor's hopes ended tragically later that year. On his next voyage to Moscow, his ship was caught in a violent storm off the coast of Scotland and became shipwrecked. Chancellor drowned in the wreck.

Sebastian Cabot was a bit more fortunate, but just a bit. In 1558 Bloody Mary died and Elizabeth I became Queen of England and began to repeal much of Mary's Catholic legislation. Immediately, Cabot retrieved the canon, which he now assumed was solely his property since Chancellor died, and presented it to Elizabeth. She was not as impressed by it as he had hoped, but she did promise Cabot a handsome reward and passed the documents on to the Royal Treasury.

Sebastian Cabot now could brag about his great discovery and he did so with much bravado to everyone he met in every tavern he entered. That is, he did so for the next two days until he died at the age of seventy-four leaving no heirs to collect the vast sum promised him by the Queen.

Evil can be found anywhere, on the darkened London streets, in the houses of commerce, in the homes of the poor and the wealthy, and even behind the palace walls. But nowhere more than in the numerous taverns scattered throughout the London area. One day after Cabot began his boasting in one of those taverns, a tall stranger arrived in London. The Stranger had many associates throughout the world who reported such stories to him. The Stranger knew this canon existed and had spent a lifetime, several lifetimes, in pursuit of it.

Cabot was easy to find. The Stranger had his men watching him, ever since his spies reported Cabot's claims.

"May I join you and buy you a brandy? I hear you have quite a story to tell," the Stranger said pleasantly to Cabot.

"Indeed, I do, friend," Cabot replied, happy to have found another person willing to listen to his story and, even more importantly, willing to buy him his next drink.

"Then you must tell it to me and don't leave out a single detail," replied the Stranger.

Cabot told the Stranger of the documents he had found and of the reward the Queen had promised. The Stranger was saddened Cabot had already turned the canon over to the Queen's Treasury, but knew that was but a minor inconvenience. Cabot described the canon as best he could recall from what his friend had told him so many years ago. It was exactly what the Stranger had been seeking.

"So where is it you found these papers?"

"On one of my many expeditions for the King of Spain."

"Precisely which expedition, and from whom did you receive these papers?" the Stranger demanded.

Cabot was taken aback by the Stranger's demand. "Does this man know I am lying?" thought Cabot. It wasn't Cabot at all who found the documents, but Chancellor. Cabot really couldn't remember where Chancellor had said he found the documents. Perhaps this Stranger is working for some long-lost heir of Chancellor. “I believe it was from a church, yes that’s right, a Catholic church. It was on one of my trips to Africa.”

The Stranger was dubious of Cabot’s response. His demeanor changed as he stared at Cabot as though he was looking right through him and into Cabot’s heart. Sebastian began to sweat profusely and his left arm began to twitch. “I’m telling you the truth,” Cabot gasped.

“Are you? Are you really?”

An unbearable pain seared Cabot’s heart as if the Stranger held it in his hand and slowly squeezed, ever so slowly tightening his grip. “I can’t remember, I really can’t remember.” Tears welled in Cabot’s eyes.

“Well, I’m sorry to hear that,” the Stranger replied, as he stood up from the table, “but not nearly as sorry as you are, I would guess.”

Cabot barely had enough strength left to turn his head as he watched the Stranger walk briskly out the door. A gurgling whistle, sounding like the last bit of air being squeezed from a bagpipe, escaped from Cabot’s throat as he took his last breath. No one in the tavern seemed to notice, or even care, as the blood trickled from Sebastian Cabot’s nose and mouth.

CHAPTER FOURTEEN

They will turn their ears away from the truth and turn aside to myths. But you, keep your head in all situations, endure hardship, do the work of an evangelist, discharge all the duties of your ministry.

2 Timothy 4:4

News of Mika'il's miraculous encounter with the Israeli soldiers spread quickly both in the West Bank and in Israel. The Israeli soldiers swore the Archangel Michael had appeared outside the house and stopped the bullets in midair, with his glistening sword protecting both them and the two Palestinian men they had tried to kill. Both soldiers vowed to never pick up their weapons again and requested to be relieved from military duty. They were sent to a psychiatric hospital for evaluation and would undergo hours of tests to see if they had suffered some sort of mental trauma or, perhaps, to determine if they were given some kind of a hallucinogenic drug that might explain their bizarre story and their peculiar behavior. Still, within days of the conflict, the supermarket tabloids in Israel and in the United States recounted the tale. The story required very little embellishment by the editors at the tabloids.

When Mika'il and his bodyguard, Ahmed, returned to Nablus, rumors of the miracle were already spreading throughout the city. The men in Mika'il's organization were very jubilant about the great victory over the Zionists. They had seen the news and heard of the destruction of the Israeli tank and of the almost total loss of the Israeli Commando unit. Several were bragging how Mika'il's plan had worked to perfection, though none of them really knew what Mika'il's plan was. Still, there was a deepening concern about these rumors being whispered about of how Mika'il allowed two of the Israeli soldiers to go free.

"Mika'il, we are glad you are safe, but we have heard fantastic stories about today," one of his men queried.

"Allah spoke to me today," Mika'il began. "Allah has shown me it is time for the violence to end. A new era is beginning, an era of peace."

"Surely you don't mean we are surrendering to the Zionists?"

"We are surrendering, but not to the Zionists. And the Zionists too will surrender, but not to us. We all are surrendering to the will of Allah, or for the Jews, to the will of their God. Allah has decided our battle is over."

"You speak nonsense, Mika'il," one of the men replied. "These Zionist's stole our land and killed our people. We must make them pay."

"Will killing them all be enough to avenge the deaths of our loved ones? Will killing them all be payment enough for the land they stole? You are seeking revenge, just as I have sought revenge. And for what? And for whom? Revenge is the right of Allah and Allah alone," Mika'il explained.

"We heard of this angel that saved you and the Israeli soldiers from the bullets and we think it is a fool's dream," the man responded tauntingly. "Prove to us Allah has chosen you as his prophet."

"I never said I was Allah's prophet. I only know what Allah revealed to me during my prayers and in the heat of the battle with the Israeli soldiers. One of his angels stopped the bullets in midair, saving me and Ahmed from certain death. It was no dream. It was Allah's wish. And I'm not angry with you for what you did," Mika'il added.

"What are you talking about?" the man replied.

"I know it was you who has been telling the Israeli soldiers of our plans. You were the only one who knew my men and I would be in the village. I told you we were going there to make bombs, knowing full well you would tell the Israelis and they would come. We went there to set a trap for the Israeli soldiers. I only regret the plan worked to perfection and so many of them died," Mika'il explained, as the other men in the room began to move away from the traitor.

The man knew there was no need to deny it. In a flash he pulled a pistol and shot several times towards Mika'il. The sparkles and flashes of blue and purple light were instantaneous, and as before, the bullets dropped harmlessly to the ground. Several of the men in the room pulled out knives to stab the traitor. Before Mika'il could order them to stop, seven fatal wounds had been inflicted to the traitor's torso. He lay dying on the floor begging for forgiveness. Blood poured out of the wounds.

"I'm sorry. I'm so sorry. Please forgive me, Mika'il."

"Forgiveness comes from Allah," Mika'il told the man as he knelt down next to him. "It is Allah you should ask for forgiveness. Will you pray with me for forgiveness?"

Mika'il took the man's hands in his own and began to pray. As he prayed a blue glow filled the room and all present witnessed a miracle. The wounds healed before their very eyes and the man began to regain his strength.

No longer were there any doubters among Mika'il's men. They had all now witnessed a true miracle.

"Allah truly is great to have performed such a miracle," one of the men began, "but why do you allow this man to live. Has he not gone against Islam and the teachings of Mohammed? If so, he must be put be death."

"It is Allah who has spared his life, not I. Perhaps we have been too quick to condemn others who do not agree with our religion. We have long been too intolerant and rigid in our interpretation of the Qur'an. Maybe a more moderate approach to our faith is necessary. I believe this is what Allah is trying to tell us. Why do we teach our children to hate the Jews and to extol jihad? We preach violence and death. We glorify martyrdom and preach of it almost from their birth. We teach the ideology of death to promote Palestinian nationalism. It must stop. We do not want our government to reward those families whose children become shaheeds. Abraham tells us 'this willful child sacrifice violates the fundamental tenets of morality and ethics. This can no longer be."

"Blasphemy!" the man shouted. "How can you speak in such a manner, Mika'il? Either you are a Muslim and follow Islam and the words of Mohammad or you are not. There is no place for moderation. There is no place for toleration. This man must die for he has helped our enemies. It is the law of our religion."

"Or is it how we as men have interpreted and twisted the words of our great prophet?" Mika'il responded. "A new beginning is upon us and now we must change if Islam and the world are to survive. You have all seen the miracles. Have you no doubt Allah is leading this change?"

Many in the room shook their heads in agreement with Mika'il. Indeed, they had seen the miracles as well as too much death and destruction over their lifetimes. Perhaps Allah was sending them a message through Mika'il. Perhaps it was time for a new beginning for Islam.

"Trickery!" the man spat at the feet of Mika'il. "You are no longer worthy to lead us in jihad. The Zionist god has corrupted your mind and your soul. It is he who allows you to trick us into believing Allah is performing miracles. I curse you and your family for eternity."

"It is no trick. Allah has performed these miracles and tells us it is time for change."

"I'll have no part of this sacrilege and any man who does is my enemy and the enemy of Islam. As a Muslim fighting this jihad, I am sworn to kill the enemies of Islam and that obligation I swear to Allah I will fulfill." The man stormed from the house. Several of the remaining men were unsure what to do. Should they follow or should they stay with Mika'il?

"You all must make your own decision of which path to follow. If you choose the path Allah has chosen for me, you are putting yourself at great risk. Allah has shown us the jihad founded in violence is over. We must follow this new path of moderation and compromise or Islam is doomed. All mankind will be doomed. I have no choice but to follow the will of Allah, but in the manner, he now directs me." Mika'il paused momentarily to allow them all to contemplate the decision before them. "You accused me of being a prophet. I did not choose such a responsibility, but it appears Allah has chosen for me. So henceforth I shall be Allah's prophet, spreading the word of Islam, but a more temperate and balanced Islam, an Islam willing to accept its place as part of a diverse religious world."

CHAPTER FIFTEEN

He replied, "The knowledge of the secrets of the kingdom of heaven has been given to you, but not to them. Whoever has will be given more, and he will have an abundance. Whoever does not have, even what he has will be taken from him.

Matthew 13:11-12

Sandro Botticelli was indeed an instrument of God. He was God's paintbrush. Savonarola told Sandro God had a commission for him and God himself came to Sandro as he sat in Savonarola's small cell. Two paintings. Two paintings representing two revelations that seemed to contradict each other. Two paintings that were the exact opposite of each other. Two paintings, both apocalyptic in subject, yet neither based on any revelation Sandro knew of. An impossible task, had it not been for the vision God shared with Botticelli. "The Ascension of Satan". Botticelli saw the setting, the image of Satan, the image of the Archangels surrounding Satan, the colors of the sky, the colors of the angel's wings, and he saw the faces, every detail of the faces. And it frightened him. Every minute detail of Satan's face came to Sandro. It shook the very core of his soul to see such a vision and to imagine such a revelation.

"How can this be true?" Botticelli asked of Savonarola. "This contradicts the very word of God. I just don't understand."

"It may be not all of God's wisdom is written as part of the Word. There are things you and I will never understand until God calls us to join Him," Savonarola explained. "I too have found what God asks of me sometimes difficult to understand. I never question his commands. I, like you Sandro, have been commanded by God to serve him in a way we may not understand, yet our faith requires us to obey."

"What do I tell my apprentices in my workshop? How do I explain it to them? And what about Lorenzo? How do I keep it from my patron?"

"The Medicis have long been too much of an influence on you Sandro. Evil resides in the house of the Medici. Lorenzo has led you down a heretical path towards paganism. Soon the hold the Medicis have on Florence will crumble and those who have taken up this life of paganism will be forced to repent. You must change your ways before it is too late. God has given you the opportunity to serve him once again. You must not fail in your task. It must remain secret. Do you understand?" Savonarola's voice was raised and his tone fiery as he lectured Botticelli.

"I understand. I do understand what God has asked. I will complete both paintings and bring them here to you. I will tell no one of my task." Sandro quietly left the cell under the stern gaze of Savonarola.

Botticelli decided to paint both paintings simultaneously. They would be on canvas of the exact same size. "The Condemnation of Satan" came to him in a vision just as clear and detailed as his first vision. The setting was different, as of course were the colors, but the vivid details of Satan's face were identical. The faces of the Archangels were also the same as in his first vision. Only this time the expressions were different. Much different! By painting both together, the anguish of painting the "Ascension of Satan" became easier to bear, for it allowed Sandro to turn and paint on the Condemnation canvas when the fear began to creep into his heart and evil threatened his soul. It took almost two months for Botticelli to complete the paintings working in secret late at night. He struggled with the details. His vision was so precise he wanted to reproduce it as true as humanly possible. Although, as Savonarola had told him, it was God who was doing the painting, Sandro was merely the instrument.

Botticelli delivered the paintings in late April of 1492, less than two weeks after the death of his patron Lorenzo Medici. Upon Lorenzo's death, and with Savonarola's warnings echoing in his ears, Sandro embraced Christianity with a newfound fervor. Savonarola had been partially correct in claiming the Medici Dynasty was doomed for Lorenzo's beliefs. The family did lose its power and standing in Florence after Lorenzo's death, but it was due to his son Piero's poor skills at running the family dynasty, not the heresy as Savonarola predicted.

Savonarola knew what was to be done with the two paintings. God had revealed this to him. The problem was the "Ascension of Satan" was to be taken to the Vatican. Savonarola was at odds with the Vatican and its present Pope. He was not happy at the path the church was taking and he called for reform. Yet God had told him what needed to be done, so Savonarola had one of the Weepers take the painting, along with the copy of the canon, to Rome. He gave it to a Brother of the Divine who had become part of the Vatican religious hierarchy. Before he did, he wrote a letter to be included with the canon and the painting. It described the painting and explained how it depicted parts of Revelation 10 which were purposely left out of the final draft of Revelation. It also contained a series of numbers which had no apparent meaning. The Brotherhood monk in turn would hide the letter with the canon copy and the painting. It was placed in the vault with the Vatican's most sacred and controversial religious icons. Few would see the frightening painting and none would see the canon and letter before it disappeared for generations.

The second painting by Botticelli, "The Condemnation of Satan", had a much different fate. On one of Savonarola's many pilgrimages throughout Italy, he had commissioned a glassblower on the island of Murano to create a special glass sheet. In fact, four identical glass sheets. Between two of these sheets of glass was placed the original epistle of John. It had been sealed in a clay tube for over a thousand years, but now was placed between the two sheets of glass and sealed to keep it from harm. Sealed between two other pieces of glass was another letter written by Savonarola. This letter was much different than the first one he had written that was sent to the Vatican along with the first painting. Several boards were cut to fit beneath the canvas of Botticelli's painting. An area was carved out of these boards and a smaller wooden box containing the glass-covered epistles were placed in this perfectly carved area. More boards were placed over the smaller box and sealed once again. The epistles were now safely hidden behind the canvas of Botticelli's "Condemnation of Satan". Savonarola ordered two of his Weepers to take the painting out of Italy and to the abbey for women at Port Royal, west of Paris. There it was to remain under the protection of the Brotherhood of the Divine until God revealed the next step in His perfect plan. Unfortunately, the two Weepers charged with taking the painting to France were robbed and killed by bandits before they even made it to Bologna. The painting was taken to Venice where it was sold to a Jewish trader. He in turn sold it to a Jew traveling to Germany, who in turn was robbed during the night by Roma, or gypsies, along his journey. They sold it to another German Jew who was at first reticent to buy it, knowing full well it had been stolen by the gypsies, but decided it would make a good present for his grandchildren. He bought the painting and hid it away in his cellar with some stolen jewelry which he also bought from the Rom, as they liked to call themselves. It stayed in the cellar for several decades until, true to his initial plan, the Jewish trader presented the painting to his grandson right before the octogenarian passed. He did warn his grandson it might be wise to keep knowledge of the painting secret just in case the original owner's family became aware of its existence. That warning was strictly adhered to for the next several generations of the family legacy.

* * *

The Stranger was not happy with the turn of events in Florence. It was he who had been by the side of several generations of the Medicis encouraging, planning, whispering, and above all tempting them. The Stranger was not happy Savonarola had come to Florence with his fiery apocalyptic rhetoric. He was even less happy when the common people began to shun these paganistic temptations that he had provided and nurtured. Soon, many began to repent, shunning these extravagances and temptations in order to live a simple and pious life. Even those who had been so close to the Medicis were beginning to turn away, all because of one man, Girolamo Savonarola.

The Stranger watched Savonarola. Not the Stranger personally, but many who held allegiance to him. And there were many. All watching where Savonarola went, who visited him and who attended his sermons. As more information came to the Stranger from his legions of spies, the more it appeared not only was Savonarola destroying all the Stranger had worked so hard to build, but Savonarola and his so-called Weepers seemed to be hiding something of great significance.

The paintings, the canon and the epistle had long since been sent to their new places of hiding. Some of the Stranger's spies reported how in the past few days several of Savonarola's Weepers went away on a distant journey to France with no plans of ever returning. Other Weepers made regular trips to Rome trying to ease the growing tension between the Pope and Savonarola. The Stranger, who had been so angry at Savonarola's crusade against the temptations, saw Savonarola's desire to reform the church as the perfect temptation to bring about his own demise. When the bonfires of the vanities began, it was the Stranger who fanned the flames of Savonarola's misguided fervor. It was the Stranger's legions who raced from building to building, door to door, ripping the paintings from the walls, tearing the whorish dresses off the women, grabbing the jewelry from the necks and wrists of the wealthy, all in the name of God, and all in the name of Savonarola. It was the Stranger who whispered words of temptation and defiance in the ear of Savonarola, making him believe he indeed had the power to change the church. When opposition to Savonarola began to grow in Florence, it was the Stranger who convinced him it was his zeal and self-sacrifice that would achieve the regeneration of religion. Thus, Savonarola remained disobedient to the Pope's proclamations. It was the Stranger who led the crowd in the attacks on the monastery at San Marcos to overthrow Savonarola. It was the Stranger who placed the noose around the neck of Savonarola when he was hanged on the 23rd of May in 1498. And it was the Stranger who burned Savonarola's lifeless body, and the bodies of Savonarola's Weepers, in the same type of bonfire and in the same square where Savonarola had burned the vanities of the Florentines.

But before the Stranger placed the noose over Savonarola's head, he had one final temptation to offer. Savonarola had been tortured and beaten for several days leading up to the choreographed spectacle of his execution. Despite the pain and agony, he maintained his faith in God. Now the Stranger was about to test that faith.

"You know who I am?" The Stranger asked, as he led Savonarola to where he would hang. Savonarola only looked without answering. This hangman was of no importance to Savonarola. But as he looked at the Stranger's face, he saw unspeakable evil, the Prince of Darkness, the fallen angel Lucifer himself, and he gasped in fear cowering backwards.

"So, you do recognize me."

Savonarola continued to stare.

"People say you are a fanatic, disobedient, a heretic," the Stranger said.

"I am a believer of God and place my faith in Him," Savonarola replied softly.

"I know you are faithful to your God. What you did for Florence was truly magnificent. Your ideas for the regeneration of the church are true to your beliefs and those beliefs are unquestionably right. But you are about to die. And with you dies all you have ever preached. All you have ever believed in. Do you want that to happen?"

Savonarola only looked at him with a pathetic bewilderment. "You are the anti-Christ, nothing you say is true."

"No, what I say is true and you know it. You are about to die, and with your death all you have ever believed and preached dies too."

"This cannot be. My God will never forsake me."

"Your God already has forsaken you. People think you are a heretic, a pagan, a purveyor of evil."

"No, that is not true."

"Your beliefs do not have to die with you. In fact, you really don't have to die either. I have the power to free you." The Stranger smiled at Savonarola. "Instead of hanging you, I can arrange to have you banished from Florence. You would be free. Then you could continue to preach your vision for revitalizing the church and restoring proper faith for millions of believers," the Stranger paused, "yes, I can do that."

He waited and watched as Savonarola considered what he had said.

"I can give you your freedom to continue spreading the word of your God. That's what you want, isn't it?" Of course, it was what Savonarola wanted. It was the perfect temptation. It made sense, it seemed reasonable, and it would save Savonarola's life. "All of this can be yours. There is only one thing I ask of you. What is the secret the Brotherhood of the Divine has protected for so many generations?"

Savonarola made no attempt to answer.

"I know of the painting." Savonarola's head lifted as the Stranger spoke. "So what Botticelli said is true. The painting is part of this secret so many have been willing to die to protect."

"Botticelli is a madman, a lunatic. He knows not what he is talking about."

"Does that mean Botticelli was a lunatic when he told me he threw his painting, 'The Ascension of Satan', into the bonfire of the vanities as he claims?"

"Tell me about this revelation, Savonarola. You are the expert on this apocalyptic scripture. What is this revelation about the ascension of Satan?"

"There is no such revelation. I told you Botticelli is a delusional madman."

"Where is this painting? I know it was not burned. My spies witnessed all that was thrown into the bonfire. Sandro did burn several of his paintings, but none depicted the revelation he spoke of, this so called 'Ascension of Satan'."

"It is in a sacred place, safely hidden away for eternity. You will never see it, never!"

"I am sorry you will not be around to witness my ascension. You have told me much, Girolamo Savonarola, more than you realize. But now you must die. And it will not be a quick death. I will make sure your rope stretches and fails to snap your neck, and as you suffocate during your struggle to breathe, I will remind you what a waste your life has been and how your God has deserted you. I will squeeze your heart until you beg me to take your soul and free you from the agony you are about to suffer."

Savonarola spat at the feet of the Stranger. The Stranger only laughed. As the rope stretched and tightened around Savonarola's neck and the monk writhed and twisted in suffocating pain, he thought he could see and feel the talons of the Stranger as he slowly squeezed Savonarola's heart, then yanked it from his body.

But it was God who collected Savonarola's soul.

CHAPTER SIXTEEN

I am poured out like water,
and all my bones are out of joint.
My heart has turned to wax;
it has melted away within me.

My strength is dried up like a potsherd,
and my tongue sticks to the roof of my mouth;
you lay me in the dust of death.

Psalm 22:24-15

The Swiss Guard had been on high alert since the strange happenings occurred with Lucy in the Sistine Chapel. The vestments found in the chapel had been taken to Kevin's office. A preliminary search of the museum and storage archives showed no such vestments were missing or, for that matter, even listed as part of the archived inventory. Even so, that didn't mean much since there were several rooms and vaults which contained treasures not listed on any inventory. Items the Vatican preferred no one knew even existed. Items locked away for centuries, items that could prove embarrassing to the Church. Items that could change the future of the Church. Items that could possibly change religion itself.

It was no more than a glimmer of a shadow that caught the guard's attention. Or possibly it was the slightest hint of a breeze in the stagnant air that filled the catacombs beneath Vatican City. Whichever it may have been, it did arouse suspicion.

"Did you see that?"

"See what?" the second guard replied. "There hasn't been anybody down here in years. You're imagining things."

The first guard continued to stare down the dimly lit corridor leading to one of the vault rooms. A large steel barred gate blocked their access to the corridor. "I know I saw something. We better check it out."

"Call and let them know what we're doing. You know the vault rooms are off limits. Tell them to send a supervisor down here with a key to that gate." A noise from the corridor startled the guards and they pulled their weapons.

They peered down the catacomb's corridor trying to see past the gate. A bird, a large black crow, hopped towards them and inbetween the bars of the gate. A sigh of relief escaped from both guards as they reholstered their weapons.

"How the hell did that bird get all the way down here?"

"Precisely!" A booming voice echoed from down the catacomb. Both guards again reached for their weapons. All they saw was a blur, as the talons of a large winged creature shot through the bars of the gate and deep into their chests, ripping out their hearts. It all happened so fast they saw their own beating hearts in the creature's talons as it screeched loudly, as though laughing at their deaths.

The Stranger was not happy at having to kill them. He knew now his time was limited. To find what he came for, he must search quickly before the guards' absence was noticed. He had just made a difficult task almost impossible.

In all the time he had spent at the Vatican, the Stranger had never been in this section of the catacombs. They were off limits to everybody, including the guards. Several vault rooms were located on both sides of the corridor. They were called vaults, but were actually large reinforced and somewhat airtight rooms with heavy wood and metal doors. Some still brandishing antiquated padlocks barring access to the rooms. No electronic locks had been fitted in this section of the catacombs, nor was there any videomonitoring of the area. Updates were planned two decades ago, but a deluge of lawsuits had siphoned the funds from the planned improvements. The locks on the doors proved to be no problem for the Stranger. The problem would be finding what he was looking for, because he really wasn't sure exactly what he was looking for. A proper search of the rooms would take hours. Hours he did not have. In each room there were crates and boxes filled with artifacts, documents, and art works. Some of the documents were extremely old and had been preserved in special sealed containers with regulated temperatures to protect them from decaying. That was what he found in the first room. The Stranger seethed with anger at not being able to analyze these documents, for he knew they held many secrets that could greatly benefit him in his battles to come. In the second room there were several locked crates and boxes, but none as large as what the Stranger was hoping to find. The third vault he entered held the kind of treasures he was now seeking. This room was temperature-controlled to protect the scores of paintings that were neatly placed in protective crates to keep them from damage. A list of all the paintings was on a clipboard hanging on the back of the vault door. There were two Sandro Botticelli paintings listed on the index sheet, but neither were what the Stranger was seeking. Time was running out. The Stranger realized he would have time to look in only one more vault before he needed to leave. But which vault? What he was seeking was meant to never be seen, or cataloged, or organized by some expert. The Stranger walked swiftly down the catacomb, passing several more vaults, all with newer locks securing the doors. As he reached the final door where the catacomb turned, he knew he had found the vault he was seeking. No new locks secured this door. The lock on this door was rusted solid, impossible to pick. It would have to be broken off. The lock shattered like glass in his steely grip. He discovered the hinges too were rusted solid. The Stranger buried his giant talons in the aging wood door and, with a mighty thrust of his leathery black wings, violently yanked the door, ripping the hinges from the wall. The noise reverberated loudly through the catacomb. The Stranger knew he must work fast. There was no electricity in this vault to power lights, only an ancient torch made of rags wrapped around a small tree limb. The Stranger lit the torch and the rags flamed brilliantly, as if they had been waiting for centuries just for this moment. There were several crates, documents and a variety of icons scattered around the room. The Stranger focused on finding the Botticelli painting that he knew had to be there. Against the back wall a dusty sheet covered several framed canvases. The Stranger hurried to the stack of paintings and threw back the sheet just as the fire alarm began to sound. Although this vault had no electricity, the catacomb outside had been retrofitted with smoke detectors. The flaming rags had produced more than enough smoke to trigger the alarm. Savagely, the Stranger rifled through the canvases, tossing them aside until he found the one he had been searching for: Sandro Botticelli's "The Ascension of Satan". It was perfect. Botticelli had painted an exact likeness of the Stranger and beside him stood the three archangels. A smile came to his face. It was exactly as he thought it would be. They all looked as they should. The Stranger was filled with glee even as the alarm continued to scream its warning.

It would be impossible for the Stranger to take the painting with him. Somehow, he had to make sure it was found and safely protected. With his giant talons he ripped and shredded the other canvases that lay alongside the Botticelli. He carefully placed the Botticelli against the door which he had ripped away from the vault. It needed to appear that whoever had broken into the vault had come for that specific painting. The alarm continued to wail. The Stranger could hear voices and the rustling of footsteps fast approaching. He smothered the flames of the torch with his wing and hurried down the catacomb away from the approaching guards. He had found proof of what he had always believed, but he knew it was not proof enough. For that, he would need to find the revelation itself, and the Stranger knew he would, for it was only a matter of time.

CHAPTER SEVENTEEN

It is the Lord's doing, and it is marvelous in our eyes.

Psalm 118:23

Elizabeth became queen when Bloody Mary's pregnancy turned out to be a large ovarian cyst. A cyst that led to Mary's failing health and to her eventual death but, even more significant, a cyst that also saved Elizabeth's very life.

Queen Mary was a tyrant whose primary goal upon taking reign was the reestablishment of Catholicism in England. She went about it with a vengeance, having over three hundred of England's most prominent citizens burned at the stake for heresy. Still, Bloody Mary met with much resistance and religious unrest dominated her reign. Her half-sister, Elizabeth, was the one threat to Mary's hold on England. She knew if she failed to produce an heir, Elizabeth would reign following Mary's death. That meant a return to Protestantism. Mary had Elizabeth brought to London and sentenced her to death. She was held pending her execution in the famed Tower of London. Whether it was a stroke of luck or a blessing from God, when Mary appeared to have become pregnant, Elizabeth was released and placed under house arrest back at her residence in Hatfield. No baby came of the pregnancy and

Mary fell ill and died, assuring Elizabeth's succession to the throne.

There was no shortage of suitors seeking to marry the Queen. And although she entertained several, managing to gain alliances and gather much wealth, she remained unmarried throughout her life, becoming known as the Virgin Queen. That by no means suggests she was not romantically involved. Two suitors in particular seemed to capture Elizabeth's heart more than any of the others. The first was Robert Dudley, the Earl of Leicester, who she loved so dearly when she was young. At that time, her life seemed so uncertain and she felt she could not commit to a relationship. When she became Queen, Dudley had already married, but he continued to be her favorite courtesan. There was one other.

Shortly after Elizabeth ascended to the throne, among the many suitors who fancied marrying the new Queen, came a stranger, the Stranger. A tall handsome and mysterious Muscovite Russian Duke named Alexis Belsky. Unlike many of her other suitors, Belsky was witty, charming, and extremely well educated and knowledgeable. Elizabeth, being considered extremely brilliant, enjoyed the company of Alexis, whom she felt was an intellectual equal.

They would spend hours together conversing in numerous languages, including Russian, which Elizabeth had learned very quickly from Alexis. He had become one of Elizabeth's most trusted confidants and advisors, as well as her lover. He was quick to advise her on how to deal with the radical Catholics and encouraged religious discussions as to the direction of the Church of England. It was Alexis who advised Elizabeth to declare herself the Virgin Queen, as the Protestant Church's equal to the Catholic Church's Virgin Mary. It was also Alexis who constantly indulged Elizabeth with sweets, which in later years would cause her teeth to rot and smell so badly she would have to keep a perfumed rag in her mouth in order not to offend guests.

It was during one of these many religious discussions that Alexis brought up the canon, the canon given to Elizabeth by Sebastian Cabot shortly before Cabot died. Alexis suggested they look at these transcriptions to see if there was anything in them that could possibly embarrass the Catholic Church. Elizabeth had no desire to inflame the religious fervor that was beginning to subside in England, but she did agree to allow Alexis to look at the papers.

There were several plots to assassinate Elizabeth throughout her reign. Her trusted aide, Sir Francis Walsingham, protected the Queen and saw to it these enemies were quickly dealt with. He was a master spy and an exacting assassin, who would go on to create Britain's illustrious secret service. He trusted no one and his sole allegiance was to the Queen and the country she reigned over. It was he who first grew suspicious of Alexis and began to question just exactly who this stranger was that claimed to be of royal Russian lineage truly. He tried to warn the Queen to be careful as to what she shared with this Russian Duke, but his words fell on deaf ears. The Queen was enchanted by her Russian lover and it would take more than words to convince her that Alexis was not who he claimed to be.

Although she didn't believe all Sir Francis told her about Alexis, Elizabeth knew better than to ignore his advice.

"My Queen," Sir Francis spoke, "you have asked my opinion as to if you should allow the Duke access to the documents given you by Cabot. I in truth must tell you I would be wary to do so. I have sent a spy to Russia to see what I can find out about the family of this Muscovite Duke. He should return any day now with his report. Perhaps then I shall think kindlier of Alexis if all he claims is true."

"Alexis tells me these documents are of great value and only he can determine just how valuable they may be," the Queen replied, in the Duke's defense.

"I dare say there are others in your realm, perhaps even in your court, that would have the same ability, and with whom I would feel safer entrusting these papers. Duke Alexis is a very shrewd man with a very clever tongue. He seems to easily sway people to achieve his desires. I have been troubled by his relentless pursuit to obtain these papers for quite some time."

"He indeed is an easy man to grow fond of," Elizabeth said, smiling coyly.

Sir Francis was one of the few people Elizabeth could joke with regarding her many dalliances in such an open manner. He also knew when it was time to give in to the Queen's desires. "Perhaps you should allow him only to look at a few of the pages of the transcript, my Queen."

"A very wise idea, Sir Francis." The Queen wrote the order on a sheet of paper, signed it, and handed it to Sir Francis. "See to it the arrangements are made at once."

"Yes, my Queen." Sir Francis read the Queen's order and smiled. She had indeed been listening. Alexis would only be given three random pages of the document to analyze, but Sir Francis knew that if the reports from Russia were favorable, the Queen would soon relinquish the entire transcription to Alexis.

* * *

Alexis had been impatiently awaiting the copy of the canon to be delivered. He knew the Queen could not turn down his request to see the documents. When a knock finally came at the door, Alexis grinned.

"By order of the Queen," the court courier said, as he handed the loose papers to Alexis.

"What is the meaning of this? Where are the rest of the papers?"

“It is as the Queen commanded,” the man said, handing the signed order to Alexis.

“This is the work of Sir Francis.” Alexis was gravely disappointed. He knew Sir Francis did not trust him and had heard from his spies that Sir Francis had sent men to Russia to inquire into Alexis’ lineage. Very soon those spies would return with news that there was no such person as Duke Alexis Belsky. At least the Stranger knew from where Sebastian Cabot had obtained the copy of the canon. The three pages were written on birch bark paper. They undoubtedly had to come from Russia, and probably from a monastery along the White Sea or the Dvina River. That was the route the ships from Cabot’s trading company used to sail to Moscow.

Sometimes even the Stranger is blessed with luck. Such was the case with the three random birch bark pages. One of the pages was from the Book of John describing the miracle of Jesus turning five loaves of barley bread into enough loaves to feed thousands. The second page was from Psalms, but it was the third that turned out to be exactly what the Stranger had been looking for. This page came from the Book of Enoch, one of the Old Testament books the Church had ordered removed and destroyed. The Stranger had searched for years for this lost book and, now in his hand he held some of the gospel he had so coveted. With delight he absorbed every single word Enoch had written. When he finished, he was like a ravenous dog desiring more than the mere tidbit the Queen had thrown him.

"Curse you, Sir Francis. Curse you, your children, and your children's children!" Alexis was beside himself with rage. He desperately needed to see the rest of the canon and had begun plotting to achieve that goal when, again, someone knocked on his door.

"Master, you must flee at once. The guards are on their way to arrest you."

The rage inside the Stranger exploded, as he threw open the door and slashed the messenger's throat with one of his giant talons. The messenger stumbled forward, collapsing on the floor where the blood pulsated out of his torn neck until his body was bled dry. The Stranger could hear horses approaching as he crossed the room, stepping in the pooled blood that now covered the floor. He grabbed the one page from the Book of Enoch, threw open the window and leaped out. His room was on the third floor and his body hurtled towards the ground right in front of the guards' horses. The astonished guards stared in amazement as, a split second before smashing into the ground, giant leathery black wings sprung from the back of Alexis and pounded the air stopping him just inches from impact. In an instant the devilish apparition lifted into the sky, startling the horses and causing the men to tumble backwards to the ground.

"Tell Sir Francis he has not heard the last from me," the creature screeched as it flew off. The guards remained cowering on the ground, afraid to move until they were sure it was gone.

When they entered the house, they found the body of the messenger and the bloody talon tracks of the creature. “At least we have some proof of what we saw. Sir Francis cannot accuse us of being drunk and concocting this story to cover our failure in not arresting the Duke.” When they told the story to Sir Francis, his first thoughts were that his men had been drinking. Not until he went to the Duke’s residence and saw the bloody prints for himself, did he believe their story. He called for the cardinal of the Church to come see the tracks and hear the story. The cardinal in turn had artists draw pictures of the prints and place paper over the bloody prints to make transfer copies to show the actual size. Some of these were stored at the Museum in London for further study. Elizabeth had of course banned Catholicism in England, but upon hearing the report from Sir Francis about what had occurred, she had some of the drawings and prints sent to the church leaders in Rome to forewarn them of possible future encounters.

The Stranger was by no means giving up his quest to obtain the rest of the canon. Like an addict, he had tasted the pleasures the transcription contained and now craved them more than ever. He had to have more. No longer would a simple rouse suffice to fool the Queen and her trusted advisor Sir Francis. It would now take more to gain possession of the documents he so dearly desired. Much more!

CHAPTER EIGHTEEN

Finally, a spirit came forward, stood before the LORD and said, "I will entice him."

"By what means?" the LORD asked.

"I will go out and be a lying spirit in the mouths of all his prophets," the said.

"You will succeed in enticing him," said the LORD. "Go and do it."

1 Kings 22:20-22

It took a couple of minutes for the security outside of the mansion to clear the people away from the gate so Kevin could get his car out. Since he had arrived for dinner at least two dozen more people had joined the vigil.

"This is unbelievable," Kevin said. He drove about a block down the street and pulled to the side of the road. He needed to talk to some of these people as part of his research concerning the miracles Lucy was said to have performed. As he was looking for a pen and notepad, the gate to the mansion opened and a red Enzo-Ferrari raced out through the crowd and past his car. He had been leaning over looking for a pen when the Ferrari rocketed past with Lucy at the wheel.

"So much for getting a good night's sleep," Kevin said, remembering what Lucy had told him. Kevin started his car planning to follow Lucy, but by the time he got the car in gear and back on the road, the Ferrari was nowhere to be seen. The crowd around the mansion gate must have realized it was Lucy behind the wheel of the Ferrari, for several of them began to wander away. Others chose to continue their vigil, hoping and praying a miracle would yet come their way that night.

Kevin tried to find which way the Ferrari had gone, but soon gave up and headed back to his office at Vatican City. All was quiet when he returned to the Vatican. Security had been tightened since the episode earlier that day and the presence of several extra guards was quite evident. Kevin had requested the extra precautions because of the man's voice which the Swiss guards were said to have heard in the chapel along with Lucy's voice. The cardinal's vestments were also quite troubling to Kevin.

Kevin spent a good forty-five minutes going over the incident reports. He also reviewed videos covering all possible access routes to and from the Sistine Chapel. The videos of course showed Lucy going in and the Swiss Guards bringing her out. It was easy to see Lucy wasn't carrying the vestments into the chapel when she entered, which meant they had to have already been there. But if that was true, why hadn't the guards found the vestments when they searched the chapel after closing? Kevin watched the video that showed the guards entering the chapel after closing and then exiting five minutes later. As

Kevin again watched the recording showing the hallway outside the chapel, he noticed a shadow that he had failed to see the first time. It seemed to be the shadow of the door into the chapel being opened, yet no one went in, and no one came out. "Lucy may have opened the door to leave and then changed her mind," Kevin said to himself. Kevin had a bad habit of talking things over with himself out loud. It was something many people found to be a little peculiar, but it did help him focus on, and solve, many a problem.

Kevin headed to the Sistine Chapel to have a look at the door which created the shadow in the video. He had to see for himself if there was any possible way to enter the chapel through that door without being seen by the camera. As he walked towards the chapel, a strobe light began to flash. Somewhere a fire alarm had been triggered. The audio warning would remain localized to the affected area until security teams determined if a general alarm needed to be sounded. Kevin was instantly on his radio.

"This is Bridges, what's the status of that alarm?"

"A smoke detector in the vault catacombs. We have two men in the area, but they're not responding," the duty officer reported.

When Kevin heard the guards weren't responding, he took off running towards the area of the alarm. "I have two fire teams heading there from different directions, only one alarm was triggered, so it can't be too bad."

"Is there a fire? I repeat, have you found the fire?" Kevin asked.

"Negative, there is no fire, just a little smoke," one of the teams reported. "Whoa. Look at that door. It looks like it was blown off."

"Or ripped off."

"Repeat again," this is Bridges.

"This door. It looks like something..."

"They're dead!" a voice screamed over the walkie-talkie. "They're both dead. There's blood everywhere. Somebody killed them." Kevin didn't need to hear that message repeated again.

"We also have what looks like a blood trail here," the first team reported.

"Both teams pull back immediately. Wait for armed backup at your entrance points," Kevin ordered.

Kevin made it to the stairway leading to the room where the two guards' bodies were found. Two armed Swiss Guards arrived seconds later.

"I want everybody to stay alert. Whoever did this may still be down in the catacombs," the operations director instructed the teams.

"Are you sure they're both dead?" Kevin asked the two firemen.

"I'm positive. It looked like something tried to rip them in two. There was blood everywhere."

"Okay, let's head in. Watch out for each other and be aware of sounds and movements," Kevin instructed.

The team headed down the stairs and stopped before entering the door to listen. They heard a strange pecking sound and what sounded like scratching.

"On three we go in." Kevin signaled his team counting down with his fingers.

The team rushed through the door and into the room, startling several black crows picking at the mutilated bodies. One of Kevin's men puked when he saw the condition of the bodies. The birds flew through the openings in the gate and down the catacombs.

"Let's have no more of that and watch where you step," Kevin ordered his team. "I don't want anything disturbed." Kevin could hear the second team working its way up the catacomb shouting "clear" as they checked each vault. "Team two, see where those birds go that are headed your way and watch where you walk. I can see a blood trail and some kind of bloody tracks on the other side of the gate heading your way. Try not to disturb them."

The birds flew past the second team then shot upward through a narrow passage that weaved towards the outside walls of Vatican City. This vent had been designed to allow fresh air to enter the catacombs, but should have had a secure grate mortared in place at ground level to keep animals from entering the catacombs.

Kevin could see that the hearts of both the guards had been ripped from their chests. He could also see both of the hearts lying on the other side of the gate.

"Get this gate open, but be very careful. I don't want anything disturbed, but I do need to see those tracks and that door," Kevin told one of his men.

"Three of the vaults have been unlocked, but seem secure," the second team leader reported. "A fourth appears to have been ransacked with several paintings destroyed. The door looks like it was ripped right out of the wall."

"This must be the torch that set off the smoke detector," another team member reported, "and look there next to the broken door, it looks like one of the paintings from the vault, but this one isn't ripped up."

"Nobody touches anything. I repeat do not touch anything. Wait for me before you enter the vault, someone could still be inside." Kevin and the second team searched and secured the room leading to the vaults and the rest of the catacomb area. "Get a forensics team down here immediately," Kevin told the security director. "We'll need lights and generators. I want all teams to secure the perimeter, but stay out of that vault room and the catacomb until forensics finishes up."

The gate had been opened, but Kevin remained to examine the bodies and the crime scene. Most of the blood that had run down a slight incline had pooled on the other side of the gate. All around the bodies were bloody prints that the crows had left as they pecked at the bodies. The chests of the two men had been ripped open as if by the claws of a giant beast. Kevin headed through the gate struggling to avoid slipping in the blood. He had been right to move his men to the perimeter for, as he suspected, the prints that led away from the bloody murder scene would have filled most men with a fear greater than what they could ever have imagined. Identical to the talon prints left by the crows were a set of talons prints almost fifty times greater in size. Kevin had seen such prints before, but only in artworks and photos from some of the classified Vatican files. It was as if his worst nightmare was coming true. As he followed the prints down the corridor, he could see where the creature had stopped and opened the vaults. The prints grew fainter the further Kevin walked.

When he reached the looted vault, Kevin immediately went to the painting leaning against the door. Picking up the painting, he could see the deep gashes in the thick wooden door which he knew were made by the same beast that had sunk its talons into the chests of the two guards. Kevin turned to look at the painting which had been left so evidently in the corridor. He was more relieved than shocked to see it was a painting by Sandro Botticelli. Had it not been a Botticelli, Kevin would have been concerned, for the events of the previous day left no other possibility, at least in his mind.

The painting was in good physical condition, having no tears, but was covered with centuries of grime. There was no doubt about the subject of the picture. Satan seemed to be ascending to a throne, wearing a crown of gold and attended to by three angels. In the background were battle scenes depicting massive devastation, pain, and anguish.

The catacomb was quickly filling with people. “I want all nonessential personnel out of the area. Let’s set up a perimeter and let the forensics team see what they can discover.” Kevin already knew what had done this, but it was not the kind of thing you spoke of. There would be no fingerprints and no DNA to link anyone to the murders, only a lot of questions with no logical explanations.

“I need that painting in my office as soon as you are finished with it,” Kevin told one of the crime scene investigators. “And get lots of photos of those bloody prints.”

Kevin went back to his office feeling exhausted. He would have to brief the head of Vatican City security first thing in the morning along with the bishop in charge of the Doctrinal Office. That was always a difficult task, for the security chief had trouble believing just how powerful Satan was. Kevin had realized this when he reported on the miracles he investigated. The chief was a devout Catholic, but even Kevin could understand how any sane person would have doubts about what really happened in the catacombs. The Bishop had a better understanding of just how powerful Satan was and was more receptive to the stories that bordered on the supernatural. He was even building quite a following among Catholics by stressing the evils that seemed to be tearing the world apart and how the church should focus more on bringing the world together.

Kevin sat down on the couch and shut his eyes for just a moment. That moment of rest turned into almost three hours and would have probably lasted longer had a knocking on his office door not startled Kevin awake.

"Come in."

"Here's the painting you wanted. The only fresh prints we found on it were yours. Kind of funny though, there were several smudge marks where someone else had picked it up. We thought they must have been wearing gloves. We can usually tell what kind of gloves they were wearing, but we just couldn't figure it out in this case. It sure has us stumped."

"Did your team notice anything else out of the ordinary?"

"Are you kidding?" the investigator replied, dumbfounded. "Everything was out of the ordinary. It's going to be one tough report to write up. I'm sure glad I'm not the lead on this one. I wouldn't know how to explain even half of what I saw."

"Just make sure I get that report as soon as you have it."

"Oh, I almost forgot. You have to sign for the painting. I was told it's worth a fortune. Also, the museum curator told me to tell you that an art restorer and historian would be coming this morning to clean up the painting just a bit. He also said, and I quote, 'whatever you do, don't try to clean any of that dirt off yourself. Wait for the expert.' He wasn't really happy that the painting was coming to you, but I guess someone higher up okayed it."

Kevin signed the paper, then lifted the painting up onto the back of the couch leaning it against the wall. He stood back to take his first clear view of the painting in its entire magnitude. Earlier he had used his flashlight to identify it as a Botticelli and to scan sections of the painting. Now as he stood before it, even as dirty and clouded as it was, the painting was awe-inspiring...and disturbing. Kevin understood why the church had kept it hidden. Such a scene would be difficult to explain to anyone. The subject of Botticelli's work, like Michelangelo's was taken from scriptures and verses in the Bible. Kevin knew the Bible and even the apocryphal books extremely well, and in none of them was there a reference to the ascension of Satan with the angels gathered around him. The dirt on the canvas hid the facial features of Satan and of the angels. Kevin pulled a Kleenex out of the box on his desk to wipe away some of the loose dirt covering those faces.

"Don't even think about it," a voice boomed, as a small bespectacled man ran into the room and dramatically placed his body between the painting and Kevin.

“I’ve just come from the vault where possibly five hundred million dollars worth of paintings were tragically destroyed. That will not happen to this one,” he said sternly, glaring at Kevin.

“I was just going to wipe a little dust away.” The man continued to glare. “Okay, okay, no problem, I’m sorry.”

“You very well should be,” replied the man, sounding a bit affected.

“I presume you are the art expert I was told was coming by.”

“I am indeed. My name is Mykos, Mykos Zorko,” he said with a flamboyant wave of his hand.

“Well, it’s nice to meet you, Mykos. Now what can you tell me about this painting?”

“Other than it’s a Sandro Botticelli, absolutely nothing, at least not yet. Neither this painting, nor any of the other items in the vault, were even catalogued as being in the archives. There is no record of any of it. It’s amazing, truly amazing.”

“At least no records you have access to.” Now it was Kevin’s turn to grin.

“I must take this painting and get it into a controlled environment before any more damage occurs,” Mykos told Kevin. “Give me a few weeks to work on it and I will tell you all there is to know about this painting. It is a brilliant work and actually in fairly good condition, considering what it has gone through. A rather peculiar, one could even say bizarre, subject matter, wouldn't you agree?"

"Indeed, I would."

"Botticelli tended to be a bit bizarre at times. This will be a real challenge. The art world will be absolutely stunned when they hear of this find."

"I'm afraid they won't be hearing about it. At least not for a while," Kevin replied, sternly. "There was a reason this and the other items were hidden away in that vault and, until I know the reason, you're to tell no one about this. Do you understand? No one!"

"I understand, you don't need to shout," Mykos whimpered, as if Kevin had hurt his feelings.

"I want you to call me as soon as you get the first layer of grime off of the painting. I want to see some of the detail in the faces of those angels and of Satan."

"I promise, I promise," the historian replied, pulling on white gloves to pick up the painting. "You know, if you're so interested in Botticelli's faces, you should go look at the frescos that he painted in the Sistine Chapel. He tended to use the faces of his patrons in most of his works. I do remember reading somewhere how the faces he painted in the chapel came about due to a vision he claimed to have had. I'll see if I can find the article if you're interested."

"I would appreciate that," Kevin replied. "Remember to call me as soon as you get that layer of dust cleared away."

Kevin had about a half an hour until he was due to brief the Bishop. He hoped to find out a little history as to why those items, especially the Botticelli, were locked away. Kevin wondered just what else he might find of interest in the vault, which wasn't listed anywhere. And he still had the episode involving Lucy in the chapel yesterday to deal with. He wondered if the two incidents were somehow connected. Then he remembered seeing Lucy race by him last night after dinner. "What was it the guard had said he heard a man say?" Kevin asked himself. "Something about my Little Lucy." He definitely needed to have a look at the Botticelli that seemed to be at the center of both these events.

He gathered some pictures from his file, along with a few of the pictures from last night's murder scene, and put them in a folder. Kevin had to hurry if he was going to have a look at the painting before his scheduled meeting. He also wanted to get there before the chapel opened to the public for the day. There had been talk about closing down all public access and tours because of the murders, but it was decided such a move would illicit too many questions which no one was prepared to answer.

On his way to the Sistine Chapel, Kevin realized he had no idea where the Botticelli paintings were located among the hundreds of frescos lining the walls and ceiling of the chapel. Actually, he did know it couldn't be on the ceiling because Michelangelo had of course painted that. Kevin remembered hearing Michelangelo was none too happy about having to paint the ceiling. Michelangelo viewed it as a punishment, of sorts, by the church for his connections to the Medicis.

Kevin was overwhelmed as he stared at the frescos covering the walls of the chapel. He had no idea where to even start looking for Botticelli's contribution to the vast display of artwork before him. Kevin remembered the vestments had been found lying in the North end of the chapel with Lucy's head resting upon them. That would be where he would start looking. The door to the chapel opened and one of the chapel docents came in to prepare for the public viewing, which was about to begin. The docent was startled to see Kevin, but saw he did have his identification badge attached to his jacket.

"Hello," Kevin said politely, "maybe you could help me find something."

The docent looked down at Kevin's badge before answering. "Mr. Kevin Bridges, from security, whoa, your badge says you've got clearance to go anywhere in Vatican City. You must be pretty important. What can I help you with?"

"I'm looking for the Sandro Botticelli frescos."

"Right above your head. It's called 'Scenes from the Life of Christ'. You can see several of the temptations of Christ pictured as well as the 'Purification of the Leper'. Probably the highlight of the fresco is the upper right-hand corner."

Kevin looked to where the docent was pointing and smiled.

"Little Lucy."

CHAPTER NINETEEN

"...she has commanded the books containing manifest heresy should be distributed throughout the whole kingdom... we are necessarily compelled to take up against her the weapons of justice... we declare the aforesaid Elizabeth to be a heretic and an abettor of heretics, and we declare her, together with her supporters... to have incurred the sentence of excommunication and to be cut off from the unity of the body of Christ."

Regnans in Excelsis by Pope Pius V 1570

Having been forced to leave England so suddenly without the copy of the canon put the Stranger in a foul and belligerent mood. He did have one important page of the birch bark copy of the canon, but he wanted possession of the entire copy. Trickery would no longer suffice to accomplish that goal. The Queen and her trusted protector, Sir Francis Walsingham, would be cautious and wary of anyone seeking to see the canon. The solution to the Stranger was obvious. The Queen and her protector would have to be overthrown, murdered, or defeated in battle. All three, if possible.

The Stranger returned to Italy where his temptation of the Medici family had been so successful. The Renaissance was now blossoming or, more aptly, festering into a complete breakdown of the morality of the Catholic Church. The proliferation of Indulgences, the collapse of clerical celibacy and of monastic discipline, and the overall corruption of the leadership of the church had brought it to the brink. Yes, the Stranger's temptations had worked well.

Demands for reformation were being heard throughout Europe and the Church was quick to react to these demands. The Inquisition had been going on for over one hundred years, torturing and killing those who were declared heretics. It reached a whole new level of brutality in response to the extensive apostasy pervading the Catholic empire. The Stranger played no small part in this madness. He was busy fanning the flames of discontent and stoking the fires of retribution throughout Germany, Switzerland, England, and Spain. Godly men called for reformation of the Catholic Church, as claims of heresy, from other godly men, came in response. The Stranger made sure of that.

* * *

Grande y Felicisima Armada, the large and most fortunate fleet, was Spain's answer to the series of England's aggressions both physical and spiritual against Spain and the Catholic Church. Or as England ironically referred to it, La Armada Invencible. The Pope had excommunicated Queen Elizabeth, calling her a heretic and authorizing her overthrow. Several plots by prominent Catholics to murder the Queen failed miserably and led to many beheadings. One of the most prominent executions was of Mary Stuart, "Queen of Scotts". Elizabeth did not want to put Mary to death, even though she was a devout and outspoken Catholic. Elizabeth avoided signing the death warrant for several years, despite the advice of her closest advisors, but finally had to acquiesce when the danger to her monarchy became too great. She knew in doing so she would put all of England at risk from the powerful Spanish empire of King Philip II. Philip was a devout Catholic and his greatest desire was to return England to what he called the true church. He wanted Catholicism returned as the sole form of worship in England. To do this meant the removal of Queen Elizabeth, exactly what the Stranger had in mind.

Privateering and piracy had also become a major concern of King Philip. English pirates like Sir Francis Drake were attacking the Spanish Galleon treasure ships coming from the colonies and disrupting the trade in the Caribbean with impunity. All of this with the blessing of Queen Elizabeth.

Not only did the Stranger convince the Pope to excommunicate Queen Elizabeth, he was able to convince the Pope to provide papal blessing and agree to financial support of the invasion of England by King Philip II and his Spanish Armada. The Pope promised a million gold crowns to help with the expense of the invasion, but only once it was successfully completed. The Pope may have been easily tempted and persuaded by the Stranger, but he was no fool when it came to protecting the assets of the Catholic Church, assets he considered his own. The Stranger had no doubt that King Philip II would quickly dispense with the English navy and overthrow and execute the heretic Queen and her loyal supporters.

The armada set sail on May 28, 1588, from Lisbon with the plan to escort an invading army across the English Channel from Parma. One hundred and fifty ships and thirty thousand men comprised the fleet's invasion force. It took two full days for all of the ships to leave the harbor. Almost immediately the armada ran into trouble when a fierce storm scattered the ships off the northern coast of Spain, forcing the armada to regroup, postponing the voyage until July. King Philip II was very displeased, as was the Stranger. Once the armada continued toward the battle, things grew even grimmer for King Philip's fleet. There were several minor skirmishes as the fleet moved through the English Channel, with minor losses for both the English and the Spanish. Sir Francis Drake broke from the English fleet just long enough to capture a Spanish Galleon filled with the funds to pay the Spanish Army in the Low Countries, proving Drake's prowess as a pirate, and his guiding principle to suspend his allegiance to the English fleet if an easy profit were to present itself. The Stranger's temptations knew no allegiance even though his desire was for a decisive victory for King Philip ii.

The Spanish were not prepared for this new type of naval battle that the English were willing to fight. The Spanish warships would come in close, fire a broadside, and then attempt to storm the English ship for hand-to-hand combat, overwhelming the English with their greater number of men. The English, on the other hand, had prepared their ships with movable cannons and taught their men to quickly reload, allowing them to exact substantial damage to the Spanish ships as the Spanish tried to maneuver. It did not take the Spanish fleet long to realize it would be wiser to flee than to fight. What they failed to realize was this new method of fighting required much ammunition for the English, something they did not have. The Spanish continued to flee, chased by the bluffing English fleet now void of ammunition.

The Spanish invasion plan had been foiled and the armada sailed north around Scotland and Ireland as they headed back to Spain. The Stranger was very disappointed and decided he would take a greater part in the battle hoping to convince the Spanish to regroup and once again attack. The English refitted their ships and waited for weeks for the Spanish to attack from the North Sea. While they waited the Stranger tried to turn the tide. The English had suffered few losses of men in the battles and no ships were sunk. Now as they waited, the Stranger worked his evilness and spread typhus and dysentery among the English sailors and troops, killing close to ten thousand of the men. Then he instigated demoralizing disputes among the men, based on England's inability to pay the troops for months due to the financial shortcomings in the government.

As the Spanish ships rounded the coast of Ireland, they were not prepared for the colder and harsher conditions. The fleet was hit by a tremendous hurricane. No hurricane had ever been seen this far north before and such an occurrence would probably not occur for hundreds of years in the future. All believed it had to have been an act of God. Several ships were sunk and over two dozen driven ashore on the coast of Ireland. Over five thousand men died from drowning and starvation or were executed by the English who were in power at the time in Ireland. More died, than had died in the naval combat with the English fleet. When the armada limped back to harbor in September, only sixty-seven ships and ten thousand men had survived. Many of them, however, would soon die from diseases and injuries suffered during the fateful voyage.

The English had defeated the Spanish Armada with God's help. Queen Elizabeth and all of England viewed the battle as proof God wanted England to remain a Protestant country. The victory gave heart to all those throughout Europe calling for the reformation of the Catholic Church. It was a blow to the Pope, although he was pleased, he didn't have to pay King Philip II the million gold crowns. Philip II had been the defender of Catholicism throughout the world, but now reformers and rebels knew

God was not always on Philip's side. The Stranger had lost this battle to gain possession of the canon, but knew there would be many more chances to discover the secret the Brotherhood of the Divine had sworn to protect. He did have the one page with some of the most provocative verses from the Book of Enoch. He knew somehow that these verses were tied to the secret the Weepers were protecting, a secret he knew would eventually lead to his ascension to the throne.

CHAPTER TWENTY

"And thereafter We said to the Children of Israel: 'Dwell securely in the Promised Land. And when the last warning will come to pass, we will gather you together in a mingled crowd'"

Qur'an 17:104 The Night Journey

Mika'il and his devoted group of followers had created quite a stir in the West Bank and in Israel. The ranks of his supporters were growing daily. It seems many Muslims had grown tired of the intifada and the unrelenting jihad. The idea of a more moderate Islam seemed to have hit a spiritual chord with Muslims tired of the bloodshed that had gone on for so many centuries. Mika'il was on a campaign to educate the world about the history of the hatred and violence that had devastated the region. He wanted people to understand how the Qur'an tells of the covenantal relationship with the Torah and the people of Israel, as well as of the right for Israel to exist, an ideology so contrary to what the vocal Muslim clerics and news media had propagandized for years. The Israeli authorities, as well as the Palestinian authorities, were not sure how to respond to this new movement. The Israelis were pleased with the message, but suspicious of the messenger. They suspected Mika'il had been responsible for many of the terrorist bombings which had killed so many throughout Israel and the West Bank. The Israeli secret service had attempted to poison him, like they had done to so many other terrorists, but with no success. They were sure they had succeeded in administering the poison, yet Mika'il showed no ill affects. Then there was the bizarre report from the two soldiers, claiming to have seen the bullets that had been shot at Mika'il, stop in mid-air. The Israeli authorities decided to back off of Mika'il and watch to see what developed. The Palestinian authorities were equally baffled at how to handle the situation. A number of Muslim clerics had called for Mika'il's immediate arrest and execution for what they considered to be blasphemy of Islam and Allah. Still, a few clerics were coming out in support of Mika'il and his new moderate ideology. The authorities tried to control the situation by tightening the borders and limiting movement within the country. They placed a strict ban on the media forbidding any coverage of Mika'il and his followers. In essence, Mika'il was under house arrest in Nablus, unable to leave the city to preach his new ideals. Still the followers came. Mika'il became frustrated at not being able to get his message out. He knew he had to get out of Nablus, for that matter the West Bank, if he wanted the world to hear the message that Allah had chosen him to share.

* * *

The jet was already waiting at the Ciampino airport when Lucy arrived. Ciampino is the smaller of the two airports that service Rome and caters to private and business jets. Much more convenient than Fiumicino or, as they now call it, the Leonardo da Vinci Airport.

It was almost daybreak when Lucy pulled her Ferrari into the hangar. She was exhausted, still feeling the affects of having blacked out the previous day. That, along with the fact she had been on the move since her dinner engagement with Kevin the previous evening. It had been a very busy night for Lucy. Astan had returned from his business meeting soon after Lucy had left the estate. He had been trying to reach her since he returned, but she either was not near her phone or she just refused to answer it. She finally responded to his text message at around 4:30 a.m.

"It's about time you checked in. Just what are you up to?"

"I don't believe that is any of your business, but if you must know I've been working."

"What kind of work are you doing in the middle of the night? Nothing sinister I hope."

Lucy was too upset to respond. She was tired of her father always questioning her. "Just what's so important that you left me four voice messages and three text messages?"

"I need you to do me an important favor. A task I believe only you can get away with."

"Nothing illegal or immoral I hope." She didn't always trust her father's motives or methods.

"I heard you're flying to Jerusalem and then going to Nablus. Some kind of accident with several people who are in comas, I believe."

"Stop right there," Lucy interrupted. "There is no way I'm going to jeopardize a medical mission for some scheme of yours. What is it this time? Do I need to sneak some artwork out of the country, or some long lost icon or document one of your so called 'buyers' have discovered? I won't put my reputation on the line for your private satisfaction of knowing you've something no one else has or can get."

"It's not an icon, it's a person, a very special person."

Lucy knew immediately whom Astan was talking about. She had heard the news reports. She knew about this alleged miracle worker, Mika'il Aslan, and his plans for a more moderate Islam. Astan had been talking about him for weeks, hoping to somehow help him with his cause. Astan felt Mika'il could be the person to finally bring peace to the Mideast if given a suitable forum in which to publicize his ideology. Astan was capable of arranging for that world stage if Mika'il would only agree to leave Nablus. Now that the Palestinian authorities had placed him under a virtual house arrest, getting him out of the country would be difficult, even if he did agree to leave.

"I know of whom you're talking about and I agree he does need to get out of the West Bank for his own protection, but why would he agree to leave with a stranger? He doesn't know you or me, or anything about us," Lucy said.

"I'm sure he has heard of you, Lucy. To him you would be no stranger. Both of you have something remarkable in common that only each other can truly understand. In truth, you're both strangers to the world."

"Wrong! I don't understand it at all. God is the only one who truly understands what's going on. It's his doing, not mine."

"And whose God is responsible for the miracles Mika'il is performing? My little Lucy, we have the opportunity to unite two religions that have fought each other for centuries. It's a historic opportunity. Can you deny this is all part of God's plan?"

"I've never known you to be such a humanitarian. What does Astan Ilves get out of all of this?"

"I won't deny I'd benefit if I were known as the man who brought peace to the world. It's a legacy I'd dearly cherish. Then again, maybe it's what God has called me to do. I've been very fortunate in my life. I've had great financial success, I've been able to pursue my passion for art and history but, most of all, I was allowed to adopt and raise you as my own daughter. You are a remarkable woman, Lucy, and I couldn't be prouder of the person you've become." Astan knew how to say just the right thing to influence Lucy.

"Okay, okay, I'll do it. You probably know I'm at the airport right now. When are you going to explain your plan to me?"

"As soon as you can get on the plane. I've made all the arrangements. One of my men will brief you when you get on board."

"Not until I take a shower, get cleaned up, and get a little sleep. I've been up all night and need to rest."

"You haven't been out all night with Kevin Bridges, I hope."

"That's none of your business."

"Well, as soon as you wake up from your nap, at least call me and tell me what the two of you discussed over dinner."

"I'll be in touch," was Lucy's only reply as she slammed closed her cell phone.

* * *

Things were becoming tense around Mika'il's compound in Nablus. There had been several attacks on his followers as they made their way to his compound. The Palestinian authorities were refusing to provide him with the necessary security to stop the attacks. Their numbers were increasing daily, but by word of mouth only since the media blackout had been imposed. To be successful in what Allah had directed Mika'il to do, he knew he had to get out of the West Bank and make the world aware of his ideas. Mika'il prayed. Surely Allah would supply him with the guidance needed to solve his dilemma.

* * *

The Al-Qasr Hotel Nablus was quiet when a stranger arrived just after one in the morning. Only fifteen of the twenty-two rooms were occupied and all of the guests were asleep in their rooms. There was one night-shift clerk busy in the office and two security guards, one sitting and reading a paper in the lobby, while the other patrolled outside the building. As the outside guard was checking to make sure all exterior doors into the service area were locked, he heard a moan come from behind a trash bin.

"Who's there?"

"Help me, please," a female voice seemed to barely call out.

The guard carefully peered behind the bin. There on some cardboard boxes was a woman. She lay partially covered by a man's trench coat. She appeared in the dim light to have been beaten.

"Help me, please. I've been beaten and raped."

The guard hurried over to see how badly the woman was hurt. He put his gun back in his holster. That move would prove to be fatal. In a flash what he thought to be a knife or a giant claw savagely slashed at his throat severing his carotid artery. The guard dropped instantly as blood spurted out all over the cardboard boxes and onto the trench coat the Stranger now used as protection from the spurting blood. Quickly the Stranger wrapped the coat around the dead guard's neck and upper torso, grabbed the set of keys hooked to the guard's belt, then dumped the body into the bin. The Stranger threw the bloodied cardboard boxes on top to conceal the dead guard.

In a matter of seconds, the Stranger had accessed the utility room containing the heating and cooling system for the hotel. With expert precision the Stranger manipulated the system to allow carbon monoxide to flow rapidly into all the guest rooms and throughout the entire hotel facility. As quickly as the Stranger appeared, the Stranger was gone, and over thirty people began to slip into a coma on their way to a silent death.

Two hours later as the first guests were beginning to die, the Stranger called the local police to report a body lying in the lobby of the Al-Qasr hotel. Police rushed to the scene in time to save over half of the people affected by the tragic accident. Those still alive were all in severe comas and showed diminished brain wave function. The local doctors had little hope for their survival, that is, until one of them remembered an article in the Journal of Medicine about Dr. Lucy Ilves and her innovative work with comatose patients. A call was placed to her foundation and late in the evening the next day she returned the call. She agreed to come the next morning. It was a simple matter for her people to arrange the necessary visas and landing clearances. She would be bringing several associates with her who would also need visa clearance. They even agreed to supply open-ended visas which would allow the names to be added later, once she had gathered her team members. The authorities assured her that they would not impede her visit in any way. Her help was an answer to their prayers.

The Stranger couldn't have been happier as things began to fall into place, just as he had planned.

CHAPTER TWENTY-ONE

Therefore, my brothers, be all the more eager to make your calling and election sure. For if you do these things, you will never fall, and you will receive a rich welcome into the eternal kingdom of our Lord and Savior Jesus Christ.

2 Peter 1:10-11

Very little escapes the notice of the Stranger. Yet much is forgotten and ignored. Such was the case of the two Weepers who traveled to France with the second of Botticelli's paintings. Overseeing all the evil in the world can be very time consuming. Never more so was this true than in the early seventeenth century. Christianity was on the verge of a complete collapse throughout all of Europe and Asia, both spiritually and financially. The Stranger had many flames he needed to fan. Chaos reigned as the divisive theologies of the reformation threatened to destroy Christianity.

The Stranger knew Botticelli had painted two paintings. He knew one of the paintings was sent to the Vatican. He had heard the second painting had been sent to France, to the abbey at Port Royal. He had his men lay in wait to ambush the monks, but for several weeks no monks appeared. Whatever the reason it was of no matter, for the Stranger knew the painting must be hidden in the abbey.

The abbey at Port Royal was founded in 1204 under the rule of St. Benedict, but later changed to Cistercian. It flourished throughout the fourteenth and fifteenth centuries, but suffered dearly during the Catholic and Protestant wars. Discipline grew lax and rules forgotten, as the nuns of Port Royal, like the monks and clergy throughout Europe, focused on worldly endeavors and philosophies. In 1602, the Pope appointed an eleven-year-old girl to be the Abbess of Port Royal. She introduced vows of poverty and seclusion and once again made the abbey a teaching institution. Within twenty years of her appointment, nuns trained at Port-Royal were spreading their teachings throughout all of France. During this period, the Stranger lost access to the abbey and waited for his next opportunity, as he continued to stir up conflict and spread confusion throughout Europe.

In 1636 a group of intellectual and learned scholars, theorists, physicians, and ecclesiasts moved to Les Grange near the abbey. Theirs was not a monastic life dictated by vows, but of a more solitaire life dedicated to religion, literary studies, teaching and manual labor. They considered themselves a community of godly men. The called themselves "The Solitaires". These were brilliant men with brilliant ideas that sometimes challenged the precepts of the Holy See. They embraced the philosophy of Jansenism. Port-Royal des-Champs became the center of this theological movement and raised the ire of both the Jesuits and the French royal government. Pope

Clement XI issued a bull condemning the Jansenists and, as hoped, Port Royal suffered. Their leaders were imprisoned and the nuns and the Solitaires were dispersed. But soon their new pious and saintly ways enabled them to reoccupy Port Royal without consequences.

King Louis XIV was not one who tolerated such insolence and zeal. Nor was the Stranger pleased with these delays that were keeping him from discovering the hidden painting. In 1709 the police arrested the nuns, dispersed the Solitaires, and took possession of the abbey at Port Royal. That allowed the Stranger's spies to search the abbey, but still with no success. The Stranger destroyed the abbey, yet people still flocked to its cemetery seeking spiritual enlightenment. The King ordered the desecration of the cemetery. The Stranger found no painting among the graves or the tombs that were destroyed, though he did find pleasure in watching the dogs fight over the disinterred remains.

The Stranger was angered. Botticelli's painting had eluded him once again. Over one hundred years wasted on another dead end. The tide was changing. He could sense it. He had found the evidence he had been searching for in England, but knew it would take more than one scrap of verse to convince the world of what was destined to be.

CHAPTER TWENTY-TWO

The end of all things is near. Therefore be clear minded and self-controlled so that you can pray. Above all, love each other deeply, because love covers over a multitude of sins. Offer hospitality to one another without grumbling. Each one should use whatever gift he has received to serve others, faithfully administering God's grace in its various forms. If anyone speaks, he should do it as one speaking the very words of God. If anyone serves, he should do it with the strength God provides, so that in all things God may be praised through Jesus Christ. To Him be the glory and the power for ever and ever. Amen.

1 Peter 4:7-9, 11

Kevin stood transfixed, staring at the face of the angel dressed in a white robe. The facial features bore an amazing similarity to Lucy. It was no wonder Astan called the angel his "Little Lucy".

He wanted to give Lucy a call and ask about the Ferrari racing past him last night. "Just where could she have been going in such a hurry?" A lot of very strange happenings had taken place at Vatican City within the past twenty-four hours. Kevin wasn't sure whom to believe or trust right now. Even Lucy was a suspect in the murders, though Kevin was convinced it was Satan.

He used his camera phone to take some pictures of Botticelli's fresco and hurried to his meeting.

"Sorry I'm late. As you can well ..." Kevin stopped in mid-sentence.

"Kevin, I understand you have already met Astan Ilves. Astan is here regarding an incident in the chapel yesterday. He says you were a little pushy with his daughter, Lucy." The Bishop waited for a response, as all eyes were on Kevin.

"I'm sorry you feel that way, Mr. Ilves, but I assure you we were only concerned for her well-being. The questions we needed to ask were regarding the voices heard coming from inside the chapel, Lucy's and a man's voice."

"Why wasn't I told about this? Was someone trying to hurt my daughter?"

"That's what we were trying to find out when you took her away," Kevin replied. "I was able to get more information from your daughter over dinner last night. By the way, I'm truly sorry you were unable to join us. I've looked forward to meeting you for quite some time. Your home is quite beautiful and your chef's cooking is simply exquisite. Perhaps you would allow me to take you and Lucy out to dinner? I would love to hear about your research." Kevin had managed to really anger Astan, just as he hoped he would do.

"I don't think that will be possible this trip. I'll be leaving for Switzerland in a few days and I think Lucy's work will keep her from returning to Rome for quite some time."

"Maybe the three of us could get together for a quick lunch before you leave town," Kevin persisted.

"Maybe you misunderstood me. Lucy has already left Italy and I doubt she'll be returning for quite some time."

Astan smiled when he sensed Kevin's disappointment. "She flew out early this morning. I'm surprised she didn't tell you that she was leaving last night when you joined her for dinner."

Kevin was taken aback by the turn of events. He was sure Lucy had enjoyed his company. He found it hard to believe she would leave without telling him. "Maybe I let my male macho ego get the best of me," Kevin thought to himself.

"Well, gentleman, I believe we've cleared up this unfortunate misunderstanding," the Bishop said, hoping to lower the testosterone level in the room.

"I'm sorry if I upset you, Mr. Ilves. I was just trying to do my job the best I know how. Oh, and by the way, I hope your business meeting went well last night." Kevin watched to see how Astan would react to his comment.

"Oh, it went well, very well indeed. Gentleman, thank you for your time. I must be going."

"What was that all about?" the director asked Kevin.

"Just a little male posturing," Kevin replied. "Nothing I can't deal with."

"Well, just remember whom it is your dealing with. Astan Ilves has been extremely generous to us at Vatican City. We'd like it to stay that way," the Bishop said sternly. "The director has already filled me in on what happened last night. It's got his investigators completely baffled. No fingerprints, no real sign of a breakin, basically few clues at all. What's your take on these murders?"

"Satan. I'm convinced it was Satan," Kevin said.

"Of course, Satan is behind all evil that happens on earth," the director said impatiently, "but these murders were committed by somebody doing Satan's bidding. We need to find out who that was."

"No man did these gruesome murders. Both guards were killed simultaneously by having their hearts ripped out. What man could do that? How do you explain those bloody talon prints? Let me show you some pictures." Kevin pulled out some drawings and what appeared to be a full-scale transfer print of the bloody talon print.

"Do these look familiar?" he asked the director.

"Sure, somebody did some drawings of the prints in the catacomb from the photographs we took last night. This one looks like somebody laid a piece of paper on one of the prints like they were taking an impression. Why wasn't I told of this?"

"You're right, it was made directly from bloody talon prints. Just not last night's crime scene," Kevin replied. "These are from a similar murder that happened over four hundred years ago in England. Compare them to the photos of last night's murder scene."

"Good Gracious!" the Bishop gasped, as he crossed himself.

The director was not quite so polite. "Oh my God! That could scare the living hell right out of you. Please forgive my language, Bishop."

"Quite alright, my son. You just summarized my thoughts as well."

"You believe the same person, or thing, who killed our two guards, killed somebody in England four hundred years ago?" the director asked.

"The evidence seems pretty clear to me," Kevin responded. "And it's not a person or a thing. Well, then again, maybe it is, but I'll give it a name, and that name is Satan."

"There's got to be a better, or at least a more rational explanation," the director declared. "What you are telling us is just too hard to believe."

"Not for me," the Bishop replied. "Satan is real; I'm sure of that but I don't understand why he'd come here to Vatican City and murder those two guards."

"I don't believe murder was part of his plan," Kevin explained. "He was looking for something in one of the vaults."

"That would explain why all the vaults had been opened," the director interjected.

"What do you think Satan, or this person, may have been looking for?" the Bishop asked, in such a way that would not offend Kevin or the director.

"Í think he found what he was looking for."

"Do you mean the painting by Botticelli?" said the Bishop.

"Yes, I believe that was part of it," Kevin replied, "but I get the feeling there's something else in that vault he wanted. I think he ran out of time when the alarm sounded."

"What else could he have possibly wanted and why the Botticelli?" asked the director.

"That is something I hope Mykos Zorko can help us answer," Kevin told the two men. "Take a look at this picture from the Sistine Chapel. I took this picture of the fresco by Botticelli."

"Talons, Satan has talons just like the prints we found," the Bishop gasped.

"I'm sorry, but blaming these murders on Satan just does not register in my brain," the director commented. "I have to believe somebody is going to a lot of trouble to throw us off their trail."

"I can only hope you're right," Kevin replied, "because if you're not, I hate to even think about the alternative."

"This is exactly the kind of thing we pay you to investigate, Kevin," the Bishop responded, "which brings me to the other reason why I needed to speak with you. I am assigning the director to handle the investigation of the murders. The Pope has suggested that you should go immediately to California and speak with this Gabe Brown, the man who allegedly speaks in all languages at the same time. If what the local priest says is true, you need to speak to this man as soon as possible. You are our expert on miracles."

"When do I need to leave?" Kevin asked, having resigned himself to the fact that he was off the case and heading to California. Investigating miracles was his first priority for Vatican City. That's what he was hired to do. He was one of the best. "In fact, this might just prove to be the best way to get back in touch with Lucy," Kevin thought to himself. "If this Gabe Brown is such the hot ticket right now, Astan won't be far behind."

"The Pope has made this a very high priority and has authorized you to take one of the papal jets. You leave as soon as you can get to the airport."

"Fiumicino or Ciampino?" Kevin asked.

"Ciampino, of course," the Bishop responded. "Only the papal jumbo jet flies out of Fiumicino," the Bishop said stumbling over the words.

"Try to say that ten times real fast," Kevin laughed, and the two other men smiled easing the tension.

* * *

Astan was not happy with the response that he received from Kevin and the Bishop. He particularly didn't care for Kevin's insinuations. What he found to be most upsetting was that Lucy seemed to find Mr. Bridges rather charming. She hadn't actually said as much, but Astan could tell.

Astan had hoped to hear about progress on the investigation into the two murders in the catacombs. Mykos had called him immediately about news of the Botticelli despite being told by Kevin to keep it quiet. He was as anxious as Kevin to see the painting cleaned and restored. He was also curious as to what other treasures might have been hidden away in that forgotten vault. Astan was sure Mykos would keep him well-informed.

Astan heard from Lucy as he was heading towards the Vatican City helipad. She had just awakened from a short nap and her plane was about to land in Tel Aviv. She needed to know what arrangements had been made for her meet with Mika'il. Astan told her not to worry, his assistant would handle all the arrangements. She only needed to take care of the Nablus coma victims. When the time was right, the meeting would take place.

"By the way, you never told me how your dinner went with Kevin Bridges," Astan said to Lucy. "I hope you were able to answer the questions he had about your fainting spell."

"Actually, it was quite wonderful. I found Kevin to be refreshing and honest," Lucy replied, inferring Astan didn't always display those traits. "How did your meeting go? Did you close another billion-dollar deal?"

"It wasn't as boring as they usually are, and in fact it did prove to be quite productive, though a billion dollars might be understating it a bit," Astan said, laughing.

"Why do I believe you?" Lucy replied. "I'll have to talk to you later. We're about to land."

"Be careful," Astan replied. "The West Bank is not the safest place these days."

Lucy had already ended the call and didn't hear Astan's warning. She couldn't seem to get Kevin out of her mind. And what troubled her even more was that she couldn't decide if that was a good thing or a bad thing.

Lucy was jarred from her daydream about Kevin by the sound of the jet engines being reversed to slow the plane. She hadn't realized the plane had landed. "This pilot is good," she said to herself, "but then again, only the best for Astan Ilves."

CHAPTER TWENTY-THREE

"Who then is the faithful and wise servant, whom the master has put in charge of the servants in his household to give them their food at the proper time? It will be good for that servant whose master finds him doing so when he returns."

Matthew 24:45-46

It was as if the circus had come to town. Two network satellite trucks were parked in the junior high school lot directly across the street from Gabe's house. They were paying the local school district several thousand dollars for that privilege. The local police had four officers dedicated to crowd control and safety. The county had assigned a paramedic squad to help with the extremely ill and elderly. It was obvious more security and more medical teams would be necessary very soon. Streets in the area had been closed down to through traffic. Gabe's wife had left after the first day of the madness to go stay with one of her sons and grandchildren. Gabe had not left the house since the FBI had dropped him off four days ago. He had quit answering his home phone and now had to even stop answering his cell phone. All personal calls came through his pastor's cell phone.

Gabe had called his pastor that first evening and asked what he should do. His pastor had seen the news showing the chaos and arranged for several members of the church to provide security for Gabe's house. He set up a media center in the parking lot of the Baptist Church about a half-block away from Gabe's house. The church was also where the pastor and his staff screened requests for interviews. It seemed everyone wanted an audience with Gabe. They also dealt with the constant requests by the city and county to somehow diffuse the situation. It was obvious to all involved Gabe had to leave the area, and leave the area soon. Very soon.

Much of Gabe's day was taken up with federal agents and scientists contemplating the military and political applications for Gabe's talent. A constant flow of high-profile clergy came seeking his help or endorsement. Some came to confirm these miracles were not some cheap parlor trick. It was the presence and influence of these priests, pastors, and rabbis who kept the government from just spiriting Gabe away. Several television evangelists wanted Gabe to appear on their shows and a few were even willing to pay him to do so. Others were trying to lay a guilt trip on Gabe, telling him it was his obligation to appear on their show. There were also three offers to give Gabe his own network evangelism show. A great opportunity had Gabe had something he wanted to say. His pastor was very helpful at knowing when to step in with an "I'm sorry, but I don't think Gabe would be interested" or "I'm sure Gabe will consider your request and get back to you soon". The pastor was turning into an agent more than a spiritual advisor. And there was no shortage of offers by agents to assist in furthering Gabe's career and take over those duties for the pastor.

"There's a man here I think you should see," the pastor told Gabe. "He's been sent by Astan Ilves. You know, the humanitarian philanthropist from Switzerland. He's very influential in worldwide Christianity, although I have never been too taken by his processed theology approach."

"I've heard his name before, but that's about all. Why's it so important I see this representative of Astan Ilves?"

"He says he has a proposition for you, but he refuses to tell anybody but you. Father Oliver from Our Lady of the Assumption tells me Astan Ilves is well-respected by the highest powers of the Catholic Church. He believes it'd be worth hearing what Astan's representative has to say. Oliver also requests you see a Mr. Kevin Bridges, Vatican City's special envoy. He should be arriving within the hour at the Ontario airport. Father Oliver suggests you see both these men at the same time. It seems the Pope is curious as to what Astan Ilves has to say as well."

"This is getting awfully complicated and awfully political," Gabe mused. "I just don't understand why this is happening to me."

"Its all part of God's Perfect Plan," the pastor replied.

"Yeah, but why me? You more than anyone know I've not surrendered my life to the Lord. My brain keeps getting in the way. There is just too much I don't understand."

"There's much nobody understands," the pastor replied. "It's your heart you must surrender and then the brain will follow. Maybe this is the Lord's way of showing you. How can these powers of tongues and healing be reasonably or rationally explained by science? They can't. Only through God can they be explained."

What the pastor had to say did make a lot of sense. The pastor always seemed to make sense to Gabe. That was why Gabe enjoyed attending the pastor's church every Sunday. Gabe just couldn't take the next step, that so-called leap of faith. "Well, if you and Father Oliver really think I should see these men, I will, but together like Father Oliver suggested. I think that would be a good idea. And of course, I want you and him with me when they say what's on their minds."

"Then I'll have someone make the arrangements. You know, Gabe, you are going to have to leave here soon. The crowd is getting too difficult to control and we're worried about your safety. There have been several threats made against your life and the police intercepted a car containing several weapons and even some explosives. You may want to consider agreeing to the government's request to place you in protective custody."

"What do I do about my job? I can't just quit. I still have bills to pay."

"I don't believe you'll ever be able to return to teaching. I can't imagine anywhere you could go that you wouldn't be recognized. People will constantly seek you out. Your life is no longer your own. You'll need bodyguards wherever and whenever you go out in public if, in fact, you can even go out in public," the pastor explained. "The Church can help with your bills for a while, but you have some decisions to make, decisions that will affect your life, your family's life, and possibly the lives of millions. We all pray that whatever path God has chosen for you, you will choose to follow." The pastor already knew Gabe's life now belonged to God. Gabe just hadn't realized it.

* * *

Kevin's jet touched down on the south side of the Ontario airport. The Church had arranged for a customs agent to meet him to expedite his passport clearance into the United States. Within minutes, Kevin was in a private car with a police escort speeding towards Claremont. Ten minutes later he was in the parking lot of the Baptist Church. Kevin was astounded at the size of the crowd. Vendors had set up booths in the junior high parking lot and in the park across the street. Several neighboring agencies had lent officers to help with the situation. Kevin had been informed that he would be meeting with Gabe immediately upon his arrival to the area. He was also told he would be doing so with another gentleman who had arrived from Italy. A man with a proposal from Astan Ilves. Kevin was not surprised.

"It's a pleasure to meet you Mr. Brown, my name is Marco Piali. I'm here to bring you an offer of assistance from Astan Ilves."

"Please call me Gabe."

"My name is Kevin Bridges, I was sent by the Pope. It's nice to meet you."

"Are you from Italy?" Gabe asked Kevin.

"Not originally. I grew up in Kansas City. I moved to Italy when I accepted the job offer. I spend about four months out of the year in Rome. The rest of the time I'm out doing my job, traveling around the world."

"Just what is your job?"

"I am the primary investigator of miracles for Vatican City."

"Keeps you pretty busy, I would guess," Gabe replied. "So, am I part of your job now?"

"Kind of looks that way. I've been following your case since the day of the train wreck. I must say, I have never seen such a chaotic scene as is happening here. You need to think about leaving here soon."

"Well, that is a perfect lead in for me," Marco interjected. "I have spoken with your pastor and I have to agree with him and Mr. Bridges. If you don't leave here soon, your government will force you to go to some military base. I don't think that's a very desirable option."

"Nor do I," Gabe responded.

"Mr. Ilves would like to invite you to his private villa in Switzerland. I assure you that you'll be safe and away from chaos such as this. He would like to offer you work with his foundation. You may bring your advisors, your pastor perhaps."

"Do you really think it's necessary to leave the United States?" Gabe asked no one in particular.

"Yes!" answered his pastor and Marco at the same time.

"What do you think, Mr. Bridges?"

"Please call me Kevin. Not wishing to make a disparaging inference regarding the United States, I have to agree that it might be wiser and safer to take Mr. Ilves up on his invitation. This is assuming of course you already have your passport."

"I do. You said I can bring my pastor?"

"Whoa," the pastor spoke up, "there's no way I can get away. I have a church to run. A lot of my parishioners are really concerned about what has been happening lately. I must be here for them."

"What about you, Kevin? Can you go with me to Switzerland? That way you could ask me whatever you need to for the Pope."

"I've no problem with that as long as Marco agrees."

"I'd have it no other way," Marco replied, very diplomatically.

"How soon should we leave?" Gabe asked.

Kevin pulled back the curtain to look at the crowd gathered outside. A portable chain link fence had been put in place around the property. Security was having a difficult time keeping people from climbing over. "I'd suggest we leave within the next five minutes based on the unruliness of that crowd."

"I can arrange that," Marco replied. "I have a helicopter on standby and I think those security men could safely get us to the soccer field behind the school."

"I guess it's up to you, Gabe," the pastor stated.

"You must have been pretty confident in thinking you could talk me into leaving to have arranged all of this," Gabe said to Marco.

"Actually, I made the arrangements while I was waiting for Mr. Bridges to arrive. If you had chosen not to leave your house, the helicopter would still be the safest and quickest way for me to avoid what I see as an impending riot."

"I assume the helicopter will take us to the airport. Then what?" Gabe asked.

"I have a jet," both Kevin and Marco spoke at the same.

"We both apparently have a jet at the airport fueled and ready to leave on a moment's notice," Marco continued.

"Yeah, but mine's bigger," Kevin said jokingly. Gabe was starting to like Kevin Bridges. They both had a similar sense of humor and both had grown up in the Midwest.

"What about clothes? What will I need to pack? What about my dogs? Who's going to feed them? It's going to take me at least a day to make the arrangements," Gabe was wavering in his resolve.

"I will arrange for someone to take care of the dogs and your household until your wife returns," the pastor told Gabe.

"We will buy you whatever you need once we are in Switzerland," Marco said. "The main thing is to just get out of here before the crowd starts destroying your house and the neighborhood. I will arrange for security to guard your house so you needn't worry about that."

"I still have a million questions," Gabe said.

"Ask them when you're safely on the plane," the pastor told Gabe.

"Then let's do it before I change my mind," Gabe said to everyone in the room.

The pastor spoke to the police supervisor on the scene and explained part of their plan. He made sure not to let the FBI men know. The pastor also informed several men from the church, who were helping with security, of the plan. Three of them came back into the house. Ten minutes later a limousine escorted by two police motor officers pulled through the barricades and into Gabe's driveway. Several people tried to rush through the opening in the fence, but the police were able to force them back. The church security people, who were all wearing bright yellow shirts, formed a tight wedge, protecting the three men as they ran from the house and to the limousine. The limousine and the motorcycles tried to pull out of the drive and head down the street, but they were quickly blocked in by the surging crowd. Four helicopters were now flying overhead. One was a county sheriff copter trying to assist the officers on the ground. Two were news copters feeding live coverage of the scene to local television stations. The fourth suddenly flew to the area behind the junior high. The group of church security people dressed in the bright yellow shirts were moving rapidly towards the gate that led to the field. A single police officer was waiting by the gate and opened it when he saw the yellow shirts approaching. Gabe, Marco, and Kevin had exchanged their clothes with three of the guards. It was three of the guards who had jumped into the limousine as a distraction. Gabe, Kevin, and Marco were now tightly surrounded by the moving phalanx of bright yellow shirts. When the pilot saw what looked like a giant yellow ladybug pushing through the crowd towards the field, he landed the helicopter. Once through the school gate the yellow blob seemed to burst apart into two dozen pieces. Three of the yellow center pieces ran to the waiting copter. Within thirty seconds the helicopter was back in the air and on its way to the Ontario Airport. A few people on the outskirts of the crowd realized what was happening, but were unable to spread the word. It would take several hours for the crowd to realize what had happened and finally disperse.

"So, whose jet are we taking to Switzerland?" Gabe asked.

"I think it best if we take Mr. Ilves' jet," Marco replied. "It already has the clearances and the flight plan filed for Switzerland. I just need to change the passenger list."

"I can go along with that," Kevin added, "but just to be on the safe side, why don't you not change the passenger list, but let me add your two names to the papal jet flight plan for a return trip to Rome. That way if your FBI friends are upset about us leaving without telling them, they'll be pulling over the wrong jet."

"Excellent idea, Mr. Bridges," Marco said.

"Please, call me Kevin. Every time you say Mr. Bridges I turn and look to see if my dad walked into the room."

Gabe laughed as he looked at the two men in the canary yellow shirts identical to his. "Looks like I'm not the only one who will need a new wardrobe when we get to Switzerland."

CHAPTER TWENTY-FOUR

We have lived a long time...without war...We have had peace when all the world has been in arms...It is I say a thing most horrible that we should engage ourself in war with another---with our own venom...we will destroy ourself!

Henry Slingsby MP from Yorkshire diary entry 1642

It had been a time of relative peace in England. The Stranger had given up his quest to overthrow the Queen. Elizabeth had died, as had her successor James I, allowing his son Charles I to ascend to the throne. The Stranger arrived in England with temptation and a poisoned tongue. Advice, along with temptation, found a most receptive ear in the trusted advisor to the King, George Villiers, the Duke of Buckingham.

Villiers joined the court of King James I in 1614. He became a royal favorite and rose rapidly, heeding the Stranger's advice. The current favorite, the Earl of Somerset, met with disgrace thanks to the Stranger. Within six years Villiers gained control of dispensation for the King's patronage. As his power in the royal court increased, so did his arrogance. In 1625 Charles I inherited the throne. The Duke of Buckingham was more powerful than ever, despite a loss of popularity with the Parliament.

His dispensation abuses and failed military expeditions were costly. Parliament impeached the Duke, but Charles I dissolved Parliament before a trial could take place. In doing so, Charles I angered the members of Parliament and they refused to grant him the monies Charles had requested.

A shortage of funds began to plague the monarchy of Charles I. The Magna Carta would not allow the King to raise taxes without the approval of Parliament. Calling Parliament into session would lead to even greater problems for the King. Several members still demanded the impeachment trial for the Duke of Buckingham, as well as demanding the King stop his illegal methods of raising money.

The King chose not to call a session of Parliament, but to look for other sources for raising badly needed monies. He decided to sell some treasures that had been given to him as gifts. Not the high-profile ones which would undoubtedly raise the ire of Parliament, but those more obscure gifts, many of which were not even considered treasure. One such gift was a large box of birch bark papers.

As during the Italian Renaissance, collecting ancient icons and documents was quite popular among the wealthy. Lord Michael Corwin was one of the MPs who had fought hard to deny Charles the money. He expected the King to pilfer the royal treasury and knew there would be good deals to be had. Corwin wasn't the only MP who hoped to prosper from the King's lack of funds. The temptation was too great for many to pass up. The Stranger made sure of that. When a not so discrete invitation soliciting bids on the birch bark canon became known, Lord Corwin feigned marginal interest hoping to obtain them at a reasonable cost. Lord Corwin had an extensive collection of ancient documents and icons and was known throughout Europe as an expert on such items. He employed several caretakers and translators to catalogue, maintain, and of course translate his numerous acquisitions. He had amassed quite a collection and housed them in a museum-like setting, allowing experts to visit and study his holdings. He knew these birch bark papers would add considerably to his collection, but the price was too high. A dealer of antiquities outbid Corwin with plans to resell them in Italy. This was not at all what the Stranger desired. No longer did he want the actual documents in his possession. The Stranger realized this copy of the canon would best serve his purpose if an expert such as Lord Corwin made them known to the world. Then there could be no doubt as to its authenticity. Still, the Stranger knew it would take more than one source to convince the Church, let alone the world, of what the Stranger was beginning to himself believe to be true.

The successful buyer was on his way to pick up the canon with a pouch full of gold to consummate the deal. Being no fool, he traveled with two of his cousins, knowing danger lurked in the streets of London. Criminals seemed to sense when a man was carrying a good deal of gold about. The trader would take no chances, but then he rarely left things to chance. The Stranger had to act fast.

He knew Lord Corwin would have nothing to do with the canon if he suspected foul play was involved in its acquisition. The Stranger would have to convince the trader to recant his winning bid, thus allowing Lord Corwin to be declared the highest bidder. The Stranger would just have to offer him something of more value.

As the trader and his cousins made their way towards Whitehall, the Stranger amassed several of his faithful servants. Their menacing presence along certain streets and intersections directed the trader and his cousins to exactly where the Stranger intended. After several unplanned turns, the nervous trio came upon the Stranger sitting on an oaken barrel outside a pub next to the Thames.

"Friend," the Stranger said to the approaching trader. "Please join me for a pint. I have a business proposition for you."

"We have no time for idle chatter," one of the cousins said harshly, as he raised his arm to shove the Stranger aside. As he touched the Stranger, he screamed in anguished pain as his body seemed to just freeze in place.

The second cousin pulled a knife from his pocket, but before he could make a move towards the Stranger, his heart was ripped from his chest so fast, he was able to watch as the Stranger threw it into the Thames. He turned to his brothers with a look of shocked horror on his face, then leaped into the river as if to retrieve his severed heart. The first cousin was still frozen in pain with his arm outstretched, but now tears began to roll down his cheeks.

The trader seemed unfazed by the spectacle before him. He remained calm returning the glaring stare of the Stranger. The Stranger burst into laughter as the cousin with the outstretched arm collapsed to the street. "Why have we not met before? You reek of evil, like the dead carcass of a man who long ago sold his soul to me."

"My soul belongs to no one," the trader declared. "What is it you want?"

"Normally, I'd want your soul or your life or perhaps both, but this evening I have but a simple request. I need you to decline the purchase of the documents you are now on your way to buy."

"And what do I get in return?"

"You get to live, of course."

"Death does not scare me. Even if it did, I know you've no intention to kill me, for if you had I'd already be dead."

"My, what a cocky little man you are," the Stranger replied, sounding surprised. "I'm sure we can reach some kind of arrangement. Maybe you would agree to my request if it meant saving your friend's life." The Stranger pointed to the cousin whose limbs began to twist horribly.

"I think not," the trader replied, as he nonchalantly pulled out his own knife and slit his cousin's throat, pushing him into the Thames to join his brother. "I did hate to see him suffer so."

Such a cold and calloused man as this trader the Stranger rarely encountered.

"I do not wish to barter with my soul, for it was committed to you long ago by my actions. I'll do as you ask and not purchase these documents. In return you must grant me what I desire."

"And what might that be?" the Stranger asked.

"I want to be a favorite of the royal court, perhaps an officer in the Royal Navy commanding my own ship so I can raid Spanish galleons of their great treasures."

"Is that all?" the Stranger said.

"No," the trader replied, "I want to live a very long time."

"Done," the Stranger promptly replied. "I'll make all the arrangements. You'll be meeting with George Villiers, the Duke of Buckingham. He will grant you the position you desire and of course your own ship."

"Then I'll go at once to Whitehall to see the Duke and to inform them I will not be purchasing the documents," the trader replied.

"A shrewd trader you are indeed," the Stranger said. The trader's soul now did belong to the Stranger.

* * *

As planned, the canon was sold to Lord Corwin, and the task of translating the Cyrillic text to English began in earnest. It would be several years before the Stranger would learn just how much of the canon was missing. When the translation was completed and made available, the Stranger was disappointed to learn the page he already possessed was the only one from the Book of Enoch. That, however, was of no significance. He knew from his page that even archangels would sometimes take human form. Valuable knowledge for the future. It was Revelation 10 of Lord Corwin's translation that revealed just exactly what the Brotherhood of the Divine had tried to protect for so many generations. God had commanded some verses of Revelation 10 be sealed and not written down. That was what Apostle John had done. At least that was what had been done in every copy of Revelation the Stranger had ever read. This copy of Revelation 10 was as all others, but contained a footnote explaining a peculiar addition in the original canon that spoke of the Ascension of Satan. "The Ascension of Satan!" The Stranger could hardly contain his glee. "Botticelli must have known of the Revelation. I must find that painting." The Stranger was pleased with this new information. There would be more copies of the verse. He was sure of that. He would search for those once he found the painting.

The trader did receive his commission and appointment as a Captain in the Royal Navy, giving him access to Charles' Royal Court. Shortly after the Duke granted him the position, the trader was accused of being a conspirator in the stabbing and murder of the Duke of Buckingham by a fellow captain, John Felton. Felton was quickly hung for his treason, but lack of evidence spared the trader's life. A life he spent locked in the Tower of London. A very long life just as the Stranger had promised. The trader was released as a very old and bitter man some fifty years later. Immediately upon his release in 1698, he returned to Whitehall and burned it to the ground. He perished in the inferno as hundreds of priceless artworks and treasures were lost forever.

"Precisely as I had planned," said the Stranger as he collected yet another soul.

CHAPTER TWENTY-FIVE

For certain men whose condemnation was written about long ago have secretly slipped in among you. They are godless men, who change the grace of our God into a license for immorality and deny Jesus Christ our only Sovereign and Lord.

Jude 1:4

Two armored Mercedes sedans were waiting for Lucy and her team when the jet touched down in Tel Aviv. So were several sick and disabled Israelis who were waiting just outside the tarmac gate. Somehow, they had found out Lucy was coming and came seeking a miracle. Today would not be the day.

It would be less than a ninety-minute drive from the airport to the hospital in Nablus. That is, if the border crossing was clear and there were no snipers along the route. If not for the occasional burnt out hulk of a military truck or tank, the scenery and countryside reminded Lucy somewhat of Greece or even possibly portions of California. Once outside of Tel Aviv there were miles of olive trees which seemed to go on forever. Past the border crossing, the olive trees gave way to acres of vineyards and the occasional Eucalyptus groves planted to suck up the swamp water that once covered the area. As they approached the city of Nablus, the team saw several Israeli military units poised on the outskirts, waiting. But waiting for what, they all wondered?

Sixteen guests had survived the poisoning at the Al-Qasr Hotel. All were in comas and, according to local doctors, had suffered irreversible brain damage. The media reported the poisoning had been intentional since one of the security guards was found with his throat slit. This made Lucy's team nervous as they drove through the surprisingly empty streets of Nablus. More than once they saw groups of people in heated confrontations arguing on street corners, sometimes throwing stones at each other. The city was on the verge of a civil disturbance that could erupt at any moment. Most of the residents had settled into their homes anticipating the trouble. Those who still wandered the streets were either the hardline Muslim extremists or the converts to the more moderate form of Islam that Mika'il claimed to be the will of Allah. It was these two opposing groups who threatened to plunge the entire West Bank into an Islamic civil war.

Lucy's medical team immediately began to evaluate the coma victims. Her research foundation had made remarkable advances in treating and curing several disabilities and diseases. She knew the therapy treatment that she and her researchers had developed to assist comatose patients was truly brilliant, but not all the results they had achieved could be medically explained. Lucy stayed out of the ward knowing what would happen the moment she entered the room. She knew it wasn't reasonable and that no science could ever explain it. The team was aware of this, but reluctant to confront Lucy with the truth behind these miraculous cures, with an emphasis on the word "miraculous". As much as Lucy wanted to deny it, there was no denying the crowds of the sick and disabled who always appeared when Lucy came. It was as if God had foretold these believers of his blessings coming to free them from their pain and misfortune. They were always waiting for her when she arrived, and it frightened her. It frightened her because she could not understand why God had chosen her. Redemption for those who truly believed. Lucy wasn't sure if she truly believed.

Her father had always said a great destiny awaited her. She thought he was referring to her groundbreaking medical research. Now she knew Astan meant much more than that. It was as if Astan always knew this age of miracle workers was coming and he had prepared for it. Lucy needed to see Mika'il as soon as possible. She had to meet another person capable of performing miracles. She left the team at the hospital and ordered one of the drivers to take her to the headquarters of this prophet Mika'il.

There was a loud screech as the Mercedes slammed on its brakes, followed by a sickening crunch as the Mercedes struck a man running from a crowd. The guards at the gate heard the crash and ran out, scaring the mob of hardline Muslims away, at least for the moment.

"I believe you've killed him," the guard said to the driver and Lucy, as they jumped out of the car to assist. "I know it was an accident, so you will not be held responsible for his death. Allah knows who is to blame." The guard pointed towards the mob gathered down the street.

"Let me help him, I'm a doctor," Lucy insisted.

"There is nothing you can do. This man is dead," the guard replied, as he stared at the two broken legs horribly twisted in an unnatural position beneath the body.

Lucy was not to be deterred. She grabbed his hand and instantly his legs untwisted and a moan escaped from his mouth. He began to regain consciousness.

"Praise Allah!" the guard shouted. "You have saved my friend. Is this some trick of the devil?"

"It is no trick," the revived man said to his frightened friend. "Allah used this woman to save me, just as he has used Mika'il to save so many others."

"I am here to see your prophet, Mika'il Aslan," Lucy said.

"That is impossible," the guard replied, "we are on the brink..."

"What is impossible?" Mika'il asked, interrupting his guard.

"Mika'il, this woman has come to see you. She has just returned my life to me. She has the power to heal the sick and injured just like you."

"Quiet," Mika'il ordered, as he looked around to see who might have overheard the comment. The mob down the street had grown larger and began to move towards Lucy, Mika'il, and his men. "Quickly, drive the car inside the compound, it is no longer safe here. What is your name?"

"Lucy, Lucy Ilves. I'm a doctor."

"You are here to help those people injured in the Al-Qasr Hotel tragedy. I have heard of you and your foundation. Your father is Astan Ilves, is he not?"

"Yes, to both of your questions. However, there is another reason I have come."

"Then come inside to talk, Lucy Ilves. It appears we have much in common and much to discuss."

* * *

Astan was confident Lucy would be successful in convincing Mika'il to leave the country. He was equally sure Marco would have no difficulty in compelling Gabe to leave California. Astan knew the United States government would never agree to allow Gabe to leave the country. He knew there was a "no-fly" label attached to Gabe's name and social security number. Gabe was under constant surveillance by the FBI. Fortunately, the government bureaucracy couldn't decide how to handle the situation concerning Mr. Gabe Brown. The party in power had strong ties and was beholden to the conservative Christian religious movement. Several of the Christian leaders at the forefront of this movement were actively pursuing Gabe for their own advantage. The military intelligence community wanted to get their hands on Gabe. Surely there were military applications for these miraculous abilities.

Astan knew that once Gabe and Mika'il were safely out of their respective countries, neither country would have any sound legal grounds requiring the two men be returned. Mika'il's country did not really want him or the grief he caused and would be pleased to see him leave. Mika'il's government feared his message would lead to a civil war between the devout hardline Muslims and this new sect. The ruling party could ill afford for such a conflict to occur. Many even believed it was a Zionist plot designed to tear the Palestinian Authority apart. The Israelis were not sure what to think of the situation. There had been the miraculous claims made by their own soldiers. Then there were the rumors of miracles being performed by this new prophet, Mika'il of Nablus, as people were now calling him. An ever-growing number of Muslims seemed to be drawn to this moderate form of Islam. Was that a good thing or a bad thing? Everyone seemed to have a different opinion. Even some Israelis were being drawn to these ideas being proselytized by Mika'il. The Israeli government was concerned about the increasing tension in the Muslim community and had sent troops to Nablus to monitor the situation. For now, they were content to just wait and see what happened next.

Astan did know what would happen next, both in Nablus and in California. That was why Gabe, Mika'il, and Lucy would all come to Astan's retreat along the shore of Lake Geneva in Switzerland. Astan would soon be on his way, but not until he had lunch with a friend of his from Vatican City. Astan had several questions he wanted to ask his friend, and he was sure Mykos Zorko would be more than happy to answer them.

* * *

When Lucy entered the fortified bunker at Mika'il's compound, she was not surprised to see her father's assistant was already there. Lucy was not the least bit happy about it either. She did not like it when her father kept her in the dark about negotiations that concerned her. Now she would have to be cautious in her conversation with Mika'il.

At the hospital Lucy's team of specialists had already administered the combination of experimental drugs through the patients' I Vs. They were beginning to attach the equipment that sent the electrical impulses throughout the brain. The prognosis was not very promising. Lucy's team knew that this treatment was very beneficial for patients with minor to moderate damage. They had seen very positive affects on both cognizant and comatose patients. The treatment had even brought several patients out of their comas. None though were in as poor of condition as these people. Then again, none were in as poor as condition as the fireman who came out of his coma after so many years. It had become an unspoken belief among the team that there was more to his recovery than this experimental treatment. The entire team knew why Lucy no longer helped in treating the patients. Every time she did assist there was a miraculous recovery. Of course, she was unable to see all the patients the team tried to help. It became awkward and painful. Who would live and who would be left to die?

* * *

Kevin had given explicit instructions to Mykos to tell no one about the newly found Botticelli. Mykos was giddy with excitement and had shared the information with Astan even before they were seated for lunch. Before the water was poured, he had passed along all the information about the break in, the murders, and how they were completely stymied in their investigation. Astan questioned Mykos about the subject matter of the painting, but Mykos refused to tell Astan any more until he had a chance to carefully clean, restore, and study it, which, he said, may be a few weeks since there was also a treasure trove of icons and other documents found in the mysterious pilfered vault. Mykos told Astan of the several other old paintings which had been so maliciously slashed in the crime. Those had been taken to another restorer who often assisted Mykos with his restorations. Mykos made Astan swear he would tell no one about the Botticelli or the crime. He promised to let Astan know if any other extraordinarily remarkable treasures were found. Astan was pleasant and gracious, as he always was with people he needed. Mykos was just such a person. A valuable asset for Astan within the walls of Vatican City.

* * *

Mika'il thanked Lucy for her father's offer to provide a worldwide stage for his message. He declined the offer expressing his need to bring the message first to the people of Palestine. Perhaps he would consider Astan's offer at a later date. Mika'il was also intrigued to learn that there were two others in the world who Allah, or God, had blessed with the power to perform miracles.

"I am deeply indebted to you for saving my good friend."

"It's not me who you owe your indebtedness. Your friend's life was saved by a higher power. Just as the many lives you have saved were not done so by your command. We're merely the instruments on whom our own Gods have chosen to bestow their blessings. What you've just told me about my father's plans was unknown to me until just now. I don't understand exactly what he has in mind, but I hope it will help make the world a safer place and bring peace to those who have battled over religion for generations. I hope you give thoughtful consideration to what my father has offered. I know I will."

The talk was formal and Mika'il could spare little time. The increasingly turbulent state of affairs in Nablus and the West Bank were being blamed on Mika'il's message. It seemed to incite near riot conditions throughout the region. He promised to meet with Lucy and Astan's assistant again. He told them he would pray to Allah for guidance as to what Allah desired, for it was Allah who guided Mika'il's future, not Astan Ilves.

***

Lucy returned to the hospital to check the progress of the patients. She still did not enter the ward where they all were located. Very little improvement had been observed. As she discussed the team's next steps in the hospital lobby, a continuous stream of patients poured into the hospital, all suffering from a wide array of injuries as a result of the religious clashes taking place in the city. In some cases, the conflict followed the injured into the hospital. Both sides sustained their share of injuries, needing immediate medical attention. Security was significantly increased, but a sense of uneasiness among the team members began to blossom into justified paranoia as gunshots were heard nearby in the streets.

That night the team stayed at the hospital, rather than risk trying to return to their hotel. Battles raged on the streets of Nablus. The hospital staff was pleased by the decision. They were overwhelmed by the number of injured and welcomed the help. The team established a triage, tended the minor injuries, and assisted in the emergency room. To most observers, Lucy appeared aloof, staying back from the beehive of activity the lobby had turned into. Her team members understood her reluctance to lend a hand, but even they were beginning to resent her non-participation.

A huge explosion shook the hospital. People dove to the floor. A mortar had hit a nearby abandoned building, damaging nothing more than the nerves of the hospital staff and patients. It was more than one of Lucy's team members could stand.

"Damn you, Lucy." one of the females said in tears. "Would you please go into that ward and heal those people. I really want to get out of here now." Everyone was quiet and staring at Lucy to see how she would react. It was something many of them had wanted to say, but none ever dared. Not even to each other did they speak of such things. Now the truth was on the table and everyone held their breath as they awaited Lucy's response.

Lucy stood silently looking towards the floor, unsure how to reply to the challenge. Suddenly she knew her time as a doctor was at its end. She hoped she still would be able to continue her research and, of course, financially support her foundation, but no longer would she be able to work with the patients directly. It was a harsh reality for Lucy to face.

"I know you're all tired and scared. So am I. I'm sorry I've brought all of you into such a dangerous situation. We were asked to come and I thought it our responsibility as doctors and scientists to do everything in our power to try to save the lives or at least give some hope to the families of those sixteen poor souls lying in comas. I want..." a second and closer bomb blast interrupted her. Several of the injured began to scream hysterically.

"Lucy, Lucy!" one of the doctors yelled, "Please, we're not prepared for this type of situation. We all want to help. We know the treatment has helped many patients in the past and given time could possibly even help these patients. We all know, but until now have been afraid to say, it's you, you and your touch that is the reason so many remarkable cures have taken place. Please. Please, for our sake and the sake of their families, please go into the ward and heal those sixteen people."

* * *

Astan's assistant had kept Astan well-informed of what was taking place in Nablus. Already Astan had arranged for heavily armed guards to help control the situation at the hospital. He was in the process of securing an Israeli military escort for the team's return to Tel Aviv if necessary. He also had arranged, through one of his more discrete acquaintances, for several armed men to inflame the situation around Mika'il's compound. Astan always seemed to know just the right kind of impetus required to achieve his goals. This would be no exception.

* * *

Concern continued to mount at Mika'il's compound as more reports of violence and deaths filtered into his camp. He watched what limited coverage CNN was able to provide of the street violence taking place in Nablus. It saddened him to see Muslim fighting Muslim, yet he knew this had been going on for centuries with the battles between the Shiites and the Sunnis. This battle was different. This was his battle. His battle as Allah's chosen warrior and prophet. His battle to make the world understand that for mankind to survive, it must change. But as he watched the news, and as he listened to the reports from his loyal followers, Mika'il felt pangs of doubt. Was he truly worthy of spreading Allah's message? It was too much of a burden for only one man to have to bear. That was when CNN showed the live video feed of what was taking place in California at that very moment.

* * *

Lucy could no longer prolong the inevitable. Every pair of eyes followed her as she slowly weaved her way through the crowded lobby and into the ward holding the sixteen comatose patients. She went from bed to bed praying for God to restore this damaged body back to health. Before she was halfway through, the first patients she had prayed for were already showing improvement. By the time she had finished praying over all the patients, two had actually come out of their comas. It would be several more days before any of the sixteen would be able to speak, but within the week the prognosis for recovery was excellent for all.

The team waited until Lucy had prayed over all sixteen of the victims before they entered the ward. Lucy spoke to none of the members as she left in near exhaustion. Word spread quickly throughout Nablus about Lucy's miraculous feat. News soon reached Mika'il at his compound. He quickly sent word that he wanted to meet again with Lucy and Astan's assistant and requested they come immediately.

* * *

"I've been told you performed many miracles tonight at the hospital," Mika'il said to Lucy.

"I did, and for the first time I can admit to having done so. I have refused to accept the fact I have been chosen by my God to proclaim his blessings to those in need. Now I have abandoned my reason and surrendered my mind to faith. For the first time in months, maybe years, I feel at peace with myself."

"Your faith in your God deeply moves me, Lucy Ilves," Mika'il replied. "Allah has shown me that I, too, must accept the unique gifts he has bestowed upon me and use them according to his word. I have spoken with your father. I have agreed to leave my compound and go with you to Switzerland."

"And did my father tell you what his plans are for us once we arrive there?"

"He only told me that by coming there, my safety would be assured. Once there, you, me, and this man from California, the miracle workers he called us, would discuss what the future holds."

"Did he say how he planned for me to get you out of the West Bank and on the jet?"

"I can handle that," the assistant spoke up. "If you remember we have several open visas from both the Palestinian Authority and the Israeli government. All we have to do is fill in the blanks and hide you among the medical team. If we dress you like a doctor, who is to say you are not a doctor. There is little risk we will be stopped. Astan has already arranged for an Israeli military escort back to the airport in Tel Aviv."

"I must insist my bodyguard accompany me," Mika'il told the assistant. "I am afraid he would not allow me to go anywhere without him."

"I'm sure that can be arranged," Lucy replied, before the assistant could take issue with Mika'il's request.

One of the Mercedes carried the team members from the hospital, while the second carried Mika'il, his bodyguard, Lucy, and Astan's assistant. The plan was to meet the Israeli military escort vehicles on the outskirts of Nablus and then race to the airport. Once there, the jet would be waiting to take everyone to Geneva. Geneva was the home of the primary research facility for Lucy's foundation. It was also near to one of Astan's very secure estates on the lake in Ville de Vevey near Montreux.

The medical team was happy to be leaving such a dangerous and explosive situation. Had any of the team members besides Lucy known the person responsible for all of the violence was now riding in their motorcade back towards Israeli, they may not have been so pleased. Though the team was unaware of Mika'il's presence, his escape from the compound did not go unnoticed. One of the CNN news crews recognized Mika'il's bodyguard in the back of the Mercedes and knew Ahmed never left the side of Mika'il. The CNN team quickly jumped into their van in pursuit of the Mercedes. They watched as the first Mercedes pulled into the hospital and stopped behind an identical car. They recognized the occupants in the other car as belonging to the medical team which had come to assist the comatose victims of the Al-Qasr attack. It was now officially being called an attack by the media. The story about the miraculous recovery was also beginning to spread throughout Nablus. No details were yet available, but people kept referring to the miracle worker.

The news van held back and tried to stay out of sight. The two Mercedes drove out of Nablus and were soon sandwiched between the two Israeli military vehicles assigned to escort and protect them. Seeing the escort, the CNN crew now knew for sure Mika'il had to be in one of the cars. As they accelerated to catch the convoy, they were delayed by several buses approaching in the oncoming lane. The camera man was filming the convoy as part of a story which they planned to file about Mika'il's escape.

A thunderous explosion shook the news van violently as a roadside bomb detonated near the convoy of four vehicles. The bomb had targeted the Israeli escort vehicle in the front, but detonated a second too early sparing the vehicle from extensive damage and saving the four soldiers' lives that were inside. The brunt of the explosion tore into a bus full of children which was heading in the opposite direction from the convoy. The bus was knocked onto its side and, although it didn't catch fire, it was riddled by the nuts and bolts packed around the explosive charge. Ten of the children and two adults died instantly as their bodies were shredded by the debris. Another twenty-one children and three adults were all seriously injured. Some with limbs ripped from their bodies. Giving no thought to possible snipers laying in wait, Lucy and Mika'il leaped from their Mercedes and rushed to help the children. As the two of them ran towards the bus, three terrorists leaped out from behind a wall and fired their machine guns. Mika'il raised his hand and blue sparkles flashed towards the shooters. The bullets from their guns seemed to stop in midair. A rage came over Mika'il. A rage he had never felt before. These men had killed children and now they were trying to kill his new friend, Lucy. With a flick of his wrist, the bullets suspended in mid-air streaked back towards the shooters with twice the velocity of the original shells. The three men were torn to shreds by their own bullets. Ahmed, along with the Israeli soldiers, stared dumbfounded at the sequence of events unfolding before their very eyes. They scurried out of their vehicles and took defensive positions to protect the rest of the medical team. In the CNN van the camera had been recording, catching the entire explosion and following events on tape. It was still rolling as Lucy and Mika'il rushed on towards the bombed bus. The cries and screams of the dying children filled the air. The cameraman was out of the van and in quick pursuit of Lucy and Mika'il, along with a newsman who began a running commentary of the events. The van was equipped with a satellite linkup system and within a minute was sending the fast-breaking story around the world.

For the next twenty minutes it was as if the world had come to a halt as millions of people watched in awe as Mika'il and Lucy healed the severely injured children and adults with their prayers and touch. Limbs that had practically been ripped from the bodies seemed to melt or morph back onto the torso. Gashing wounds, some torn completely through the bodies, began to heal right before the camera. Lifeless bodies suddenly jarred back into existence as if shocked by a bolt of lightening. And then, the cries and the screams stopped. An eerie silence fell upon all who had witnessed the miracles. Even the CNN commentator was unable to continue his broadcast as the significance of what they had just witnessed left him and the others speechless.

"Everyone back in the cars," Astan's assistant ordered, "we have to leave now."

Stunned, the medical team did as they were ordered. Ahmed grabbed Mika'il by the arm and dragged him back to the Mercedes, as did the assistant with Lucy.

"Forget about the escort, just get us out of here," the assistant yelled at the driver. Within seconds the two Mercedes were traveling in excess of one hundred and twenty kilometers an hour as they raced for the Tel Aviv airport. The assistant knew if they were not out of the country within the next hour, chances were they never would get Mika'il out of Israel. The two military vehicles and their crews remained on the scene securing the perimeter and controlling the ever-growing crowd. The CNN news van was unable to get around the crash scene to pursue the two escaping Mercedes. They remained at the scene to followup with the children whose bodies had only moments before been bloodied and mutilated but now were restored anew.

The two Mercedes were not stopped as they crossed from the West Bank into Israel. They continued at a slightly slower pace now that they were in Israeli territory. They went straight to the airport and prepared to board the jet which had been fueled and readied. Security and customs agents were waiting to check the visas and passports of all those leaving the country. Mika'il and Ahmed's names were added to two of the open-ended humanitarian visas. Everything appeared to be in order and the passengers boarded the plane. The jet was cleared to taxi onto the main runway to prepare for takeoff. The pilot waited patiently for his final clearance, expecting it any second, but it didn't come. He requested permission again, but was advised to continue to hold. Out of the window the pilot could see several military vehicles approaching the plane and he notified Astan's assistant. A check of the names on the visas revealed Mika'il and Ahmed were both wanted terrorists responsible for the past deaths of several Israeli military personnel. Regardless of what Mika'il may be doing now, or the fact he had just saved the lives of so many Israeli children on worldwide television, he was a wanted man.

"Don't wait," the assistant ordered, "you have got to get us into the air. Do you understand?"

“Yes sir.” the pilot replied. He knew where his loyalties laid. Astan paid him extremely well and, without hesitation, complied.

“Roger that tower… you are breaking up, but believe you said I was cleared for takeoff. Thank you tower… and we will see you soon. This is …” the pilot interspersed a crackling noise with his voice as though there was static on the radio. He revved the engines and rolled down the runway for a picturesque takeoff. He left the radio off as he raced to leave Israeli air space. Before he was able to do so, two Israeli military fighter jets appeared to his starboard side and signaled for him to land. He pretended his radio was dead and couldn’t understand them. He called back to the assistant.

“They’re signaling for me to land, sir. What should I do?”

“Do nothing. We’re almost out of their airspace and they wouldn’t dare shoot us down.”

“Well, let’s hope you’re right,” the pilot replied, then smiled and waved at the two combat jets sent to force it down. Seconds later they were out of Israeli airspace and the two combat jets were on their way back to base for a not-so-pleasant reception.

The Israeli bluff did not work. Of course, they couldn’t shoot down a private plane belonging to Astan Ilves, especially knowing who was on board and what the world had just witnessed them doing. Several people would lose their jobs because of what had just occurred.

The head of Shabak, also known as the GSS (General Security Service), swore to never again allow such a lapse in territorial security to occur. He, along with the head of the Aman, the military intelligence service who had supplied the two combat jets, agreed this would be the last time anyone would dare to call their bluff. Next time it wouldn't be a bluff.

CHAPTER TWENTY-SIX

The boundary lines have fallen for me in pleasant places;
surely I have a delightful inheritance.

I will praise the LORD, who counsels me;
even at night my heart instructs me.

I have set the LORD always before me.
Because he is at my right hand,
I will not be shaken.

Psalm 16:6-8

James Bruce came upon the three soldiers when he and his party of traveling companions reached the river. The soldiers had been herding one of the many pure white cows the herdsman tended throughout this part of Ethiopia. The cow was tied to a tree to allow the men to prepare for dinner before crossing the river. They invited Bruce to join them. Bruce in turn offered the soldiers honey and bread made from dhurra, a type of millet. They in turn offered to share their meat with James Bruce. One of the soldiers pulled out a knife from beneath his robes and cut several large pieces of meat from the flanks of the cow. He folded the cow's skin down over the wounds and used small skewers to refasten it. He passed the hunks of raw meat to his comrades and to Bruce who forced himself to eat it out of courtesy. The soldiers finished the meat, untied the cow, and headed on across the river. Along his journey James Bruce would see many more cows with the skewers holding the skin together. Eating raw meat cut from living animals was the only way Ethiopians enjoyed it.

James Bruce had come to Gondar, the capital of Ethiopia, in a time of civil unrest. He had come seeking the source of the Nile. He also wanted to collect ancient religious icons and documents which he had heard existed in Ethiopian churches. Ras Michael was the advisor to the fifteen-year-old ruler of Ethiopia, King Takla. Ras Michael, though not the King, was the real power and ruler of the land. Ras Michael returned to Gondar leading the parade of his victorious troops. The procession featured the stuffed skin of one of the rebel chiefs who had been flayed alive. Ras Michael took a liking to Bruce, thinking Bruce might prove to be a powerful ally. He agreed to allow Bruce to seek out the Nile's source. However, it was what he would discover along his way that would prove to be the true find of his six-year ordeal.

* * *

The epistle and canon arrived in Axum in 1333 AD. Three monks of the Brotherhood of the Divine protected them along the treacherous journey from Smyrna. The Stranger's spies were everywhere. He had inflamed unrest resulting in war for most of Northern Africa and the Middle East, making the Weeper's journey perilous. In Axum the three brothers found a fellow monk who knew the Brotherhood of the Divine was charged with a sacred and dangerous task. This monk too, had an important and divine task. He, like several monks who had come before him, was "The Guardian of the Ark of the Covenant." His entire life had been spent in a secluded room at St. Mary's of Zion Church, the only human allowed to view the sacred relic he was sworn to protect. He agreed to place the box containing the copy of the canon and the epistle in the room with the Ark. Instructions as to who could retrieve the vessels that had been placed in the box were attached, in case he was to die before his replacement was trained. It was here the canon and epistle would remain until 1535 AD, when "the Left Handed," Ahmed Gragn's cultural annihilation, swept towards Axum. The Muslims were attempting to wipe out Ethiopian Christendom. They looted and destroyed the churches along with the icons and manuscripts held inside. Two days before his raiding army reigned destruction on Axum and burned the city to the ground, the priests and monks took the Ark, the box of manuscripts left by the Brotherhood of the Divine, and other treasures from King Solomon's Temple to one of the remote islands on Lake Tana. Gragn's march across Ethiopia finally came to an end in February 1543 AD on the shores of Lake Tana. Fifteen years of devastation would put a pall on Ethiopia which would last for centuries.

* * *

Bruce began his journey sailing across Lake Tana, stopping at several of the islands along the way. One of those islands, Tana Kirkos, held the very treasures Bruce had come to Ethiopia to find. When the priests and monks escaped from Axum, they made their way to this small isolated island. Several years before, a very devout sect of monks had come to Tana Kirkos and dedicated their lives to prayer, meditation, and worship. Now they were given the task of protecting the most Holy of Holies, the Ark of the Covenant. It, along with the other treasures, remained hidden on the island until the mid 1600's when the Ark was returned to the newly rebuilt St. Mary of Zion Church. For some reason, several items and documents were left behind on the island. One such item was the box containing the canon and epistle which the Brotherhood of the Divine had entrusted to the Guardian of the Ark. Of course, that had been several guardians ago and no longer was there a Weeper to watch over the canon. One of the monks on the island began to translate the canon from the original Greek to Ge'ez, the local language. After several years he had completed his task. The additional Revelation he found puzzling until he translated the epistle. It was then that he realized the magnitude of significance that the canon and epistle held for the world. A second copy of the canon was made in Ge'ez for use in the church on the island. The original Greek canon along with the first Ge'ez translation was placed back in the box and sealed. The epistle and its Ge'ez translation were sealed in a separate container and hidden away in the hope that God would reveal to the monks just how this copy of the epistle would play its part in his perfect plan. Bruce was the answer to part of the monk's prayers.

James Bruce was a giant of a man standing six feet four inches tall with bright red hair, towering above and striking awe in most Ethiopians. Bruce always wore the robes of the local people, could speak and read Ge'ez and, although he did have quite a temper, was usually a gentle and likable man. God had answered the prayers offered by the monks of Tana Kirkos and had told them that such a man would come to take the canon from the island. They were only to give him the Ge'ez copy of the canon, but not the epistle. God had other plans for the epistle and the original canon. This was exactly what Bruce had hoped to find on his trip to Ethiopia. He could read Ge'ez and knew this canon contained the Book of Enoch, as well as other books the Council of Nicaea had ordered banned and burned. Such a find would surely guarantee Bruce much praise and recognition when he returned to England and Scotland.

Bruce eventually did discover the source of the Blue Nile, but his notes, the canon, and the drawings his companion had made of their adventure were almost lost on his return trip out of Ethiopia. The King, as he had done once before, refused to allow Bruce to leave. Bruce was forced to escape with four others who were being held. They set out across the desert with five camels and full water skins. Running out of water and near death from the dryness and the dreaded simoom that nearly suffocated them, the men had to kill the camels and drain the water from their stomachs to survive. The men continued on, leaving all of Bruce's journals, drawings, and collected documents behind. A few days later, God in his mercy, delivered Bruce and his companions to safety in Aswan, just as all hope was turning to despair. Deathly ill, Bruce's first action was to borrow camels and retrace his steps to recover the possessions he had left behind in the desert. Once he had recovered his baggage, he returned to Cairo, then on to France to seek medical help. When he eventually returned to England, he did not receive the reception he had expected and many doubted the tales of his extensive travels. He returned to Scotland, humiliated, and didn't even look at his journals for several years.

The Stranger heard tales of Bruce's discovery and hoped such a find would help prove that the revelation detailing his ascension to the throne was intentionally left out of the Bible when John first wrote down the Revelation. It was not until 1821AD that the Stranger's hopes were finally realized. That was when William Laurence published the first English translation of Bruce's find. Now the Stranger had the most complete version yet of the Book of Enoch. He would learn just how the angels had been, and still could be, coerced and manipulated. More importantly, here was the first confirmation he had been seeking of the tenth Revelation, "The Ascension of Satan." Just like in the Russian birch bark copy belonging to Lord Corwin, the revelation appeared in Laurence's translation. In Lord Corwin's translation, it too had been left out of the actual translated text, but was footnoted in its entirety. He knew it would take more than two references to the missing verses in Revelation 10 to make the world believe they were deliberately deleted from the Book of Revelation and the New Testament. He also knew that in time he would find the additional proof necessary to convince the world God knew, and tried to hide, word of the Stranger's inevitable ascension. He would offer temptations and send his spies to Ethiopia to search for the original canon. Finding that canon would bring him ever so closer to his destiny.

CHAPTER TWENTY-SEVEN

And the one most high sent his archangels to the earth to live as men, cleanse the earth of corruption, bring peace to all generations of men, with miracles bestow the blessings which are known in heaven.

Book of Enoch 11:4

Mika'il sat in silence as the plane streaked towards the planned rendezvous in Vevey, Switzerland. He was having great difficulty comprehending what he had done to the three terrorists. It was against everything he had been preaching. Lucy and Ahmed stayed silent, allowing Mika'il to sort through the events of the past three hours. The rest of the medical team sat in an area in the rear of the private jet away from Lucy, Mika'il, and Ahmed. They were thankful just to have gotten out of the West Bank alive. Unlike their fellow passengers, they could not stop talking about what they all had just witnessed.

Just as stunned and amazed were Gabe and Kevin who had watched the entire event unfold live on CNN. They, like millions of other viewers, sat in utter disbelief as they not only saw Mika'il reverse the bullets and massacre the three men with but a flick of his wrist, but also sat spellbound in front of their television sets as Lucy and Mika'il went from victim to victim healing them with their touch and prayers. Every television station in every country around the world was running the CNN video again and again. One religious' expert after another was paraded before the news cameras to give his or her interpretation of the events which had occurred in the West Bank.

Sitting in his library at home, Astan could not stop smiling at what he was seeing, although it was not going exactly as he had planned. He could not have been more pleased by this turn of events. Here was incredible free advertising, far superior to what he had been planning to pay millions to achieve. Paid programming could never have the impact this live CNN news coverage provided. Now his only challenge would be to get all three of these miracle workers to agree to his plan, a plan he hoped would unite the world in support of his vision. He knew there would be many who would never support what he had in mind, but that really didn't matter. The only support he really needed was the three miracle workers who were all on their way to Switzerland at that very moment.

Kevin's phone began to ring not ten minutes after the first rerun of the CNN live footage. It was the Bishop from the Doctrinal Office calling to make sure Kevin was watching CNN. He also wanted to know why the Vatican jet was returning to Rome without Kevin. Kevin explained that he was with Gabe Brown and the two of them were on their way to Astan Ilves' house in Switzerland. The

Bishop knew they were together, for he had seen the news coverage of the three men escaping from Gabe's house in California. He was surprised to hear where they were headed. The Bishop advised Gabe to keep him updated and to call the security office for an update on the murder investigation. Kevin assured him he would. Kevin was curious as to what new information the security office might have for him and was preparing to call when Astan's assistant came out of the cockpit and joined the two men in front of the television.

"Well, they made it, but it was close."

"What do you mean, close? It looked like they got away safely on TV," Gabe responded.

"I'm talking about their jet. The Israeli's tried to keep it from taking off. Two jet fighters threatened to shoot it down if it didn't land. The pilot called their bluff and won. The two Israeli jets backed off and Lucy's plane made it out of Israeli airspace."

"Where's her plane now?" Kevin asked.

"I'd say it's about an hour behind us. That'd make it about two hours from touching down in Geneva."

"Precisely." Gabe just blurted out in a peculiar way.

"What'd you say?" Kevin asked.

"I was just figuring our distance to Geneva and, along with our air speed, and I came up with exactly one hour till we land. That would make the other jet precisely two hours from landing. So, I said 'precisely.' I have no idea why I chose that word."

Kevin got the feeling Gabe was hiding something, but did not want to labor on it.

Kevin walked to the back of the jet and called the Vatican City security office as the Bishop had advised. They had found no leads as to who murdered the two guards. He knew there was no way they would ever believe his theory. They had done a careful match of the talon prints with the four-hundred-year-old ones and found them to be identical. There was still no word about anything yet from Mykos regarding the Botticelli or the inventory of the other items found in the vault. They did have one rather curious bit of information that deserved to be followed up. It seems the Rome police had ticketed a car parked illegally very near to where the vent opening for the catacomb was located. The car was registered to Astan Ilves. It was a red Enzo-Ferrari. Kevin's interest in what the investigator told him suddenly picked up. "What would she be doing near Vatican City?" Kevin said to himself, forgetting he was still on the phone.

"What would who be doing where?" the investigator asked.

"Just thinking out loud," Kevin replied. "You know I'm always holding discussions with myself." The investigator knew that peculiarity about Kevin Bridges. Everyone in security knew he was a little bit out of the ordinary, but they all agreed he did get the job done. Kevin hung up the phone now with even more questions that he needed to ask Lucy when he saw her. According to Gabe, that would be in "precisely" one hour and forty-seven minutes.

The escapes of both Gabe from his house in California, and Lucy and Mika'il from of the West Bank, had been televised by CNN. The crowds at Gabe's house had for the most part dispersed once they realized he was gone. The violence surrounding Mika'il's compound in Nablus had also slowed to almost a stop. Most of his followers had blended back into the cities and villages to wait for the time when Mika'il would call for them to rise up and follow. No doubt several thousand more Muslims, Christians, and Jews would all submit to Mika'il's message after seeing the miracles he and Lucy had performed.

Kevin had questioned Gabe for most of the flight from California to Switzerland; that is, until the breaking news caught their attention. He listened as Gabe explained what had occurred on the commuter train, first with everybody thinking he was speaking their native language simultaneously, then about the prayers and the train car landing out of harms way. Gabe purposely left out the part about the Stranger and the dreams he had. He told Kevin how he had inadvertently healed that woman with the broken jaw and how several friends whom he had been in contact with since the incident had told him how they had never felt better in years after coming to visit. Some claimed to have been cured of their cancers or damaged backs. Gabe gave Kevin a list of the ones he could remember. Kevin would followup on them at a later date.

Kevin was fluent in several languages and asked Gabe questions in each language, always receiving the answer in the language in which he had asked the question. Gabe said that he had heard every question Kevin asked in English. He also said he answered each question in English. This miracle was rather difficult for Kevin to grasp. He did recall the story in Acts about the day of the Pentecost and knew such a miracle was not unprecedented.

Soon after Lucy and Mika'il's plane was safely away from the fighter jets, lack of sleep caught up with all the passengers on board. All were soon asleep, all but Lucy. She didn't need much sleep. She had never needed much sleep even as a little girl. Two or three hours a night was the most she ever got and it suited her just fine. She sat trying to decide exactly what the future held and, even more importantly, what her father had in mind for her and her two miracle working companions. She was anxious to know more about this Gabe Brown from California. He was said to have displayed some remarkable healing powers. She wondered if this man could possibly have healed those maimed children the way she and Mika'il had. She respected Mika'il for his abilities and how he used them. She even respected the religious message he was now promoting. But something... something made her a bit wary of him. Perhaps it was that Mika'il reminded her of her father. Or maybe it was the outburst of anger when he killed the three men responsible for hurting those little children. He seemed deeply troubled by what he had done, but was it just an act? Lucy couldn't tell for sure and even having the slightest shred of doubt made her wary.

"If only Kevin were here," she thought. She found herself in a most unfamiliar situation, desiring male companionship. Ever since her dinner with Kevin, she couldn't seem to get the thought of him out of her mind. She had thoroughly enjoyed their conversation that night and hated to see it end. She wished he was there so she could feel that happiness again.

"Your father is on the phone for you," the co-pilot said to Lucy. "Why don't you take it in the forward galley where you won't be disturbed?" Lucy thanked the co-pilot and headed to the galley.

"I guess you got your wish. My career as a doctor and research scientist is definitely over. Things have gotten completely out of control."

"It didn't look that way to me," Astan replied. "It appeared that you and Mika'il had things completely under control."

"What do you mean by 'look that way'? How do you know what it looked like? Your assistant could only describe it to you."

"Are you telling me you didn't know the entire episode was being sent live around the world on CNN?" Astan asked, astonished. "They're still showing it over and over as we speak. You two are the biggest stars in the entire world right now."

"Oh my God. I do remember seeing a cameraman there."

"Turn on the television and see for yourself. You're on every channel in the world right now."

Lucy quickly turned on the television and stared without saying a word. Astan knew what she was doing and remained quiet as the reality of the situation began to sink in.

"Oh my God," she repeated, "what am I going to do now?"

"You're going to come to the house in Vevey. Then you, I, Mika'il, and Gabe are going to discuss my plans for our future. This is our chance to finally bring the world together."

"Is that Gabe person already there?"

"No, but he will be within a couple of hours. Their plane is about an hour ahead of your plane's arrival time."

"You said their plane. Is there another miracle worker you forgot to tell me about?"

"Good gracious no. There's just the three of you. Gabe is being accompanied by someone. I don't like it, but he insisted he be allowed to bring this person along. I really couldn't say no, although I really wanted to. He is being escorted by your good friend, Mr. Bridges."

"Kevin? Kevin Bridges from the Vatican is with him?"

"Unfortunately, yes," Astan replied.

Lucy wasn't sure how to react to the news. She had promised Kevin she would include him in whatever her father was planning and now it was actually happening. With the miraculous healing of those children by her and Mika'il being plastered on televisions around the world, she wasn't so sure if seeing Kevin right now was what she wanted even after, not more than ten minutes ago, wishing for exactly that.

"I just thought you should know that Mr. Bridges will be here when you arrive," Astan said, softening his tone.

"I appreciate that," Lucy replied. "Did you know the Israelis threatened to shoot down our plane?" she asked, hoping to veer the conversation away from Kevin.

"I was told about it. Believe me, I'll be talking to my friends in the Knesset and, if I don't get the proper response, you can be assured the Israeli economy will feel the fury of my wrath." Lucy had no reason to doubt Astan's word or his ability to follow through on his threat.

"You do know Mika'il also has a traveling companion who he refuses to part with. It's his bodyguard. A man named Ahmed. Actually, a very nice man from what I can tell," Lucy explained.

"I already have my people checking on him. I do know he's been with Mika'il for years. I really don't think there'll be a problem, especially if you think he's a nice man."

"I need to rest before we land, so we can continue our discussion when I arrive. See you then." As she usually did when talking on the phone with Astan, she hung up before he could respond and get in the last word.

Lucy returned to her seat, leaned back, and closed her eyes. She knew she wouldn't sleep, but she needed to relax and think about what she was going to say to both Kevin and her father. One thing she did know, it was bound to be a very interesting conversation.

* * *

The Stranger could finally see all the pieces of the puzzle beginning to fall into place. His time was growing nearer, ever so nearer. The pieces were all nearly in his grasp. Just a little more manipulation was all that was needed. Then the world would witness what for so long had been denied and secreted away. "The Ascension of Satan," no longer could it be denied. Soon, so very soon.

CHAPTER TWENTY-EIGHT

Dear friends, do not be surprised at the painful trial you are suffering, as though something strange were happening to you. But rejoice that you participate in the sufferings of Christ, so that you may be overjoyed when his glory is revealed.

1 Peter 4:12-13

It took very little effort by the Stranger to instigate the "War to End all Wars." A few broken alliances, one simple assassination, the sinking of a ship, any of these things could be said to have started it. Once it began, they all became insignificant. In the end, there was no clear winner. Just a temporary peace, leaving plenty of fuel for the next major conflict to begin. Just the way the Stranger liked it.

Joshua's father had died from the mustard gas in one of the trenches on the western front along with tens of thousands of others. Joshua was but a baby at the time, the first and only son born of his Russian father and Jewish mother. After his father's death, Joshua's mother moved him and his two sisters from Smolensk to Poland. With her she took a painting passed down through her family for generations, along with a warning to keep the painting hidden and never to tell anyone but family of its existence. The painting was by Sandro Botticelli. She had heard of the artist but knew nothing about him. She was told the painting depicted a verse from the Christian Bible. She was not familiar with the Bible at all. As a child, Joshua would spend hours staring at the violence depicted in the painting. Most of the gore and scenes of death were painted in the background and showed what appeared to be soldiers. Some were on horseback, some floated in the air, and some were on the ground destroying a vast array of beasts and grossly disfigured humans. In the foreground was what Joshua believed to be the devil. It was a large, horrific looking angel with huge black wings and large spiked talons instead of feet. There was an angel draping chains across its body, a twisted pained look was on its face. It was being cast into a deep crevasse. Joshua found a second scene to be even more fascinating. Two men, one dressed like a church official, one in a tunic, were being thrown into a flaming pool full of beings, all in different stages of melting and burning. Joshua was sure it was the pools of Hell. Three angels all seemed to be watching piously. Joshua imagined his father had died in such a battle of good versus evil. That was why, when he was old enough, Joshua joined the Polish military.

He advanced quickly and served near his home village. On September 16, 1939, the Russian Army occupied half of Poland. His village was located in the part the Russians now claimed. Several Russian soldiers came to his mother's home and demanded to be garrisoned. Joshua was taken prisoner and moved back to a gulag near

Smolensk in the Katyn Forest. It was there that he became one among the thousands of Polish soldiers Stalin ordered massacred and buried in mass graves. His family would eventually be wiped out, not by the Germans who were systematically exterminating the Jews throughout Europe, but by the Russians who would blame their massacre on the German Army. The Russians would eventually join the fight against the Nazis, but not till many more were to die in Poland.

* * *

Viktor Gorkin was one of the soldiers who occupied Joshua's mother's house. He was no more than a boy of eighteen. He had been conscripted into the Russian Army from one of the many youth athletic training camps designed to prepare the Russian youth for the inevitable war with Germany. For now, the Russians and the Germans were on the same side, both occupying their portions of Poland. It was an alliance that could not and would not last. When he and his comrades moved into the house, he was appalled at how the older men sexually brutalized the mother and daughters. He refused to have anything to do with it. He would run to the basement and stay there until the screams of the women finally stopped. It was there that he discovered the Botticelli hidden away behind a shelf. Looking at the painting would take his mind away from the horrors taking place above him. It was his secret that he refused to share with anyone. It did not go unnoticed by his comrades that Viktor never participated in the raping of the three women. Each had their turn on the women, so they were equally culpable for atrocities, guaranteeing each to silence. His comrades grabbed Viktor, holding him down while others undressed him. They forced all three of the women to sit upon Viktor until he no longer could claim to be a virgin. The mother in her anger lashed out at one of the Russian soldiers with a pair of shears. A second soldier shot her in the head. The game the soldiers had been playing had suddenly turned very ugly. Viktor was released and one of the men pulled the girl away and locked her in an adjacent room. Her sister would not stop screaming. Viktor rolled onto his side and puked several times on the floor. A comrade threw him a towel to wipe the blood, brains, and vomit off of his body. Viktor hurriedly dressed without saying a word. They were busy cleaning the mess of the dead mother. No one noticed Viktor was gone.

Viktor was ill from what his comrades had done and had forced him to do. He wanted to get away. He had to get away. He ran down the steps to the basement and grabbed the painting from its hiding place. He ran out the cellar door with the painting in hand and stole a motorcycle belonging to a mail courier. He placed the painting in the sidecar attached to the cycle. Seconds later he was racing down the street headed back for his home town in Russia. It would take him two weeks travel time and the assistance of many farmers and storekeepers, giving him food and money for petrol, before he reached his small dacha on the outskirts of Molotov. He hid the painting in a work shed, drove the cycle into the Kama River, and went to work at a munitions plant using the name of a deceased cousin. Here he would remain till the end of the war, when he would move into the city, marry a young woman, and raise a family. Twice a week for the rest of his life, Viktor would return to his dacha. He would tend to his garden and gaze upon his painting.

* * *

This was Jacob's third missionary trip to Perm. He came to visit and bring food, clothes, and supplies to the orphanages located in the surrounding countryside and smaller towns. Since the fall of Communism several Christian organizations had began coming to Russia on such missions. Few came to an area as remote as Perm. For years, Russia denied the existence of Perm. It appeared on no maps. Perm was the military industrial center for much of Russia. During the Cold War, the less anyone spoke of Perm, or knew of Perm, the happier the government. Perm was a thirty-hour train ride east of Moscow. It was the debarkation point for those going to Siberia and there were always several going there. The Russian gulags and prisons were a popular destination.

Jacob had grown familiar with the area and was out walking past a row of older dachas in the countryside near Zakamsk. As he passed by one of the small dachas, he greeted an elderly *babushka* out tending her strawberries. She was thrilled to meet an American and invited Jacob into her yard to share some of her strawberries. She was amused by his feeble attempt to speak Russian and took a liking to him, offering him tea. The *babushka* was extremely poor with few possessions. The house itself was immaculate, everything set perfectly in its proper place. She had but two changes of clothing and one blanket for her bed, not nearly sufficient for the long cold Perm winters. The kitchen cabinet held two glasses, two tea cups, and two plates. There was no refrigerator in the tiny kitchen, but she did have a sink and running water. Her bathroom was an outhouse located no more than ten feet from her back door. Still, even the thought of traveling ten feet in the darkness of winter, with fifteen feet of snow on the ground, seemed utterly mind-numbing. Jacob was appalled by her meager living conditions and promised to bring her some clothes and a quilt the next day. She said she was just fine and that wouldn't be necessary, but Jacob insisted.

When he returned with the quilt, some clothes, and a box of groceries, the *babushka* had prepared a strawberry cake and had tea ready to share with her new friend. They talked together, as well as they could, she showing him pictures of her late husband, and he admiring the Russian Orthodox art icons on her walls. Jacob had an eye for that sort of thing. He had been an art history major in college and now owned a small antique store. Jacob was always searching for a good bargain. Unfortunately, there were few antiques to be found for sale in Russia and it was illegal to take religious icons and artwork out of the country. The *babushka* offered one of the crosses to Jacob, but he declined explaining the government policy. She cursed her government and told Jacob she had a painting which her husband had told her had come from Poland. She didn't know the circumstances of how he had come to own it. She asked Jacob if he might be interested in it. She said it was wrapped in several layers of canvas and stored out in the shed. He offered to take a look at it and, with her permission, brought it in from the shed. Together, they unwrapped the painting. Jacob couldn't believe what he saw. It was filthy and had a strange wooden frame and back on it, but there in the corner was the unmistakable signature of Sandro Botticelli. Jacob could not imagine such a painting was an original Botticelli. Even so, it was a very old and exceptional painting. It had all the characteristics one would expect to find of the Florentine school of painting. Jacob asked if she would be willing to sell the painting and she told him he could have it. Jacob couldn't believe his good fortune, but refused not to pay her for it. He pulled out all the rubles he had, almost four hundred American dollars worth, and handed it to the *babushka*. She had never seen so much money in her life and began to cry. Jacob could not stop thanking her, and she him. He hurried to leave before she changed her mind.

When he got back to the center where he was staying, he carefully wiped some of the dust off of the painting and took several pictures with his digital camera. He sent an email and the pictures to whom he knew to be one of the world experts on Botticelli's work, Mykos Zorko. He then started to figure out how he was going to get the painting past customs and out of Russia.

Mykos' computer received Jacob's email and sent an acknowledgement informing the sender Mykos was on a very important project and unavailable for several days. Jacob was disappointed, but not too concerned. He was more concerned about sneaking the painting past the Russian authorities. Last year they didn't bother to open any of his bags, but the year before they had searched through everything. His plan was to stick the painting in the empty trunks that had been filled with supplies for the orphans and, if they found it and questioned him, he would tell them it was not a Russian religious icon, or for that matter, even a piece of Russian art. He was ready to argue the point and raise a big stink if necessary.

When the day finally came for the missionary team to leave from the Moscow airport, it was as if they were expecting Jacob. They went right to the trunk that held the painting and opened it up. They took the painting, making Jacob so irate that he was arrested and placed in a holding cell at the airport for two days. Someone from the

American consulate finally came and had Jacob released. When he asked about getting his painting back, the authorities played ignorant as to what he was talking about. That made Jacob even more irate and he filed a formal complaint of theft. He included copies of the photos as part of his complaint. He convinced the consulate to take the case seriously and managed to get a formal letter of protest sent by the ambassador. Jacob decided if he was going to go down, he would go down swinging. The Russian Ministry of Culture quickly got involved when they heard it could possibly be a Botticelli and within hours the painting had miraculously reappeared in a back room at the airport. It was soon on its way to the Hermitage in St. Petersburg where Russian experts would evaluate it. Jacob insisted on a receipt, but only received a trip to the airport where he was informed, he was no longer welcome to visit Russia in any capacity. The consulate told Jacob they would continue to monitor the case, but not to get his hopes up. Chances were slim he would ever see the painting again unless it was hanging on a wall at the Hermitage but, since he could no longer even enter Russia, there was no chance of that happening.

"Just be thankful they're allowing you to leave the country," the consulate attaché told Jacob. "The last American who tried to sneak religious icons out of here is still in jail."

"It's not an icon," Jacob yelled at the attaché, as the two Russian security men hurried Jacob towards his plane.

CHAPTER TWENTY-NINE

Praise belongs to God, the Lord of the worlds, the Merciful, the Compassionate, the Lord at the Day of Judgment. Thee we worship and Thee we ask for help. Guide us on the straight path, the path of those to whom Thou showest kindness, not those upon whom Thou wrath rests, nor those who go astray.

Qu'ran, the Fatiha

It had been three days since he had begun the inventory on the vault and Mykos had barely slowed to catch his breath except, of course, for his luncheon meeting with Astan. Mykos and his assistants had removed all the items from the vault and placed them in his workshop. Twenty-four hour armed Swiss Guards protected the artifacts and did security checks of everyone going into and coming from the vault and Mykos' workshop. Kevin had insisted on that. If someone, or something, wanted an item in the vault bad enough to kill two men for, then there was plenty of reason to believe they might try again. Kevin asked that there be a priest always on duty with the guards. The guards found that rather peculiar, but the Bishop from the Doctrinal Office insisted Kevin's request be followed. The Bishop himself informed the priests of why they were to be there and told them under no circumstances were they to tell anyone the reason. Even the Bishop took a turn, keeping the guards company while he looked over the wealth of recently rediscovered treasures.

Mykos had gone back to cleaning the Botticelli and was carefully removing years of dirt from around the faces of the angels. He was at least following one of the requests Kevin had made. Soon the faces on the painting would be clear enough to photograph and email to Kevin. Several of his assistants were busy analyzing and translating other objects and documents which had been removed from the vault.

"Mykos...Mykos," one of his assistants called, "I've found a peculiar letter included with this copy of the canon. It refers to the Botticelli painting you are cleaning." Mykos put down his brush and rushed over to read the letter.

"The painting is called the 'Ascension of Satan'. My goodness!" Mykos suddenly exclaimed. "This letter was written by the monk Savonarola. Incredible. Simply incredible," Mykos said, excitedly. "The letter says the painting depicts verses in Revelation 10."

"Wait a minute," one of the assistants interrupted, "there are no such verses about the ascension of Satan in Revelation 10."

"Savonarola says there were additional verses in Revelation 10. They were purposely left out of the Book of Revelation because they were so frightening," Mykos continued to read. "He says in this copy of the canon that all of Revelation 10 is included. He claims Irenaeous ordered it removed from John's writings soon after Apostle John's death. Savonarola also claims there are at least three other early copies of the canon that include all of Revelation 10. A group of monks known as the Brotherhood of the Divine have guarded and protected the secret of the missing Revelation for centuries. Savonarola claims God had spoken to him and the other Brothers, telling them these deleted verses of Revelation 10 must never be destroyed, but kept hidden from Satan and the fallen angels. It was God's infinite wisdom that instructed John to not write it down as part of the Book of Revelation. There are also a series of numbers at the bottom of the page. I have no idea what they stand for."

"I've heard about those additional verses to Revelation 10," one of the assistants spoke up. "I read about two other canons that had a different version of Revelation 10. One is in the Library at the Lord Corwin Museum outside of London. It came from a birch bark copy made in the tenth or twelfth century. I can't remember the date, but I do know it came from northern Russia. I believe they said they had traced its origin back to the Archangel Michael monastery in Russia."

"That's right," Mykos replied, "I remember reading that as well. And as I recall the other canon with the altered Revelation 10 was found by James Bruce during his explorations in Ethiopia in the late 1700s. He found a copy of a canon written in Ge'ez that contained the Revelation along with several of the apocryphal books. I believe it is in Scotland somewhere."

"Mykos, do you think it is really possible some verses of Revelation 10 were deliberately left out of the New Testament?"

"As incredible and as blasphemous as it sounds, based on this letter, it might very well be true. I want one of you to immediately translate that canon. I need someone else to head to England and get me a copy of those other two canons that contain the complete version of Revelation 10. I will make all the arrangements, but I want you to leave now. This is a priority. I bet this just might be the reason someone broke into the vault in the first place." Mykos was bubbling with excitement. He couldn't wait to tell Kevin Bridges he had figured out the motive for the breakin and murders. Even more exciting was the thought of having discovered that parts of Revelation 10 were purposely left out of the Bible. He had uncovered Christ's words that were originally meant to be part of The Book of Revelation. But before he emailed Kevin with his discovery and with pictures of the Botticelli, he had to tell his friend Astan Ilves the exciting news. Mykos headed to his office to make his call to Astan.

* * *

A limousine was waiting for Kevin, Gabe, and the assistant when the plane touched down at the Geneva airport. Since they were friends of Astan Ilves, there would be no need to be cleared by customs. The limousine took the three men directly to an exclusive clothier shop where two suits, four sports jackets, several shirts and slacks had been prepared for them. The assistant had phoned their measurements ahead during the flight. Three tailors were available to do any alterations necessary. By the time the three of them had changed out of their yellow shirts and into something more suitable, Lucy's plane had landed. She, Mika'il, Ahmed, and the other assistant were all on their way to Astan's lakefront estate. Both parties would arrive at the same time, making it quite an interesting, if not awkward gathering.

As tired as she was, Lucy still looked beautiful, at least she did to Kevin as he watched her climb out of the limousine. He and Gabe had arrived just a minute before Lucy's car pulled through the heavily guarded gate. Lucy smiled at Kevin when she saw him approaching.

"I told you I would invite you to the gathering of miracle workers," Lucy said.

"I believe it was my friend Gabe here who did the inviting. Gabe, I would like to introduce you to a very special lady, Lucy Ilves, our host's daughter."

"It's a pleasure to meet you," Gabe said politely, shaking Lucy's hand.

"And allow me to introduce the two of you to Mika'il and Ahmed, two friends we were able to help escape from a rather tense situation in the West Bank."

"So, we hear..." Gabe started to say, but was interrupted.

"...and saw on CNN live," Kevin said, interrupting and completing Gabe's sentence.

Everyone politely exchanged handshakes and headed inside the main house where Astan was impatiently waiting to greet his three miracle workers.

"What do you mean, 'saw on CNN live'?" Mika'il asked, as they walked towards the house.

"You didn't know about it?" Kevin said, incredulously, as he looked towards Lucy.

"I only heard about it right before we landed. You were still asleep Mika'il. I knew there would be plenty of opportunity for you to see it."

"To see what?" Mika'il said. Ahmed automatically tensed in reaction to Mika'il's serious concern.

It was Gabe who spoke up. "It was live. We watched you and Lucy saving the children. It was all live on CNN. The whole world watched. It was unbelievable."

"I must say you speak the Palestinian Arabic dialect remarkably well," Mika'il said, "where did you learn our language?"

Gabe really didn't want to talk about his new language ability so was very happy when Kevin spoke up.

"A CNN camera crew must have found out about you leaving the West Bank and followed your convoy. They were filming when the bomb exploded. They caught everything on camera and went live while the two of you were tending to the injured children."

"Everything?" Mika'il asked, very concerned. Kevin knew what he was referring to.

"I believe I understand your concern but, yes, they even captured that on video as well."

"I'd have killed them had you not done so, Mika'il," Ahmed replied, quickly.

"Thank you, my friend, but I allowed my anger to overcome my faith, and I alone now must deal with that."

The group continued inside where they were all greeted as old friends by Astan, even Kevin.

"You all must be exhausted. I've had rooms prepared for you. I'm sure you would like to rest for a while. I'm Astan Ilves, Lucy's father and your host. Anything you need feel free to ask for. Make yourselves at home, but please, if you need to go outside the house, stay behind the walls and away from the lakefront. There are already several boats with film crews plying the waters just outside of the breakwater," Astan explained. "I was just about to have lunch in the conservatory if any of you would care to join me."

They all were starving and thought lunch was a splendid idea. It'd also be a good way for everyone to get to know one another before the talks turned serious.

They adjourned to the conservatory and were beginning to be served, when one of the butlers came into the room and approached Astan. He spoke softly, but not softly enough for Kevin and Lucy not to hear.

"There is a Mykos Zorko on the phone for you. He says it is urgent." Astan looked to Kevin to see if he had heard the name. He had. Lucy also turned to look at her father when she heard the name, for she too knew Mykos. Astan was not sure how to respond to the butler's message and just sat there as Lucy and Kevin stared, awaiting his response.

"Sir, what should I tell Mr. Zorko?"

Astan knew this conduit to inside information at the Vatican had just been severed. "I guess my secret is out. Mykos has assisted me with dating and analyzing many paintings and documents in the past. He keeps me well informed about historical discoveries."

"Even when I've given him direct instructions to keep certain things secret it appears," Kevin said.

"In the past we've often been of mutual assistance to each other. Perhaps he's calling to seek my expertise."

"Why don't we see, then?" Kevin responded. "Take his call, but put it on speaker phone for all of us to hear."

No one dictated terms to Astan, especially some insignificant Vatican City investigator sitting in Astan's own home. Astan glared at Kevin, who in turn glared back. Lucy began to smile.

"I think that'd be a splendid idea," Lucy responded, taking advantage of her father's very uncomfortable situation.

"So be it," Astan finally huffed. "Please bring me a phone," he said, turning back to the butler.

"Yes sir, as you wish sir."

"Hello Mykos," Astan said. Before he could tell Mykos that several people were listening to their conversation, Mykos was off and running with his giddy nonstop talking.

"Astan, you won't believe what we've discovered that goes along with the Botticelli painting, which by the way is entitled the 'Ascension of Satan,' named after missing verses in Revelation 10."

"Mykos..." Astan tried to interrupt.

"I know, I know, there are no missing verses to Revelation 10, but that was before we found the copy of the canon and the letter from Savonarola explaining everything. You know there are two other canons, one in England and one in Scotland that contain this other version of Revelation 10 as well."

"Mykos..." Astan tried again to stop his friend from talking.

"Oh, I'm just quivering with excitement." Mykos still wouldn't stop talking. "I've already sent one of my assistants to get me a copy of the Revelation from the one in the Lord Corwin Museum and..."

"Mykos..." Astan had now raised his voice, but it still didn't silence the incredibly excited Mykos.

"Astan, please don't raise your voice with me, it hurts my feelings. Aren't you excited by all of this? I know

I'm just beside myself with glee. I mean how often does one get the chance to..."

"Mykos, this is Kevin Bridges," Mykos stopped mid-syllable.

"Astan?" Mykos said coyly.

"Yes Mykos?"

"Astan is there somebody in the room with you?" Everyone in the conservatory was smiling, including Kevin.

"Yes Mykos. There are several people here with me. I tried to tell you, but you wouldn't stop talking."

Astan, please tell me one of them is not Kevin Bridges."

"I can't say that Mykos. Mr. Bridges is sitting right across the table from me."

"Astan, you better be kidding because I just peed in my pants," Mykos said, in tears. Everyone in the conservatory burst into laughter.

"Mykos," this is Kevin Bridges. "I think you and I need to finish this conversation in private."

"Ohhhhh...Ohhhhhh my...Ohhhhhh..." Whimpering and moaning was all that was heard over the phone and then suddenly a thump followed by the sound of the receiver hitting the carpet. In the background you could hear the voices of people calling Mykos and then the sound of running footsteps approaching the phone.

"I think you just gave him a heart attack," Lucy said to Kevin. They heard the sound of someone picking the phone off of the floor.

"Hello, hello is anyone there?" one of the assistants asked.

"This is Kevin Bridges from Vatican security. Is Mykos all right?"

"We believe he fainted," another voice was heard in the background. "His pants are all wet, what the heck?" The first voice came back on. "I'm afraid Mykos is in no condition to finish this conversation. Should I tell him to call you back?"

"No, tell him I will be in touch very soon. Until then, tell him to make no more phone calls. Do you understand?"

"I'll let him know," the man back in Mykos' workshop replied.

"Well, that was very interesting," Lucy said. "Are there really missing verses to Revelation 10?" Nobody answered right away.

Mika'il and Ahmed had continued eating during the phone conversation, paying little attention to the drama and amusement it seemed to give to the others in the room. Mika'il was the first to respond to Lucy's question. "Unfortunately, I have not studied your Bible as much as I probably should have, but the 'Ascension of Satan' that this man refers to seems absurd."

Ahmed looked at Mika'il, perplexed, but did not say anything. How could Mika'il say he had not read the Bible? Ahmed knew Mika'il was well-versed on the writings in both the Old and New Testament. Perhaps Ahmed had misunderstood Mika'il's comment.

"I beg to differ," Kevin replied, "Satan is as real as these miracles you all have been performing. I do find it implausible that a revelation referring to this ascension was deliberately left out of the Book of Revelation by Apostle John."

"I know of this revelation," Astan spoke. "I have seen the copy of the canon in Ge'ez that James Bruce brought back from his expedition to Ethiopia and the translation that was done several years later. The copy from Lord Corwin's Library that Mykos mentioned is one I have done much research on. As a matter of fact, I even own a page from the original birch bark copy Corwin obtained. My page is from the Book of Enoch which you all know was removed from the canon and ordered destroyed."

Kevin suddenly took a greater interest in what Astan was saying. In the letter from Queen Elizabeth's court that had included the talon drawings and prints, the scribe mentioned this evil winged creature who had escaped with a page of the birch bark canon that has never been recovered. "Just how did you come about obtaining that page?"

"I gave it to him," Lucy responded, "it was a birthday gift several years ago. I bought it from an antiquities dealer in Beirut, Lebanon, of all places."

"How thoughtful of you," Kevin replied. "What does your page of the Book of Enoch talk about?"

"I didn't know you had such an interest in the apocryphal writings, Mr. Bridges," Astan replied, "but, since you asked, it tells how God sent his Archangels to inherit the bodies of humans for the good of mankind. It also tells how the good angels, even God's own Archangels, can suffer the fate of the fallen angels as described in other parts of Enoch if they aren't careful. If the rumours are true, I believe you have some first-hand experience with some of these fallen angels, do you not?" The room became very tense at what seemed like a challenge by Astan.

"I believe you are referring to those stories about Nephilim in Spain which I investigated," Kevin replied tersely. "Perhaps you should ask the Bishop about it. I'm not at liberty to discuss the findings of my investigations without proper authorization."

"Perhaps I shall," Astan grumbled.

"Gentlemen and Lucy," Mika'il spoke, sensing the tension, "if you would please excuse me, I think I'll retire to my room for some needed rest." Mika'il and Ahmed stood and headed towards their adjoining bedrooms. Ahmed insisted that he be next to Mika'il even though Mika'il always wished not to be disturbed when resting, even by Ahmed.

Everyone agreed that they all should take a rest and begin their discussions over dinner later that day.

Astan tried to catch his daughter's attention, but she was already in a conversation with Kevin as they exited the conservatory.

"I've missed seeing you," Lucy told Kevin. "I've been thinking about you a lot."

"You wouldn't believe how happy I am to hear that. I've had a hard time keeping you out of my thoughts as well."

"Good thoughts, I hope."

"For the most part," Kevin replied.

"What do you mean, 'for the most part'?" Lucy snapped back.

"I wasn't going to bring this up until later, but the other night after our wonderful dinner, you said you were heading to bed. When I left I had pulled over outside the gate to talk to some of the people waiting to be healed. As I was looking for a pen, you pulled out and raced past me in a red Enzo-Ferrari. I was curious as to where you were headed at such a late hour?"

"Jealous kind of curious or business kind of curious?" Lucy asked.

"A little of both. When I first saw you leaving that night, I was hurt that you had lied to me and, a little jealous, as I tried to figure out whom you were in such a hurry to go see. I tried to follow you, but my old car was no match for your Ferrari. I drove around hoping to find your car, but gave up when I realized how immature I was being."

"You said a little of both," Lucy reminded Kevin. "What about the business part?"

"Well, as you now know, thanks to Mykos, there was a breakin at the Vatican City vaults the other night. What you don't know is that two Swiss Guards were brutally murdered during the breakin."

"That's terrible," Lucy replied, sounding genuinely shocked at the news. "Have you caught the person who's responsible?"

Kevin didn't answer for a moment as he tried to figure out how to phrase his next question without ruining any possible chance of having a future relationship with Lucy. He decided to avoid asking the question for a moment. "No, and as bizarre as it sounds, I don't believe we're even looking for a person. I think Satan is responsible." Kevin paused, to see how Lucy would react. "Did that sound crazy?"

"No, not really, you are Catholic, aren't you? I mean, all Catholics believe in Satan, don't they?" Lucy replied, smiling. "Who am I to say what's real and isn't real or even possible anymore. You saw the CNN coverage. Is what the world witnessed Mika'il and I doing any more logical than believing in Satan? I don't think so."

"Lucy, where were you going that night you left the mansion? The Rome police reported ticketing your Ferrari for being illegally parked very near where I believe...", Kevin paused momentarily, trying to phrase the rest of his statement, "did you see anything strange when you parked your car that night?"

"Nice try, covering your butt. Are you afraid to ask, or afraid of the answer?" Kevin didn't reply. "No, I'm not Satan, and I wasn't anywhere near an entrance to the Vatican. If you'd bothered to check, you'd have found out my car was parked outside one of my foundation offices. I had some last-minute preparations to make for my trip to the West Bank."

What Lucy had said did make sense, but why hadn't she said anything about her trip during dinner? He remembered her specifically telling him that she wanted to get to bed before her father got home that night.

"By the way, what time did your father finally return that night?"

"I have no idea. I never returned home after going to the office. I went straight to the airport and headed for the West Bank."

Lucy was trying to hide something, but Kevin wasn't sure exactly what. Either she was lying to him or she was trying to cover for her father. He would call his office at the Vatican to have her story checked out, and to try to get phone records for the mansion and her cell phone. He just couldn't let her know about it. He also needed to have someone follow up on that missing birch bark page from the Lord Corwin canon that seemed to have circuitously ended up in Astan Ilves' possession. There couldn't be too many antiquities dealers in Beirut.

He would get one of the investigators to check on that as well.

By this time all the other guests had gone to their rooms. Lucy kissed Kevin softly on the lips. "I really need to get some rest right now, but perhaps after dinner we can take a walk together along the lakefront."

"I would like that very much," Kevin answered, squeezing her hand affectionately. The two parted, Lucy to her room and Kevin returning to the conservatory to speak with Astan.

When Kevin entered the conservatory it was empty, except for several men cleaning up after the luncheon. Astan was nowhere to be found and no one seemed to know where he had disappeared to. Kevin would just have to question him later. For now, he would call his office and get them busy following his leads. He also needed to give Mykos a call. That is, if Mykos had recovered from his shock of being exposed as the "Deep Throat" of the Vatican. There was no doubt Mykos had much explaining to do, even though his deliberate disobedience inadvertently provided leads and a much-needed boost to Kevin's investigation. Unfortunately, those leads seemed to imply that Lucy or Astan just might be Satan. Kevin shivered at the thought. "Maybe I don't want to become romantically involved with Lucy after all," Kevin said to himself. "Nah..., just kidding." Kevin couldn't wait until the two of them could go off alone.

Kevin called the security office to get investigators working on the leads he now had. He warned them of the importance of keeping what they were assigned to do quiet. If it got out, not only would he be really mad but, if Astan Ilves were to find out, Astan could probably get them fired. The last part of his warning did the trick. They all knew the power Astan seemed to wield at Vatican City. There was a message from the Bishop requesting an update. Kevin decided that could wait. It was a different story, however, when he called Mykos back at his workshop.

After almost five minutes of Mykos apologizing on the phone, he finally retold all the information about the letter written by Savonarola which they had found along with the accompanying canon. What Mykos hadn't said during the call to Astan was that there was a series of numbers written on the letter which made absolutely no sense whatsoever. They appeared to just be random numbers, but they did have someone trying to figure out if they had a hidden meaning. Then Mykos had a most peculiar story to tell Kevin. He had done a preliminary cleaning of the faces on the Botticelli painting just as Kevin had requested and was about to email Kevin the pictures of the faces. While he was downloading the pictures from the camera to his computer, he decided to check his e-mail.

"I received an e-mail from an American visiting in Perm, Russia. He claims to have discovered what he believes to be a Sandro Botticelli. He didn't tell me many details of the painting or of the story behind how he came across it. He did send several dozen photos of the painting. The framing was extremely odd, but what I found unbelievable was that it seemed to be the exact antithesis of the Botticelli we found in the vault."

"What do you mean by 'antithesis'?" Kevin asked.

"Exactly what it means," Mykos responded, as if reprimanding Kevin. It was obvious the old prissy Mykos was back and his faux pas already forgotten. "This Botticelli is the exact opposite of the one we have. It appears to be the 'Condemnation of Satan' rather than the 'Ascension of Satan'. The paintings had to have been painted at the same time. They go far beyond the typical classically inspired work Botticelli is so known for. The formal balance, the symmetry, the perspective. They are identical in both paintings." Mykos seemed to have fallen into a poetic flow as he described the paintings. "Each background scene is the antithesis of the scenes painted in the other painting. In one, the forces of evil are winning the battle, while in the other the same characters are fighting in the same scene but with the opposite result. Good triumphing over evil. It's difficult to make out the faces of Satan and of the angels in both paintings, but from what I can tell they are both the same. Just in a different order and with different colored wings. It's astonishing, truly astonishing."

"Can we get in touch with this American?" Kevin asked.

"I dearly hope so. I have already responded to his e-mail seeking more information and asked if I could come see the painting. He wants me to authenticate it for him. From the pictures he sent, I have no doubt it's a Botticelli. I'm sure it was painted at the same time that ours was painted. It's remarkable."

"Mykos, you must tell no one of this. Do you understand? No one, especially Astan Ilves. For if you do, I will personally arrest you, lock you up in a vault in the catacombs, and throw away the key. I'm not kidding."

"I promise to tell no one, not even my staff. I've learned my lesson."

"Let's hope so. I want you to send me the pictures of our painting and the pictures the American sent you of his Botticelli. Try to arrange for the two of us to see it as soon as possible," Kevin told Mykos, then hung up the phone.

Kevin was still sitting at the desk when he suddenly got the feeling he was being watched. He turned and saw the door to his room was open and Gabe was standing in the doorway smiling.

"Sorry, I didn't mean to frighten you, and I didn't want to interrupt your phone conversation. Could you tell me where the bathroom is around here? I thought they said there was one in my room, but for the life of me I can't figure out where it is."

Kevin stared for a second before he answered. How much had Gabe heard about the painting? Kevin was beginning to suspect everyone. "I know all these curtains hanging on the walls can be very confusing, but I believe the bathroom will be behind one of them. I'll help you find it."

"Oh, that won't be necessary. Now that I know where to look, it will be like that old TV show *Let's Make a Deal*. I should be okay. Have a good nap." Gabe turned and hurried back to his room.

Kevin went and looked up and down the hallway to see just what other surprises might be awaiting him. He saw no one and slowly closed the door to his room. Even if Gabe had heard his conversation with Mykos, he wasn't overly concerned. He had gotten to know Gabe reasonably well over the past two days and had the impression that Gabe was just a normal guy caught up in an extremely abnormal situation. At least that's all he hoped there was to it.

He turned on the television to see if CNN was still running the Mika'il and Lucy video. What he saw made him even more nervous. Satellite photos were showing a massive buildup of Chinese and Russian troops along their common border. Reports of tens of millions of Chinese soldiers amassing along the border, far outnumbering the Russian troops, had prompted tens of thousands of the Russian proletariat to head towards the border to help defend the "Mother Land". The world was quickly spinning towards what could very well be World War III and a nuclear Armageddon. Leaders from around the world were gathering in an attempt to avoid the impending disaster. Still, if given a choice, Kevin would rather see the world deal with a war between governments than a war against Satan, which he believed beyond a shadow of a doubt was coming, and coming soon.

* * *

The Stranger had fanned the flames of war in the East. It was all going precisely as he had planned. He needed some time to begin the next phase of his plan. A restful afternoon would be plenty of time to achieve this next step. It was all moving so fast. Soon, very soon, the world would see his "Ascension to the Throne", just as he always knew it should be. Not God, Apostle John, nor the Brotherhood of the Divine could any longer keep the Stranger from the destiny he felt he so dearly deserved.

CHAPTER THIRTY

"A rudderless ship is at the mercy of the waves and the wind, drifts wherever they take it and if there arises a whirlwind it is smashed against the rocks and becomes as if it has never existed. It is our firm belief that a soul without Christ is bound to meet with no better fate."

Excerpt from Haile Selassie's "One Race, One Gospel, One Task," address to the World Evangelical Congress, Berlin, October 28, 1966.

Two hundred mules and sixteen elephants were needed to haul off the treasures and manuscripts of Emperor Theodore II of Ethiopia, which had been hidden away in the mountain fortress at Maqdala. As the procession of British soldiers wound their way down the mountain back towards the Red Sea with the plundered goods, hundreds of natives pounded their chests as if at a traditional Ethiopian funeral, mourning their loss. Others attacked the caravan only to be unmercifully killed by the heavily armed British contingent. Before the victorious troops sailed for home, they held an auction for the senior officers who bid on and bought many of the treasures in order to raise "prize money" to reward the soldiers. Over five thousand pounds were raised and distributed to the troops. The officers were able to buy priceless treasures for a mere pittance.

Much of the plunder ended up in London's British and the Victoria and Albert museums but other parts of the pillaged treasure just vanished into the private studies and libraries in the estates of these officers' descendants. During the auction, the Stranger was there, always watching for the next piece of the puzzle that would bring him closer to uncovering the secret the Brotherhood protected.

* * *

Haile Selassie, the King of Kings, Lord of Lords, the Conquering Lion. Some even believed he was the Messiah returned to earth. Selassie was crowned Emperor of Ethiopia in 1930. He was a devoutly religious man who brought a new hope to Ethiopia. In 1935 that hope was temporarily destroyed by the invasion of the well trained and equipped Italian army. Unlike the British whose plunder was limited to Maqdala, the Italian invaders pillaged treasures throughout all of Ethiopia and forced Selassie to flee to Britain in exile. He had little time to gather documents or treasures. As his army retreated from battle in disarray, Emperor Selassie risked possible capture as he secretly visited the Church of Our Lady at the distant summit of Mt. Asheten. Here he took time to pray but, more importantly, retrieved from the monks of the Church the original canon and epistle, as well as a translation of the epistle into Amharic that Emperor Selassie knew to be of major religious significance, not just for Ethiopia, but for the world.

While in England, Selassie used the fame he had suddenly received following his dazzling and eloquent plea for help before the League of Nations, to win friends and support for his eventual return to power in 1941. After the war, the country went though great change and development, focusing on modernization and education, but always keeping Ethiopian traditions in mind. Selassie's fame and power continued to grow as he toured the world expounding his vision of bridging cultures and bringing all races together.

Troubling to Emperor Selassie was his designation by the Rastafarian movement as God incarnate, the Black Messiah. It was said that Haile Selassie was descended from King Solomon himself, and the titles he was given were the same as those given to the returned Messiah in the New Testament. When he once visited Jamaica, two hundred thousand Rastafarians arrived at the airport to greet their Messiah. Emperor Selassie was afraid to even get off the plane. He was finally convinced that he would be safe and the trip turned out to be a success. However, Selassie believed these Rastafarians were misguided and in deep need of Christianity. He did not judge or condemn them for their beliefs, but saw powers were at work that could challenge the foundation of Christianity. He scheduled a meeting with Pope Paul VI in Vatican City. Emperor Selassie was not Catholic, but a devout Ethiopian

Orthodox Church member. He did realize the best defense against Satan would be through the Catholic Church. It was at his audience with the Pontiff when he surrendered the canon, original epistle, and the Amharic copy of the canon he had personally guarded since ascending to the throne. Pope Paul VI assured him that he in turn would guard and protect it until the day came when God, in all his wisdom, would reveal what to do with these sacred documents.

The minions, loyal to the Stranger, would try one final time to find the canon he knew was in Ethiopia. The BBC ran a documentary exposing the famine that devastated parts of Ethiopia and almost immediately Selassie's popularity in his own country plummeted. The Dergue was a small political movement desiring the overthrow of the Emperor. In 1974, with the backing of the Soviet Union, they staged a bloody coup deposing Emperor Selassie. All the democratic rights which Emperor Selassie had worked so tirelessly to provide to the citizenry were suspended and martial law was declared. He was placed in an abandoned officer's house at military barracks of the 4th Division on Denbre Road. He was taken to the grounds of the Imperial Palace when the military leaders behind the coup decided to claim the Emperor's Palace as their own. Selassie was placed in a small house on the palace grounds and was under constant guard and subjected to relentless questioning. Most of his interrogators wanted information about the billions of dollars Selassie was rumored to have stolen, but one inquisitor was interested only in the canon. Selassie's faith was stronger than the Stranger's temptations and the Stranger left without what he so desired. Others could not refuse the Stranger's temptations and a division arose between the coup participants culminating in a night of bloodshed. Hundreds of Selassie's family members, and loyal supporters including the church clergy, were rounded up and killed in a barrage of machine gun fire, then buried in mass graves. Not the outcome the Stranger originally desired, but one that pleased him nonetheless. Emperor Selassie did not die in front of a firing squad. The government reported he had died from complications following prostate surgery. This was denied by his doctor who claimed Emperor Haile Selassie was suffocated in his sleep. Selassie was given an Imperial funeral by the Ethiopian Orthodox Church. The current post-communist government refused to allow Selassie's funeral to be given the status of a State Funeral.

Emperor Haile Selassie's death would remain a mystery to everyone but the Stranger. It had fallen upon the devout Emperor Selassie to protect the secret of the Brotherhood of the Divine. The Ethiopian King of Kings had found strength in God's promise and died knowing the words in Apostle John's epistle still remained safe.

CHAPTER THIRTY-ONE

Then I saw three evil spirits that looked like frogs; they came out of the mouth of the dragon, out of the mouth of the beast and out of the mouth of the false prophet. They are spirits of demons performing miraculous signs, and they go out to the kings of the whole world, to gather them for the battle on the great day of God Almighty.

Revelation 16:13-14

"Mika'il," Ahmed called. Ahmed was troubled at what was happening in the house and had had difficulty falling asleep. "Mika'il, I feel evil in this house. We know nothing about this man they call Gabe or of his friend Kevin. I feel this Gabe may be a 'jinn', just like Suleiman the Magnificent, he seems to have the ability to speak and communicate with all creatures."

"Ahmed, does he appear to you to be made from the smokeless fire? Did he come out of a lamp like Aladdin's 'jinn'? Have you seen him transform into another creature? Has he done evil? From what I have been told, he has done only good. That would make him more of an angel than a 'jinn'."

"Still, they speak of the devil Satan, and the Qur'an says the devil was a 'jinn', yet these people call him a fallen angel. Kevin says he is as real as you and I. This troubles me much, Mika'il. Why did you tell them you do not know the Bible this afternoon? You studied it thoroughly. We have discussed it on many occasions."

"Sometimes it is wiser to listen to a conversation than to participate in the conversation. I was trying to learn the wisdom of these people whom our fates are tied to," Mika'il explained. "We should go down to dinner and join the others. It is time to learn what Astan Ilves has in mind."

Mika'il was troubled as well, but did not want Ahmed to know. He was unconcerned by Lucy or Gabe, who both had the ability to perform miracles. Neither of them seemed to have an agenda, or even a message they wanted the world to hear. Astan on the other hand seemed like a man driven by a purpose. He planned to use the three miracle workers to get that message across. Mika'il too had a message he wanted to tell the world.

Gabe was almost jovial, whistling as he headed down to meet his companions for dinner. This had been the first time in two weeks he actually wasn't worried about what the future had in store. Having seen Lucy and Mika'il on CNN made him feel a lot better about the limited amount of healing he had done. He knew healing people was not the primary reason Astan Ilves had brought him to Switzerland. It was his ability to say something and have everyone, in every language or variant of that language, understand. He knew how important that would be in broadcasting a message to the world. Gabe was well aware that Astan had a media conglomerate that covered the world with both television and radio. Whatever Astan had planned, Gabe would be the voice that spoke to the world. He actually hadn't figured that all out on his own. Kevin had given him much of the information on the trip from California. Gabe also had found out quite a bit about Kevin. Kevin had studied to be a forensic scientist and actually had a psychiatric medical degree. He told Gabe to tell no one else that secret. For a while, he had worked for the FBI as a crime scene specialist and profiler. Once he even spent time living undercover with monks while investigating a serial murder case. He solved the case and made quite an impression with the Catholic Church hierarchy. When the Vatican needed a miracle investigator, Kevin was the perfect choice, even though he was an evangelical Christian. Since he had come to work for the Vatican, he had resolved several mysteries involving alleged miracles and was instrumental in helping to solve an international serial murder case.

Lucy did very little resting either during the afternoon. She had several phone calls to make to her research and medical teams. She too had been watching CNN and saw the escalation of military might along the Russian and China border. She had dozens of doctors who worked for her foundation and wanted to be sure all her people were out of the region. She had put the team that had gone with her to the West Bank through too much danger and was not willing to take such a chance again. As she left her room to head to dinner, Kevin was waiting in the hallway.

"Did you sleep well?" Kevin asked.

"Not really, but I rarely sleep much anyway. I did have some business calls I needed to make."

"Same here, that and write up some reports. Funny thing, every time I typed your father's name in my report the computer would try to change Astan to Satan and Ilves to lives. 'Satan lives'. Your father's name is an anagram for 'Satan lives'."

"You just now figured that out? Some investigator you are. School mates, friends, and colleagues have been teasing me about that since I was a little girl. Lucy was teasing Kevin for his lame epiphany. "My father has been haunted by his name his whole life. He never forgave his parents for purposely naming him that. Why do you think he's so adamant about showing the world us miracle workers? It's like he has to prove he's the exact opposite of what his name implies. I'm told he was an angry young man."

"How did your mother deal with your father's anger?"

"I was adopted when I was just a baby. My father was never married. I never knew my biological parents and Astan and I didn't ever discuss them."

"I never knew that. Why did Astan, being a single man, and an extremely busy man at that, decide to adopt a baby?"

"That's a question I think you should ask Astan, don't you think?" Lucy replied, sounding a bit miffed. They finished their walk to dinner in silence.

All the guests had arrived. Astan had instructed his chefs to prepare a variety of ethnic and international cuisine to please everyone's palate. The chefs performed to perfection, as did all of Astan's employees. He expected nothing less. After dinner the group adjourned to the library to begin what would prove to be a very spirited religious and moral discussion.

Mika'il's desire to promote a moderate Islam was met with some skepticism from Astan and Kevin who joined in the lively debate.

"I don't understand how it is possible to be a moderate Muslim, or a moderate Jew, or even a moderate Christian," Kevin explained. "Faith is absolute. Faith is life. How can someone be moderately alive? For me, a man is either a Christian or about to be an ex-Christian. There is no compromise with faith. I'm sure it is the same with Islam."

"I do admit Islam has always had the 'convert or die' attitude, but societies have greatly changed. Globalization is threatening the very existence of Islam. If it doesn't change, I fear it is destined to fail," Mika'il explained.

"At the name of Jesus every knee shall bow, and every tongue confess that Jesus Christ is Lord, to the glory of God the Father. Philippians 2:9-11," Astan quoted. "Will these moderate Muslims bow to Jesus Christ our Lord?"

"I'm sure changes will have to be made to your Bible as they will have to be made to the Qu'ran," Mika'il told Astan.

"That's absurd," Lucy replied, "the word of God cannot be changed. It is perfect as it is."

"Then why has it undergone so many changes in the past?" Mika'il challenged. "From the conversation with that Mykos fellow on the phone yesterday, it sounds like even your God has changed or at least purposely left prophecies out of his own Word. I find this very puzzling."

"As do we all," Kevin replied, "but Mykos will sort through that mystery and, when he has, I will tell all of you. That is, if he doesn't tell you first." Kevin looked at Astan.

"I can see the value in your belief of a moderate form of Islam as long as it tolerates other religious beliefs," Astan said, "and I'm willing to let you proselytize that belief on my broadcasts, as long as you agree to support our Christian message as well. I also expect all three of you to do some televised healings to generate interest and help build a following for our presentations. My ultimate goal is to help bring the world together in peace. I believe that with the three of you, we can achieve that. Gabe, you of course will be our spokesman because of your unique miracle of languages."

"Like the day of the Pentecost," Mika'il added.

"Precisely." Astan interjected, causing a chill to run down Gabe's spine.

How could any of them argue with achieving world peace? There would be many details to work out, but Astan already had hired some of the best producers, writers, and directors to handle that part of the presentations. The three miracle workers, along with Kevin and Ahmed, all wondered what Astan was getting out of this. Nevertheless, all three agreed to Astan's plan. Kevin and Ahmed were not so convinced. Ahmed was troubled that Mika'il seemed to agree so readily without discussing it with him. He seemed too anxious to compromise his new beliefs which Allah himself had ordered Mika'il to share with the world. Kevin, although agreeing that world peace was a noble cause, knew the three miracle workers, with the power of Astan's media empire, could convince millions to become followers to their message. He felt Astan was usurping the religious power of the churches and God's own message in doing so. That was just too much power for one person. Power that could be abused or molded to reflect Astan's message and not God's.

Kevin's plan to be with Lucy later that evening fell apart when Astan insisted they all prepare for and record their first television special. They would explain their goals and intentions to the world. A brief history of each of the miracle workers would be presented showing clips from the CNN video. The footage of Mika'il killing the three attackers would of course be edited out. Some local news footage from California stations would be shown, telling about Gabe, and a brief explanation about his miraculous language ability would be made, although most viewers would not understand. The professionals Astan had hired had already prepared most of the footage for the special. Only brief interviews with the three, along with Gabe's narration, would be necessary. Astan knew he was walking a fine line with how much on-screen filming would be done of Gabe. Gabe's narration was the integral part in making Astan's plan work. It was important not to make Gabe's face the primary image associated with the message. It would be necessary to make sure Mika'il's image did not dominate the broadcasts either. It was finally decided that Gabe's image would be reduced to a small corner of the screen as he read the script. Lucy's participation would be limited to healing, talking about her foundation and her research in curing world health issues.

The broadcast was flawless. It was one of the most watched shows in the history of television. It was done commercial free as would be all of the broadcasts of Astan's miracle workers. The show was well choreographed, with just the right number of sick and injured to be healed by the miracle workers. Even Gabe was becoming more at ease with that portion of the presentation and found himself beginning to ad-lib during these healing sessions.

Kevin was awed by the miraculous healings he was able to observe during those first few days of the broadcasting. He was troubled by the way Astan seemed to downplay the role of God in his message. He also felt Mika'il's proselytizing of a moderate Islam that would work "hand in hand" with Christianity was overdone. Even more troubling to Kevin was that since his walk to dinner that first night, he had been unable to see Lucy without twenty other people in the room. He still had much he wanted to ask and to say to her, but he never seemed to get the chance. Astan was working everyone extremely hard, and the pressures were beginning to show.

Ahmed had been relegated to nothing more than a "gofer" for Mika'il and Astan. His patience was beginning to wear thin. Mika'il was insulating himself with a new group of protectors. Ahmed had dedicated his life to protecting Mika'il and was unhappy with the change. Mika'il seemed caught up in his image more than his message and was constantly at odds with Astan. The world was buying their message, for hundreds of thousands of dollars were pouring in, even though no request for funds was being made on the broadcasts. Astan was fast becoming the most liked and trusted man in the world except, with the Jews and the Fundamentalist Christians who believed he was distorting God's word to make it fit with the masses. Mika'il's following of moderate Muslims continued to grow, but at a much slower pace. Violence seemed to follow all those who announced their belief in Mika'il's vision. Cities and entire regions throughout the Muslim world were becoming split between the hardline Muslims and these new moderate believers, with scuffles and confrontations becoming the norm. Several Islamic countries were more accepting of the new moderate Muslims than others and had opened their borders to those wishing to follow the ways of Mika'il. Syria, the West Bank, Turkey, and Iraq were the first countries to do so and seemed to attract an ever-growing number of followers. Even Iran was beginning to show a tolerance for these moderate Muslims. Astan's message of bringing the world together was making sense to a lot of people. Peace was becoming more important than any one religion. The Stranger wasn't so sure he liked that idea. Still, things were going just as he had planned and soon, he would ascend to the throne and rule over the world. For it was indeed written, and there was now proof supporting that written word, God's own Word. Proof positive Satan was always destined to ascend to the throne.

Like Mika'il, Lucy seemed to have an increasing number of protectors around her. This made it difficult for Kevin to see her let alone talk with her. Kevin had been in contact with Mykos, and Mykos was very concerned about what he had discovered about the authenticity of this new version of Revelation 10. He had informed the Bishop, who in turn told the Pope. The Bishop also told his good friend

Astan Ilves. Mykos wasn't the only leak at Vatican City. Mykos informed Kevin he had contacted this Jacob fellow who had sent him pictures of the alleged Botticelli. It seems the Russian government confiscated the painting when Jacob tried to leave Moscow for the United States. The painting had since been shipped to the Hermitage in St. Petersburg. Mykos tried to call his friend Vlade, who was in charge of restoring and authenticating art for the Hermitage, but he was on a holiday in France. Mykos told Kevin he would followup as soon as his friend returned.

Kevin had been busy observing the healings and carefully documenting his findings and his reactions to what was happening with Astan's scheme. Kevin did view it as a scheme because the more he watched and listened, the more it seemed like things were spinning perversely out of control. Astan was moving away from what Kevin thought was the original plan of using God's Divine Grace, manifested through the healing of these miracle workers, to help achieve world peace. It was as if Astan was attempting to establish a new world religion and order.

One morning after filming, Kevin was able to find Lucy and discuss a few matters that were weighing heavily on his mind. "I've wanted to speak with you for days, but you are always filming or too busy to talk."

"I've been very busy with Astan's project and my own medical research. Haven't you been watching the news? A new strain of bird flu has reached epidemic proportions along the Russian and Chinese border.

Millions are expected to die. I have been working day and night to find a vaccine and I think we finally have."

"That's fantastic!" Kevin exclaimed.

"I'm not so sure. Why should we heal them? If we do, they will only kill each other off in a war that is on the verge of erupting at any moment. The only thing stopping it is the bird flu."

"Maybe helping them save lives will help avoid the war."

"And maybe Astan will achieve world peace with these ridiculous broadcasts," Lucy replied. "The chances seem about the same to me."

"It sounds like you have soured on your father's plan. I still don't understand what his motive is and what he hopes to get out of all of this."

"I think it's an attempt to make amends for his name. You asked me why Astan adopted me. I asked him that same question one day. He told me he had a spiritual vision telling him to quit focusing on his media empire and to devote himself to studying ancient sources of the Bible and religious art. This spiritual vision also told him to adopt a child. I was chosen because of the name my parents had given to me. The name on my birth certificate is Lucifer Raphaela Sexton. Astan had it officially changed to Lucy Raphaela Ilves. He thought I should keep my middle name Raphaela. I'm sure you know it is the name of the archangel of healing. Rather ironic, don't you think?"

"Why did your parents put you up for adoption?"

"They didn't. The orphanage did. Both of my parents were mysteriously murdered in Scotland. I was just a baby."

"I'm so sorry. That's just awful."

"You know I hadn't even thought about it for years, but it all came rushing back when your friend Mykos said there was a copy of the Revelation in Scotland. Then my father mentioned James Bruce. Hearing that name after so many years sent chills down my spine."

"The word Scotland brought back such bad memories?"

"Of course not, the name James Bruce did. My parents both worked for the museum that housed many of his documents and diaries. At least that is what Astan once told me as a child." A light went off in Kevin's head and he made a mental note to have the murders checked out. The murders sounded just a little too suspicious in light of all that had been going on lately.

"You know I've really missed you these past few days," Kevin said

"And I've missed you as well. I've given it a lot of thought and I just don't think I could handle getting involved with someone right now."

"I'm not asking you to get involved with someone. I'm asking you to get involved with me," Kevin said, as he took Lucy's hand into his own. She did not pull it away.

"I'm sorry, but I feel something is about to happen. What, I really don't know. I just don't want you to be hurt."

"How can you be so sure?"

"The same way I know that if I touch a sick child he will be healed. God is guiding my life right now and I must follow his Word."

Kevin knew he couldn't argue with that logic. Most people seemed to use God's Word or God's calling as a convenient way to justify their actions, when they really had no justification for what they did. A bit misguided, but based on what Kevin had witnessed these past weeks he had no reason to think Lucy fell into this category.

"I'm deeply saddened, but I do understand. I really do. You know I originally wanted to tell you the Pope has called me back to Vatican City. I'm to leave as soon as transportation can be arranged."

"How convenient, Astan is leaving this very morning to handle some business in Rome. He's picking up a supply of the bird flu vaccine and is taking it to China. Mika'il and I are leaving tomorrow afternoon to take a shipment produced here in Switzerland to the Russians. You can ride with Astan. That'll give you the opportunity to ask him all about his plans," Lucy told Kevin. "You'd better get your things together because he is leaving within the half-hour. I'll let him know you'll be joining him on the Geneva to Rome portion of the flight." Lucy was off before Kevin could get in another word. It would give him the chance to really talk to Astan. Astan always seemed to disappear when Kevin tried to speak with him. On the jet Astan wouldn't have too many places to hide. Kevin was devastated at his rejection by Lucy, but he'd seen it coming. All three of the miracle workers seemed to be gradually isolating themselves from the people around them. Actually, it was more like they were being isolated by a growing number of zealous supporters who seemed to have become their protectors, their own guardian angels.

Kevin grabbed the clothes Astan had bought for him and headed down to the foyer to meet him. As he approached, he could hear Mika'il and Astan arguing over the most recent television production. Mika'il wanted more air time for his message and Astan insisted he already had enough time to proselytize. When they saw Kevin, they agreed to continue their discussion later in the week after they had both returned from their humanitarian missions delivering the bird flu vaccine. Neither seemed pleased. Mika'il immediately walked away, not saying anything to Kevin. Lucy purposely avoided seeing Kevin off. She knew she'd cry which could send the wrong message. She really did believe she may be falling in love with him. Gabe and Ahmed were both waiting to say goodbye. Gabe was concerned he was being left alone by the one person he trusted the most. Kevin promised he would return as soon as possible and warned him not to be misled into things he truly didn't believe in.

Kevin knew Gabe was still on the Christian path, but had not yet given his life over to Jesus. Kevin gave to Gabe his own personal Bible to read to help Gabe grow spiritually. Kevin knew Gabe had to be really special to have such miraculous powers and yet was not a Christian. Then again, neither was Mika'il, but he had given his soul over to another God, or at least God of a different name, or so he claimed. Gabe had his own group of protectors that did seem very godly which made Kevin feel better about leaving him. Ahmed was also there to see Kevin off. Kevin had found Ahmed to be an honorable, delightful, and honest man. Ahmed had admitted to Kevin that he really regretted participating in the terrorist activities associated with Mika'il. He personally had never killed anyone, though he admitted by association he was just as guilty as those who had. He also expressed his concern for the changes that seemed to be coming over Mika'il. He had many reservations about this plan by Astan for achieving world peace through these miracle workers. Kevin assured him it all would work out in the end and asked him to keep an eye on Gabe.

With all the goodbyes finally said, Astan and Kevin climbed into the limousine and headed for the airport. Astan could not stop smiling when he realized Lucy would not be coming to say goodbye to him or Kevin. She rarely would say goodbye to Astan but, by not coming to see Kevin off, she was definitely sending a message, a message that pleased Astan greatly.

Kevin was able to ask Astan at least a few questions on the flight to Rome. When he asked Astan some of the same questions he had asked Lucy, like why Astan adopted her and why he started his broadcasts with the miracle workers, Kevin got answers that were almost identical to the ones Lucy had given him; in fact, answers so close to the same answers that Kevin had no doubt they had been scripted. Whether it was Lucy or Astan who had prepared the answers, he wasn't sure. Kevin did get Astan to admit much of the information Mykos had supplied to him. It was more information than Kevin had imagined but probably much less than Mykos actually shared. Astan told him of his plan to take the bird flu vaccine to China in hopes of convincing the Chinese to stand down from their impending war with the Russians. Astan was very aware of the significance of this new Revelation 10. He told Kevin that he feared Satan was indeed planning to use this Revelation to ascend to power. Astan's hope was that his group of miracle workers could bring the world together to stop Satan. It was a great story, but Kevin just wasn't sure he could buy it. If Astan truly did feel that way, why hadn't he mentioned it prior to getting embarrassed by the phone call from Mykos? The story seemed just a little too contrived. The question now on Kevin's mind was just who was making up these stories, and who actually was in charge? He also needed to talk to Mykos. Astan seemed to know just as much about Mykos authenticating these different versions of Revelation 10 as Kevin did. He only hoped Mykos had said nothing about the Botticelli that was now at the Hermitage.

When the plane landed, two limousines were waiting to whisk the men off to their separate destinations. Astan was taken to his mansion in Rome and Kevin was taken to a direct meeting with the Pope at Vatican City. Kevin had wanted to first visit Mykos and the security office for updates, but was told that would have to wait. When he entered the Pope's office, the Pope asked everyone else present to leave. This stirred a few complaints from the Bishop and from the Pope's personal secretary but, in the end, Kevin and the Pope were left alone. Mykos had informed the Pope and the Bishop that several copies of a different Revelation 10 had surfaced over the past several centuries, the newest one being from the Vatican's own vault. Mykos had no doubt that it had been purposely left out of the Book of Revelation in the New Testament. With the rise of these miracle workers and Kevin's belief that Satan was behind the murders, the Pope had summoned Kevin to share with him some documents Haile Selassie had given to one of the Pope's predecessors, Pope Paul VI. These documents consisted of a very early copy of the canon in Greek, an epistle in Greek written by the same scribe, and an Amharic translation which Emperor Selassie had personally translated into English. Haile Selassie had told Pope Paul that only he and two monks from a remote church on Mt. Asheten knew of these documents. These monks were members of a secret sect known as the Brotherhood of the Divine whose service to God was the protection of these sacred documents. The Pope handed the English translation of the epistle to Kevin. Kevin read the epistle. The blood seemed to drain from his face.

"Have you heard of the Brotherhood of the Divine?" the Pope asked.

"I've heard the name. I thought they'd died out years ago."

"I understand all the remaining brothers did die right after Emperor Selassie gave these documents to Pope Paul the VI. I believe it is necessary for someone to complete the task the Brotherhood began almost two thousand years ago. I'm entrusting you with that task. Deal with these papers as you see fit in order to fulfill the task outlined in Apostle John's epistle." The Pope paused to allow Kevin to think about his command. "Is there any information you've found out from these miracle workers or from the murder investigators that may help us in this matter?"

"Did Mykos tell you of the painting at the Hermitage?"

"No, neither he nor the Bishop mentioned anything about a painting," the Pope replied. The mention of the Bishop sent up a red flag in Kevin's brain.

"Was it Mykos or the Bishop who told you about the authenticity of the Revelation?" Kevin asked.

"It was the Bishop. Why do you ask? I sense this troubles you."

"It very much does. I believe Astan Ilves was informed of this information as well," Kevin explained. "Normally, I would suspect Mykos as the one leaking such information, but I had caught him doing so earlier and threatened him to never let it happen again. He would not have ignored my threat. I also found Astan speaking with the Bishop right before I left for the United States. Even then I had my suspicions. Now I believe they are justified. I think we need to keep the Bishop uninformed about what is happening."

"Does that mean you suspect Astan Ilves to be involved in Satan's plot?" the Pope asked.

"I do, to what extent I have no idea, but I'm sure he is involved somehow."

"What about these alleged miracle workers, are they too part of Satan's plan?"

"Not alleged miracle workers, actual miracle workers, and to answer your question, I'm not sure. At least not sure about all of them. This man, Gabe Brown, whom I went to see in America, could not possibly be involved. Lucy, I'm not sure about. I know she's lied to me, but for what reason I don't know. The third one, Mika'il, could very well be involved, although he seems to be constantly at odds with Astan. I really need to get back to Switzerland to watch them."

"Then you should return as soon as possible, but don't forget about these papers. They may be our only salvation."

"They will be our salvation if Mykos is as good as he claims to be," Kevin replied.

The Pope thanked him for coming and called his secretary and the Bishop back into the room. As Kevin left, the Bishop walked with him asking for an update on the investigation and what the Pope and he had discussed. Kevin told him as soon as he learned anything, he would give the Bishop an update.

Kevin headed directly to see Mykos to scold him in person about supplying private Vatican information to Astan Ilves. He also wanted to see if Mykos was the one who gave the latest information to Astan, or if it was the Bishop as he now suspected. Mykos had assured him he told absolutely no one about the Revelation except the Pope and the Bishop. Kevin decided not to tell Mykos to keep the Revelation information a secret from the Bishop. He did stress the importance of keeping the information about Savonarola's letter and the Botticelli painting in Russia in the strictest confidence. No one, not the Bishop, nor even the Pope, was to be told of that information.

"I promise to tell no one. You need not worry, Kevin."

"Then let me reward you for your promise," Kevin said, as he handed the Greek copy of the Ethiopian canon to Mykos.

"Oh m-m-my goodness gracious," Mykos stuttered. "Is this what I think it is?"

"If you think this is the original Greek canon the Ethiopians copied their Ge'ez version from, then it is what you think it is."

"This is simply amazing. It appears the Book of Revelation in this version was written by a different scribe than the rest of the canon. And look," Mykos yelled, running across the room and grabbing the canon that was found in the Vatican vault, "both of these were written by the same scribe. The calligraphy is identical. That means these deleted verses of Revelation 10 really should be included in the Bible. This, along with the others we've found, is proof positive. That's just awful. Satan really will ascend to the throne."

"He will unless you and I can prove otherwise," Kevin replied, "but, for now, I want you to tell the Bishop you've absolutely no doubt these additional verses to Revelation 10 do belong in the Book of Revelation."

"Well, I don't have any doubt, at least not yet."

"Then tell that to the Bishop, but leave out the part about not yet. Do you understand?"

"No, I don't understand, but I'll do as you say."

"Good, that's all I ask. You continue to clean up that Botticelli, but hide that letter from Savonarola in the vault and tell your workers to tell no one about it."

"As you say, it'll be done," Mykos responded and, with a flip of his wrist, he turned to get back to work. Kevin was confident Mykos would do as he was told. This time.

The Stranger was elated by the news that Mykos had authenticated all the copies of this new Revelation 10. He no longer had any doubts it had been purposely left out of the Bible by Apostle John or one of his scribes. The Bishop in charge of the Doctrinal Office affirmed Mykos' research. Things were almost in place for the Stranger. Soon his ascension to the throne would be complete. The prophesy was coming true.

CHAPTER THIRTY-TWO

Then there came flashes of lightning, rumblings, peals of thunder and a severe earthquake. No earthquake like it has ever occurred since man has been on earth, so tremendous was the quake. The great city split into three parts, and the cities of the nations collapsed. God remembered Babylon the Great and gave her the cup filled with the wine of the fury of his wrath. Every island fled away and the mountains could not be found. From the sky huge hailstones of about a hundred pounds each fell upon men. And they cursed God on account of the plague of hail, because the plague was so terrible.

Revelation 16:18-21

It was early in the morning. Tisha was out for her morning jog with Zeke. On these days when the sun shone for almost twelve hours, they always ran early to avoid the heat. It was the same jogging trail they had taken every morning for the past two months. Tisha was trying to keep in shape and Zeke was trying to get Tisha to sleep with him. So far only Tisha was reaping the benefits of the early morning exercise. The trail they followed wound in and around the foothills just outside Pano Lefkara village, east of the Troodos mountains in Cyprus.

"Did you feel that one?" Tisha asked Zeke.

"No, I didn't feel that one either," Zeke replied, sounding a bit skeptical.

Tisha had been telling him she had felt small earthquakes all morning. Zeke was yet to feel one and was beginning to rethink these early morning runs with Tisha. The last thing he needed was to get into a relationship with another paranoid woman.

"Look out!" Tisha screamed, grabbing Zeke by the back of the shirt and yanking him to a stop.

"What? What's the problem?"

"That snake is the problem," Tisha said, pointing up the trail.

"Don't you mean snakes? Holy Christ, there are snakes everywhere," Zeke yelled, "let's get out of here."

The two of them started running down the trail leaping over snakes, lizards, and every kind of beetle and bug imaginable.

Suddenly hundreds of birds took to flight simultaneously from the surrounding trees. Dogs began to bark in the village below. The earth gave a loud crying moan as if gasping its final breath, then began to shake violently.

Muslims in masjids throughout the Middle East were in the middle of their Subah prayers. Without warning the foundations snapped and the walls and ceilings came roaring down upon their heads, crushing their bodies below tons of rubble. Islam's most sacred shrines were instantly destroyed, including the Dome on the Rock in Jerusalem. Dozens of ancient Byzantine churches fell to ruins from the shaking. Entire cities were instantly reduced to piles of rubble, burying hundreds of thousands if not millions of souls beneath them. Few would be left alive to mourn, let alone recover and bury the dead.

Giant fissures split the earth like a knife tearing through an overripe melon. The fissures extended well into the Mediterranean Sea, sucking billions of gallons of sea water deep into the earth's crust. Such a massive displacement of water created a tsunami of historical proportions, killing millions more as it raced onshore in Egypt, Italy, Greece, Libya, Tunisia, Syria, Lebanon, and Israel. In Turkey, the damage from the tsunami was miniscule compared to the damage and deaths caused when a series of long thought dormant volcanoes exploded back into life with unimagined fury. The Aegean and Turkish plates collided with previously unknown ferocity, all compounded by the influx of the billions of gallons of sea water. The day turned to night as ash blocked the sun from shining upon the fractured earth. Tons of ash and rock rained down on the decimated land below. Thousands more would die as a scalding cloud of pyroclastic gas and debris raced down the sides of the volcanoes into the already devastated populated areas, killing those who had somehow survived the initial quake.

Tisha and Zeke were both knocked to the ground as forests of giant trees snapped liked toothpicks at their base. Huge sections of the earth welled up into the sky and came crashing back down, reshaping the landscape forever. One such violent upheaval smashed and trapped Zeke's foot and ankle under a slab of rock. Tisha disappeared as a giant vacuum of space opened beneath her and the earth seemed to swallow her, then slowly closed, leaving no trace of what it had done.

Millions were killed in the initial devastation. Tens of millions were left homeless. Almost two million more would die from injuries, disease, and starvation as they waited for help to arrive. For most, help would never come.

Zeke was knocked unconscious when the slab of rock crushed the lower part of his leg, pinning him to the ground. He awoke to his own screams as the excruciating pain pounded through his weakened body. He looked around, but the world had changed. The village was gone, just a pile of rubble remained, surrounded by several new vertical outcroppings of rock. Zeke was alone. He knew no one would come looking for him. The throbbing in his leg continued, though little blood seeped out from beneath the slab of rock. Below him was more rock, making it impossible for him to dig his crushed leg out from between the two slabs gripping his leg like a vise. He had no choice but to wait, which he did for two days of continuous aftershocks and searing heat. On the third day Zeke knew if he could not free his leg he would die. His only alternative was to attempt to amputate his own leg. The only tool available that might possibly work was the metal covering to his I-pod. It was still attached to his arm, although the earphones were nowhere to be seen. He broke apart the I-pod and attempted to sharpen the metal case on the rock that trapped his leg. He grasped the metal casing in his right hand, then stuffed his T-shirt into his mouth and bit down. Tears filled his eyes and began to run down his face as he started to slice his skin and flesh, just inches below his knee. He continued to rip and tear at his muscles until he finally reached the bone. His chest was heaving as he bit down hard and screamed into the shirt. He fell back on the ground in exhaustion. He was unable to cut through or even cut into the bone with the flimsy tool. Tears again began to pour down Zeke's face. This time they were not tears of pain, but tears of defeat. It was impossible for him to free himself from the rocks that held him prisoner. Zeke lay back down and stared up into the sky and prayed. He had never been a religious man. Actually, he had not been to church since he was a little boy. But that day, on a hillside just outside of what used to be the village of Pano Lefkara in Cyprus, Zeke surrendered his life to Jesus Christ. Tens of millions of people lay dead and suffering from nature's fury, yet Jesus was there by Zeke's side holding his hand, welcoming him into the kingdom of God as Zeke took his final breath.

CHAPTER THIRTY-THREE

Then I saw another beast, coming out of the earth. He had two horns like a lamb, but he spoke like a dragon. He exercised all the authority of the first beast on his behalf, and made the earth and its inhabitants worship the first beast, whose fatal wound had been healed. And he performed great and miraculous signs, even causing fire to come down from heaven to earth in full view of men. Because of the signs he was given power to do on behalf of the first beast, he deceived the inhabitants of the earth.

Revelation 13:11-14

Kevin spent the evening researching the death of Lucy's real parents in Scotland. He had contacted the local Scottish police who said they would have somebody search for the file in the storage room and fax him what information they had about the murders. The officer on the phone said most of the older records were lost when the police station burned to the ground about twenty years ago.

"Some of the older blokes tell me t'was an arson fire, but no culprit was e'r found. Tink it 'twas Bob told me that," the chap on the phone explained to Kevin.

"Is this Bob around?" Kevin asked.

"Nah, He's awa on the ran-dan," the Scotsman replied.

"He's what?" Kevin asked.

'He's out a drink'n and a tear'n up the town."

"Well, any help you can give me will be greatly appreciated."

"I'll see what I can do for you, Mr. Bridges. We have your number and you'll hear from us, one way or the other," the officer replied.

Kevin was too tired to head back to his apartment and decided to spend the night sleeping on his office couch. The next morning, he would get Mykos to try to find his friend Vlade to see if they could get a look at that Botticelli at the Hermitage. Until then, sleep is what Kevin needed.

* * *

Astan arrived back at his mansion and began preparing for his trip to China with the bird flu vaccine from the lab in Rome. They had been working around the clock preparing as much vaccine as possible. Astan knew it would not be enough to stop the Chinese outbreak. There were by some estimates over a hundred million soldiers encamped near the Russian border. The flu was already at pandemic proportions and had killed upwards of a million people. The research lab told Astan they should have all the vaccine prepared and loaded by mid-morning. Astan was satisfied with that schedule. It would allow him time to meet with his other mole within the Vatican. He had arranged for a late-night dinner and conversation with the Bishop.

The Bishop commanded quite a following of ardent supporters, but he desired greater power than he already wielded at the Vatican. He knew Astan could help him gain that power if he kept Astan informed. A mutually beneficial arrangement, or so the Bishop thought. Only it wasn't mutual at all. He was not even in the same league as Astan when it came to scheming and manipulating. He, like so many others, would be used and left to suffer the consequences of their naiveté. Astan was the master of seeing to that.

Mykos had called the Bishop to inform him that he now had absolutely no doubt these verses to Revelation 10 were purposely left out of the Book of Revelation. This new Greek canon given to the Pope by the Emperor of Ethiopia erased any doubt anyone could raise concerning the authenticity and veracity of these verses.

"Seeing what the true Revelation 10 discloses, it's no wonder Apostle John, or one of the first scribes copying his Revelation, left it out. It's simply unthinkable," Mykos told the Bishop.

"Yes, my son, it's true that it might be unthinkable, but they are Christ's prophecies. No one, not even Apostle John, had the right to alter his Word. It should have been written," the Bishop explained to Mykos, "and may God have mercy on our souls if it is ever written."

That night over dinner the Bishop shared this information with Astan.

"I have feared this for a long time," Astan told the Bishop. "That's why I wanted all of the miracle workers together to help deal with this Revelation. We must bring the world together to help stop this from happening."

"But Astan, it is God's will. It should have been written in Revelation from the very beginning."

"Yes, but it wasn't written. Maybe God purposely allowed that to happen. I think that, with your help, Bishop, we can still stop what is unthinkable," Astan explained.

"I will do all that you ask of me."

"You will do all that my miracle workers ask of you as well," Astan said, purposely. "They know the truth even though they yet might not realize it. When they do realize what must be done, listen and follow them."

The Bishop was a little puzzled by Astan's last request, but knew he must do as asked.

Before he went to bed that evening, Astan gave a final call to Switzerland and spoke with all three of the miracle workers. They were preparing to leave the next day for Russia with their supply of the bird flu vaccine. So far, the bird flu had only taken a minor toll on the Russian troops that manned the border with China, but inoculations would be necessary to prevent the flu from spreading.

* * *

The next morning both Astan and Kevin were awoken by the motion of the undulating ground. Even though the epicenter was over twelve hundred miles away, there was no doubt Rome was experiencing an earthquake. When the news services pinpointed the epicenter as being in Cyprus, the magnitude of the disaster became apparent. The quake registered a 9.8 on the Richter scale and had unleashed a series of volcanoes and a tsunami of monstrous proportions. Millions died during the initial quake and millions more would die from the aftermath. Countries from around the world would send financial assistance and personnel to help assist in the rescue. It would make virtually no difference, except to a very few fortunate areas, where teams would come to help. Several major cities, along with their historic buildings and shrines, were totally destroyed. The destruction of the Dome on the Rock in Jerusalem would become an issue of major significance. Mika'il told the producers to broadcast a special message to the world saying the miracle workers pledged to do everything in their power to help the world recover. Mika'il went on to say that maybe this was God's and Allah's way of telling the world they must work together in peace. Along those lines, he proposed an immediate rebuilding of a new temple where the Dome on the Rock had stood. Mika'il envisioned this new temple with three separate but equal rooms of worship. One room would be for the Jews, one for the Christians, and one for the Muslims where each could hold their own religious ceremonies and rites. Many people who saw the broadcast applauded this innovative plan offered by Mika'il. Others, particularly the Jews and the fundamentalist Muslims, were outraged by such a proposal. The fundamentalist Muslims insisted the mosque be rebuilt just as it was for the Muslims to continue to worship there. The Jews, on the other hand, saw it as an opportunity to return it back to its rightful origin as a Jewish house of worship, the Bait Hamikdash, just as it is written. They were tired of people meddling in their internal affairs, especially a proven enemy of the state like this alleged miracle worker, Mika'il.

A medical team from Lucy's research center in Italy was quickly organized and Astan agreed to take them to Cyprus on his way to China. They left just after noon on the day the earthquake occurred. Astan was so busy preparing for the trip that he did not see Mika'il's broadcast or even hear about it until he was almost to Cyprus. He tried to call Mika'il or Lucy back in Switzerland, but the earthquake had knocked out several communication centers and his call did not go through. This seemed to make Astan as irate as Mika'il's broadcast had. The one thing Astan hated the most was not being able to reach people when he needed to.

* * *

In Israel, The Shabak, Israel's general security service, was focused on trying to get emergency personnel, equipment, and supplies to where they were most needed after the earthquake. Even though communications were sketchy at best, one call that did get through was an anonymous call to the head of the Shabak, who in turn contacted the head of the Aman, the military intelligence service. The caller warned them that the Palestinian terrorist and now miracle worker Mika'il was planning to drop several hundred canisters of the toxic nerve agent Sarin in the waters off the coast of Israel and on Israel itself. He would be flying over in another of Astan Ilves private jets. The caller said the plane Mika'il would be using was a large Boeing 747. The head of the Aman wasted no time in ordering four fighter jets to intercept the terrorist.

Astan's jet had landed in Cyprus and the medical team and their equipment were off-loaded. Astan, his assistants, and another medical team which had been scheduled to distribute the vaccine, left Cyprus and headed across the Mediterranean Sea. They had not even reached their cruising altitude when four military jets boxed them in. Astan saw the jets outside his window and rushed to the cockpit.

"Ask them what they want."

"They want to know why we are carrying a weapon of mass destruction and plan on using it in Israel," the pilot relayed to Astan.

"Tell them that is absurd. We are carrying vaccines of bird flu victims in China. Tell them Astan Ilves is aboard and there will be hell to pay if they don't move away and allow us to go on unhindered."

The head of Aman and Shabak were monitoring the conversation between the two pilots.

"What do you think, my friend, should we believe this pilot or our anonymous caller?" the head of Shabak asked his associate.

"Ask them if Mika'il the miracle worker is aboard the plane," one of the men told the fighter pilot, who also followed orders well.

When told the fighter pilot's question, Astan was beside himself with anger.

"Tell that SOB it's none of his damn business who is on this plane, because this plane is nowhere near Israeli airspace, so get the hell out of our way."

Moments later, the Israeli jets all peeled away from the jumbo jet.

"You see," Astan said, "they know better than to mess with Astan Ilves." Just then a buzzer went off in the cockpit signaling an eminent collision. Before the pilot could react, the jumbo jet was blown out of the sky by two Israeli stinger missiles. The wreckage splashed down on top of the warm Mediterranean Sea. No survivors were found.

CHAPTER THIRTY-FOUR

In the last days, God says, I will pour out my Spirit on all people. Your sons and daughters will prophesy, your young men will see visions, your old men will dream dreams.

Acts 2:17

Anatoly Katz arrived in Ozersk in 1954. He had been recruited by one of his former professors with wondrous promises of research freedom, a supportive government, and unlimited financial backing. What his professor failed to tell him was that it also included a life sentence of confinement within the Chelyabinsk oblast, or region. Barbed wire fences and heavily armed guards were both plentiful to assure no strangers entered the closed city but, more importantly, that no one got out. Anatoly had accepted the position at the Mayak Chemical Combine. This plant was responsible for making almost all the weapons grade nuclear material required for Russia's burgeoning nuclear weapons program. Anatoly would play a key part in the functioning of the reactors, making sure the needs of the Russian military were met. Not even the several accidents that poisoned the ground and many of the people in the oblast slowed down the plutonium production from Anatoly's reactors. He performed his job flawlessly until the graphite reactors were closed down in the 1960s. After the reactors were shut down, Anatoly was moved to the storage tanks that kept and cooled all of the high-level wastes, the same tanks whose cooling system had failed in 1957, causing Russia's worst nuclear disaster up until that time. When the Cold War ended, neither Anatoly nor his wife were allowed to leave Ozersk. They had been able to send their children back to Israel to be raised by relatives. Had the children remained with them, they would have been destined to the same confinement as their parents. Those children who did stay almost all ended up with alcohol or drug problems; that is, if they didn't commit suicide. Twice his son and daughter had been allowed to come to Ozersk to visit, but these visits were always closely supervised to ensure no state secrets left the country. On the second visit, Anatoly and his wife saw their only grandchild Amichai Katz for the first time. "Amichai," their son's only child, meant "my people are alive" in Hebrew. His father had named Amichai in honor of his grandparents who were still confined in Ozersk, but were not and would not be forgotten. The old couple dreamed of one day returning to Israel.

Amichai was a troubled child. He was in elementary school when he first began to hear the voices which came at night when he was trying to fall asleep. These voices told him to hurt animals and even to hurt himself. At first his parents were very concerned by his claims and had several doctors treat him. The doctors blamed the voices on the Ritalin Amichai had been taking for hyperactivity.

These same doctors would then prescribe a variety of other medications to counteract the Ritalin. He began to have visions and bizarre dreams but still the voices continued. Actually, it was only one voice, the voice of the Stranger. The Stranger knew just what words to whisper to prepare Amichai for the part he would someday play.

By the time Amichai reached high school, he had learned not to tell anyone about the voices. Instead he created a façade of craziness. He became known as the joker, the trickster, or "crazy Katz." As the voices became louder, requiring his response, Amachai would respond, but play it off as a hoax or as a game. He began dressing in bizarre costumes, often coming to school dressed in all yellow as the character Pikachu. He claimed it kept him safe from the voices when he dressed this way. As his strange behavior persisted and even increased, his parents had no choice but to take him out of school. He was able to pass a high school equivalency exam that gave him his diploma, but his continued strange behavior would not let him keep any job for more than a couple of weeks. His parents were at their wits end when news came of the death of Anatoly's wife in Ozersk.

The Russians would still not allow Anatoly to leave the closed city of Ozersk. It wasn't that Anatoly knew too much about the Russian nuclear capabilities, but that they feared he knew of too many incidents that could bring unwanted grief to the Mayak Chemical Plant. The government was not completely heartless and agreed to allow a relative of Anatoly to come care for him. Amichai was the perfect choice.

* * *

Rusted and broken barbed-wire fences still surround the city of Ozersk. The signs on the main road warn visitors that they are not welcome and must obtain permission before approaching any further. The signs were written in both Russian and English. To back up the warning signs, just a short way up the road, was a checkpoint with a security gate and heavily armed Russian soldiers. That, however, is where the security seems to stop. Anyone with an old worker's badge can easily pass through this security checkpoint, and those without a badge can usually bribe the guards with a few hundred rubles to be let through. Those not wishing to deal with these bored men with machineguns could easily find a hole along the exterior fence. Once in the town, the same worker's badge would allow you to pass through the gates into almost all the sensitive areas that either store or manufacture plutonium as well as the waste storage areas. The United States had been working very hard at trying to get Russia to improve its security of nuclear facilities such as Mayak. Congress grew reluctant to keep pouring money into Russia, when so many pressing issues called for substantial financial commitments at home. Russia was also reluctant to accept the conditions that were attached to this money for security improvements. An ingrained mistrust and fear of losing state secrets that had matured during the Cold War still lingered, making negotiations difficult. Security improvements were slow in coming.

Amichai had been issued a special pass from the local authorities allowing him to enter the city and stay with his grandfather for up to two months. When Amichai arrived, he found not the proud Jew he expected but a bitter old man, angry at the world and whose only solace in life was his dreams, an old man's dreams never to be fulfilled. Amichai was appalled that the elderly Jews who still resided in Ozersk were so scarred by the fear of Communism that most would not leave their houses until after dark. They all expected and waited for the return of Communism into their daily lives. This was not the vision Amichai had imagined. His people, the Jews of Ozersk, were dead. Not literally dead, but dead to the rest of the world. Russia had taken his people, his Jewish people, squeezed from them all they had to offer, then devoured them.

"They must be punished," the voice echoed inside Amichai's head. "You must punish these evil Russian warmongers for their hatred of the Jews." Visions of a better world filled Amichai's mind as he saw his grandfather free from the oppression that he had suffered throughout his confined lifetime.

Amichai knew what must be done. The Stranger's voice tearing through his brain told him what must be done. His visions, a young man's visions, showed him how to do it. Over the next few days he learned much from his grandfather, much about his grandfather's dreams, and much about the Mayak Chemical Combine. He also learned anything can be bought in Russia for the right price, from American cigarettes to Russian nuclear warheads. It's not difficult to find someone who will sell them to you. Such was the case when Amichai purchased several hand grenades from a soldier in a local bar. He knew it was likely that the soldier would have him arrested within a couple of days and then confiscate the grenades to sell to another unsuspecting buyer. The Stranger's voice in Amichai's head had warned him of this. He knew that if he were to succeed, he had to act immediately.

That afternoon, Amichai wrote several letters to major newspapers around the world, complaining of the plight of Jews in Russia and elsewhere. The letters were little more than the ranting of a madman, but made it clear that what Amichai was about to do was for, and in the name of, Israel and Jews everywhere. He mailed the letters and gave second copies to a trusted Russian friend of Anatoly's. That friend agreed to take them to Yekaterinburg that afternoon and mail the second copy from there.

Later that evening, when it was still light, Amichai entered the Mayak facilities using his grandfather's badge, carrying the hand grenades and his grandfather's old pistol. From listening to his reminiscences of his work at the plant, Amichai had learned exactly where to go to inflict maximum punishment on these Russians who had ruined the lives of his people, his Jewish people. There was a large cement warehouse with thick steel doors that had recently been constructed with money supplied by the United States. To enter it required complex key codes and at least three different individuals with different codes all entering their codes at the same time. Several video cameras monitored the warehouse to ensure no one could approach it unnoticed. It was state-of the-art security where none had been before. Unfortunately, the Russians had been remiss in transferring the several tons of plutonium from the old warehouse to the new secure structure, which sat a few hundred yards from the old warehouse. This warehouse had wooden doors each secured by a padlock. This is where Amichai would make his final stand. First, he would visit the cooling plant. Several million gallons of highly radioactive wastes were kept in a dozen giant cement holding tanks. These tanks were constantly cooled by a massive series of pipes which ran through these tanks and carried chemicals designed to keep these tanks of nuclear waste from overheating. It was a similar tank that overheated in 1957, resulting in an explosion which led to the contamination of several hundred square kilometers and thousands of people. Exactly how severe the contamination was had never been, and would never be, told by the Russian government. When the new tanks were built, a large single cooling facility was designed to service all of the nuclear holding tanks. That made it much easier to monitor, but much more vulnerable if something were to go wrong. It was at this facility Amichai that made his first visit.

There was but one guard at the door as Amichai approached. He took no notice as Amichai entered the cooling plant. There were always a minimum of a dozen men monitoring and mending the pipes and equipment that controlled and cooled the monstrous vats of nuclear waste. Amichai knew he would have to blow up both the control room and the main coolant pipes if he wanted his plan to succeed. That presented no problem as he casually lobbed two grenades into the control room where most of the workers were located. He ran down the hallway and into the main facility that housed the coolant pipes. He arrived just in time to see a bright flash, followed by a thunderous roar, as the windows of the control room overlooking the main facility disintegrated into a million shards of glass, killing everyone inside and demolishing the sensitive equipment and computers. He then casually rolled three more grenades beneath the myriad of pipes that filled the room. He thought he would have to shoot the guard whom he had seen on his way in, but the guard was nowhere to be found as Amichai hurried out just before the three grenades exploded. The cooling facility had been completely destroyed by Amichai who now rushed to the storage warehouse. Sirens began to wail throughout the plant and the city of Ozersk. No one took notice of Amichai as rescue and fire suppression teams rushed towards the cooling plant. That made it extremely easy for Amichai to break open the lock on one of the wooden doors of the storage warehouse without being seen. What his grandfather hadn't told him was that the storage warehouse, though easy to enter, was alarmed and had video monitoring on the inside. Even with all the chaos the guards in the security center were quick to notice the breach of security at the warehouse. Security was dispatched to intercept the intruder. Had the congestion of the fire suppression teams not delayed the guards from reaching the storage warehouse as quickly as they should have, they may have been able to stop Amichai before he could detonate his next three grenades. There was row after row of buckets lined up on the floor of the warehouse. In each of these buckets was a quantity of plutonium. Amichai quickly tossed several of the buckets into three piles and then rolled a grenade into each pile. He was running out the door when the security team arrived and cut him down with a burst of machine gun fire. As Amichai's body dropped to the ground, the three grenades went off in quick succession blowing the roof off of the old warehouse and raining down plutonium over a wide area of the Mayak property. The chief of security on duty panicked when he realized plutonium had been spread all over the vicinity and ordered the fire suppression teams, security teams, and all workers out of the area. It wasn't the plutonium they needed to fear. It was the ever-increasing temperatures of the millions of gallons of nuclear waste in the storage tanks. It would be almost two hours until Mayak officials realized this. They also knew they had no way of stopping the inevitable catastrophic explosion as the temperatures continued to rise unabated. An attempt was made to evacuate as many people as possible, but when the explosion did come, hundreds were killed and tens of thousands would eventually die from radiation poisoning.

Newspapers around the world printed Amichai's "declaration of intolerance" that he, as a representative of Israel and the Aman, put forward to the world. A long-deserved justice for the thousands of Jews who for decades had been used, looked down upon, and unjustly treated by the Russian authorities. "No longer would Jewry or the people of Israel tolerate such treatment."

Normally such ravings would have been laughed off by the editors of the world's most prestigious newspapers. However, the magnitude of the atrocity Amichai committed, along with the malicious assassination by the Israeli military of the great Astan Ilves and his medical team on the way to save millions of lives in China, demanded front page coverage. The Russians had no doubt Amichai was an Israeli agent. How could anyone but a highly trained agent be able to so efficiently and effectively breach their security? How else could he have gotten the grenades in a closed city like Ozersk? According to Russian news dispatches, analysis of explosive residue showed the grenades were Israeli made munitions. Never before in history had so many nations and peoples expressed such anger at the brazen actions of the Jewish state of Israel. Even though Israel now lay in ruins from the massive earthquake, people demanded revenge and the Stranger was there fanning the flames of hatred at every opportunity.

CHAPTER THIRTY-FIVE

They are spirits of demons performing miraculous signs, and they go out to the kings of the whole world, to gather them for the battle on the great day of God Almighty.

Revelation 16:14

Lucy was devastated when she heard of her father's "murder," as the world press was now calling it. So far Israel had offered no statement of regret or admission acknowledging what they had done. The country was in such disarray from the massive devastation caused by the earthquake, that there was no way the government could convene to deal with the shooting down of Astan's plane. Lucy was in flight to deliver bird flu vaccine to the Russian troops positioned along the border with China. From there they had planned to return to the Middle East to assist with earthquake recovery. Now all of that would change. Everything would change now that Astan was dead.

The jet arrived at a military base just south of T'ungur near the Chinese border. The base had gone into a high security alert. The Chinese had heard about Astan and his supply of vaccine being shot down by Israel. Vaccine meant for them. They also knew of the Russian supply of the vaccine scheduled to be delivered that evening. Chinese troop movements into Kazakhstan had been reported by satellite imaging. Several units were quickly moving towards T'ungur just above the Russian-Kazakhstan border. It was believed that they were a rogue division with the intent of stealing the vaccine from the Russians. Of equal concern to the Russian troops was news of an Israeli attack on a nuclear facility in the southern Ural mountain region. This information was sketchy, but it had been confirmed. An attack was now being planned on the advancing Chinese troops. Such an attack could spark the conflict and ignite the battle which could lead to a nuclear holocaust. Mika'il insisted he be flown by helicopter to meet the advancing column of Chinese troops, he and his video crew of course. Mika'il saw his opportunity to usurp all the power and the following Astan had amassed with his television broadcasts of the miracle workers. At first, no pilot was willing to risk his life flying Mika'il to intercept the Chinese. Mika'il had learned well from his brief association with Astan and made one of the Russian helicopter pilots a financial offer impossible to refuse. They soon were in the air and approaching the Chinese. The video crew was of course filming as the helicopter came under fire. Just as before, flashes and sparkles of silver and blue created a barrier protecting the helicopter from harm. A missile was shot at the copter and, with a flick of his hand, Mika'il reversed its direction, sending it back destroying the launcher and the soldiers who had launched it. The copter landed in front of the Chinese troops, but the Chinese refused to give up so easily. They continued a non-stop torrent of automatic weapon fire at the copter only to have the bullets drop harmlessly to the ground before reaching the intended target. Mika'il realized it would take more than just stopping the bullets to put an end to this Chinese advance. He reversed the barrage, sending the bullets back toward their points of origin. As soon as a soldier fired his weapon, his own bullets would rip his body to pieces. Several hundred Chinese had to die before they fully understood the futility of their attack. One of the Chinese officers approached Mika'il who, through an interpreter, explained that if the Chinese gave up their planned invasion of Russia, he would guarantee more vaccine would be delivered. He also warned them to abandon their plans of conquest or he would stay and help the Russians defend their border. The officer couldn't agree to such demands, but he would stop his advance and pass the message on to his superiors. The officer didn't know about Satan or God, but he did know for sure that the ying and the yang were no longer in balance in the world. It seemed evil reigned over good and the world had become an even more dangerous place than it already was.

"Give them this video," Mika'il said, handing the officer a copy of the futile Chinese attack.

"They can also watch it on the news later today," Mika'il said smiling. "Make sure you let them know the consequences if they persist in this invasion."

When they arrived back in T'ungur, Lucy insisted they leave the medical team with the vaccine, and return immediately to Rome. She wanted to coordinate the search for survivors from the attack on Astan's plane. Mika'il had other ideas about what needed to be done.

* * *

This was the first time Mika'il had traveled without Ahmed accompanying him and Ahmed was not too pleased about it. He had seen it coming. Over the past several days, Mika'il had pushed Ahmed aside, slowly at first, as Mika'il's new protectors seemed to arrive and gather around him, insulating Mika'il from unnecessary contacts. Lately, Ahmed had rarely even seen Mika'il, let alone stand by his side as he had done for so many years. Ahmed always knew this time would come. Even before Mika'il had begun performing miracles, Ahmed knew Mika'il had an important date with destiny. Ahmed had thought of himself as a guide in getting Mika'il to that journey's end safely. Now it appeared he had failed at that task, for others now wielded the influence as to which path Mika'il would follow, a path that seemed to be headed the wrong direction.

* * *

Gabe was enjoying the break from the hectic schedule he had been on the past several days. He was constantly reading some script the producers prepared for him. Most of the time he paid absolutely no attention to what it was he was reading. A couple of times they had asked him to participate in healing the sick. He did so, and was successful in the healing, but lacked the persona and flair the directors were looking for. A decision was made that Gabe would be best used just narrating the programs. Gabe couldn't have been happier with the decision.

At the last minute he decided not to join the other two miracle workers on their mission to Russia. Instead, he would stay in Vevey for some needed rest.

Gabe and Ahmed had been spending more time together. They had become friends and, oddly enough, a group of protectors had seemed to grow around both of them. Gabe's protectors were understandable since he was a miracle worker and godly people had been attracted to his presence since that day of the train wreck. Ahmed was vexed at why these protectors were beginning to gather around him. It had started just about the time Mika'il began shunning Ahmed. Now the number of these protectors seemed to be increasing daily. No longer could Ahmed take those quiet walks alone along the shore of Lake Geneva or through the quiet and quaint streets of Vevey. Now his protectors were always there waiting to accompany him wherever he went.

Ahmed had never been a fanatical Muslim. In fact, had it not been that he was born in the West Bank where worshipping Allah and practicing Islam was expected of everyone, that along with hating the Jews, Ahmed would probably have chosen a different path. He was, in fact, on his way down that opposed path, when as a child he met Mika'il. Something he didn't understand at the time, and in fact he still couldn't understand to this day, bound him to Mika'il from that moment forward. Whether it was a voice telling him what he must do, a vision, or a dream, Ahmed knew his destiny was tied to this charismatic leader. Now it was all changing. Ahmed realized his job as protector, nobly standing by the side of Mika'il, was completed. Yet, just as he knew his life would be spent with Mika'il, he now knew he had yet another part to play in this saga. His adventures were not over nor being his heroic deeds at an end.

Ahmed found much spiritual meaning in his long discussions with Gabe. Gabe had been on the Christian path for quite a long time, unwilling, or unable to make that final commitment to Jesus. Gabe and Ahmed talked in length about God and His perfect plan for mankind. For years Gabe had asked countless questions of his pastor and friends, all of whom had given their lives to Jesus Christ and had accepted Him as their savior. They had given him many answers, but Gabe was still unable to understand just exactly what the Word was and what it meant for him. Ahmed had no trouble understanding God's message. He knew you received Jesus Christ into your heart, not in your mind, a choice he readily made. It was a beautiful awakening for Ahmed whose life suddenly seemed to blossom before him. He could not wait to share his happiness with Mika'il. That is, if he could even see Mika'il when he returned from his mission to Russia.

Gabe was very happy for Ahmed and his newly chosen path. He couldn't understand how Ahmed could find his salvation in Jesus Christ so quickly, when Gabe had been struggling for so long. Their happiness was soon dimmed when they turned on CNN and watched Mika'il turn bullets into a rain of fire killing hundreds of Chinese troops. Then there was the mind-numbing news that Astan's jet had been shot down by the Israelis in what the media was calling an unthinkable assassination.

"That is not how God meant his gift to be used," Ahmed said to Gabe.

"Where is Lucy?" Gabe said. "I don't see Lucy anywhere. I wonder what she thinks of all this? I'm even more worried about how she's taking the death of her father."

"I'm sure she's fine," Ahmed said, trying to reassure Gabe.

"What do you think will happen to us now that Astan is dead?"

"I'm really not sure," Ahmed replied, "but I would guess Lucy and Mika'il will both try to take Astan's place."

"Well, I sure wouldn't mind going back to California."

"I wouldn't count on that happening anytime soon. I think now, more than ever, you are needed and are going to be playing a bigger role than you imagined as a miracle worker. For some reason I sense a change is upon us, and you are a part of that change."

Gabe didn't respond, but just watched CNN as it went from Mika'il's encounter with the Russians, to the devastation from the earthquake, tsunami, and volcanoes, to the horrific tragedy in Ozersk, which was being blamed on Israel along with the shooting down of Astan's jet, apparently killing all on board.

"Yes," Ahmed said as he watched the news, "things are changing quickly and we both need to be prepared to help as God has intended for us to do."

* * *

Kevin had slept in the clothes he had worn the previous day. It was not the first time and undoubtedly would not be the last. He had turned on the news and was just finishing washing his face when his phone rang. He was hoping it was Lucy or even Mykos with some good news about the Russian Botticelli, but it was a man with a thick Scottish brogue.

"You must be Bob," Kevin said to the Scotsman.

"Aye, and you must be Kevin. What kin a do fo ya?"

"I'm trying to get some information on a murder of a Mr. and Mrs. Sexton that happened in your town around thirty years ago. I was told all the records were lost, but the other officer said you may remember the case." There was only silence on the phone. "Bob, are you still there?"

"Aye, just away in a dwalm. T'was a terrible murder as I recollect. Neva' found out who killed the three of thaim."

"Three? Lucy said only her mother and father were killed."

"Awa ye go," Bob responded in disbelief. "Lucy you say. T'was the middle name of the deid l'il lass found with her mither and dad."

Now it was Kevin's turn to be shocked. "Are you telling me their daughter Lucy was killed as well?"

"Truelins. T'was I that fand the three morts."

Kevin wasn't sure what to ask or even say next. He could not understand how that could be. "Was there anything really unusual about the murders?" he finally got the courage to ask.

"Awa ye go! There's aye a something," Bob responded, surprised by Kevin's question. "Thay aw haed thaer herts riven oot."

The accent was thick, but Kevin didn't need a translation of what he had just heard. He couldn't believe it, but it all seemed to make sense. He was going to ask if there were any bloody talon prints, but he already knew there had to be. "Thanks for your help," Kevin replied, "can I call you later if I need to?"

"Atweel, mak a kirk or a mill o' it," Bob replied and hung up. Kevin wasn't quite sure what he said, but it really didn't matter. His brain was already going a mile a minute trying to figure out what it all meant. Either Lucy was lying to him, or somebody had lied to Lucy. Astan was sure looking suspicious, although Kevin was by no means ready to call him Satan, at least, not quite yet. And he for sure wasn't going to accuse Lucy of being the devil, although the thought did cross his mind.

Kevin turned to the television to try to find out about the earthquake that had awoken him that morning. The devastation was horrific. Then he saw Mika'il's broadcast calling for the rebuilding of the destroyed Dome on the Rock with a church that included the Muslims, the Jews, and the Christians.

"What the hell is he thinking?" Kevin said to himself. "I can't believe Astan allowed him to say that or for that matter even allowed Mika'il to make a broadcast without Astan in town." Kevin knew things would be getting more interesting between those two. Kevin next received a call from the Bishop at the Doctrinal Office wanting him to come to a meeting to discuss the new Revelation 10. Kevin knew it would be a waste of his time, but at least he would get a better idea where the Bishop stood in relationship to the Pope. The Bishop had disagreed openly with the Pope recently and aligned himself with a more Orthodox point of view. The Pope was afraid to discipline him, for the Bishop seemed to have quite a few powerful followers of his own within Vatican City. A lot of political wrangling was occurring in the Catholic Church and if the Pope wasn't careful, the Catholic Church would be split in two.

By the time Kevin left the meeting with the Bishop, breaking news was on CNN that hit Kevin like a brick. CNN had obtained the recording of the conversation between Israeli military intelligence and Astan Ilves' aircraft just prior to what they were calling Israel's second unforgivable act of world terrorism. Israel shot down Astan's 747 jumbo jet, as he and a team of doctors were on their way to China to administer life saving bird flu vaccine. It would be impossible to produce more vaccine in time to prevent millions of people from a certain death. The previous night Israel's first egregious act of terror occurred when an Israeli covert agent sabotaged a nuclear facility in Ozersk. This alleged spy had sent a letter to several newspapers throughout the world, outlining Israel's anger over the historically disgusting treatment of Jews by the Russian government. Israel was of course denying having anything to do with the bomber, but after the unwarranted and brutal missile attack on Astan Ilves, absolutely no one believed Israel's denial of the Ozersk attack. Russia considered it an act of war and was taking their case to the United Nations. Russia already knew it was a crazed relative of one of their Jewish scientists acting alone who had caused all the damage, not an Israeli agent. The Russian soldier who had supplied the Jewish man with the grenades had already been put to death for his part in the tragedy. They had no plans of invading Israel and were just hoping to get world opinion on their side for some needed financial aid and support in their impending fight against the Chinese.

Kevin sat dazed in front of his office television trying to sort out all that was happening. That was when the first broadcast of Mika'il's clash with the Chinese soldiers in Russia was aired. It was skillfully put together by Astan's team of producers, showing Mika'il to be a righteous and worthy leader who would not tolerate what he perceived as injustice, nor did it leave any doubt that those responsible for these injustices would be punished. It was crafted to perfection, endearing Mika'il to all who watched the confrontation and subsequent massacre of Chinese troops, all in the name of righteousness. Kevin now knew who his enemy was.

* * *

Lucy had been furious when Mika'il left to confront the Chinese on his own when they arrived and she was prepared to battle him when he returned to the Russian airbase. All her planned arguments came to naught when Mika'il agreed that they should immediately head to Rome as she desired. Mika'il suggested they use the money that had been sent in support of the miracle workers to have plane loads of food and supplies delivered to those affected by the tragic earthquakes. Lucy was shocked at his suggestion, but agreed it was an excellent idea. Mika'il said he would arrange for it to happen, knowing Lucy had other more pressing concerns. Lucy was surprised at how truly saddened and despondent Mika'il seemed because of Astan's death. She thought she may have judged him too harshly. When she saw the first CNN broadcast of Mika'il's confrontation with the Chinese, she rethought her moment of compassion. The production of the program showing the confrontation left no doubt that Mika'il was positioning to become leader of the miracle workers if not leader of the entire world. At least it seemed that way to Lucy. For now, she had other more pressing concerns, but she knew that soon the two of them were destined to clash.

* * *

The Stranger chuckled sinisterly as he saw all the pieces of the puzzle finally falling into place. His time was growing near, ever so near. His ascension would be validated by the highest authorities. There could be no question as to his rightful place as leader over mankind. There would be those who would still try to deny him of what he knew was rightfully his. Battles would have to be fought, but his destiny was written in the verses of Revelation 10. Christ's words. The words Apostle John tried to deny. The words the Brotherhood of the Divine tried to hide, the words that would shake the world like never before. The Ascension of Satan was about to become a reality.

CHAPTER THIRTY-SIX

And I saw a beast coming out of the sea. He had ten horns and seven heads, with ten crowns on his horns, and on each head a blasphemous name. The beast I saw resembled a leopard, but had feet like those of a bear and a mouth like that of a lion. The dragon gave the beast his power and his throne and great authority. One of the heads of the beast seemed to have had a fatal wound, but the fatal wound had been healed. The whole world was astonished and followed the beast. Men worshiped the dragon because he had given authority to the beast, and they also worshiped the beast and asked, "Who is like the beast? Who can make war against him?"

Revelation 13:1-4

Kevin tried to contact Lucy, but had been unsuccessful. He did talk to Gabe in Switzerland who told him Mika'il had called and asked him to meet the other two miracle workers in Rome. The production team in Switzerland was also ordered to move to Astan's mansion in Rome. They, along with Gabe and Ahmed, were preparing to leave that afternoon. Gabe told Kevin he had no idea when Mika'il and Lucy would be arriving in Rome. Kevin tried Astan's Rome mansion, but no one answered the phone. The staff had been fielding nonstop phone calls from the media since Astan's death, and Lucy had ordered them to stop taking the calls. Kevin drove by to see if anyone would answer the door, which they also had been instructed not to do. As he approached, he knew Lucy had to be on her way because a crowd of ailing and disabled people were gathering by the gate. Kevin went back to Vatican City to meet with Mykos. Mykos had found his friend Vlade by leaving a message for him at a bath house in Nice, France. Vlade would not be returning to St. Petersburg for several days. His staff had told him about the alleged Botticelli, but having not seen the pictures that Mykos had seen, Vlade was very skeptical as to its authenticity. He instructed them to lock it in a vault until he returned in another week. Mykos tried in vain to convince Vlade to cut his holiday short and return to Russia. Mykos offered to meet him so they could look at it together. Vlade was tempted, because he was attracted to Mykos even though Mykos had spurned his advances in the past. But Vlade explained that he had met the nicest man from San Francisco, who by the way was just a bronzed Adonis, and Vlade was very content to remain in Nice until his scheduled holiday was over. Mykos knew there was no point in trying to change Vlade's mind. Vlade did offer to allow Mykos to look at the painting in a couple of weeks, after he returned from his holiday in France and had a chance to get his own look at it first. Kevin was not happy to hear this news, but was pleased to hear Mykos had done more cleaning on the Botticelli from the vault. Mykos took him into a private room off of his workshop to show it to him.

"I compared the faces of the angels and of Satan in this painting to the one in the Sistine Chapel. I believe the angels painted in each are the same, even down to the clothes they are wearing. Satan's face is a little too dark and distorted in the chapel painting to really tell. They appear the same, but I cannot be sure. Of course, the wings of the angels are much darker in the Ascension of Satan painting than in the chapel painting. It's as if in this painting the archangels belong to Satan. And you know the face of the angel dressed in white even looks more like Lucy Ilves in this painting than in the one in the chapel."

"Jeez Louise!" Kevin said in surprise. "You're right, it does look just like her." Then Kevin looked carefully at the angel dressed in the green robes. I know that face too." He said pointing to the angel in green. "That looks just like Gabe. The miracle worker from California."

"You're right, it does. Look at this photo from the chapel. You can tell it's him in this painting as well. I've seen him on television several times narrating those miracle worker specials." He looked carefully at the third angel. "That angel looks nothing like the other miracle worker Mika'il," Mykos said, pointing to the angel dressed in gold.

"It sure doesn't, but he does look familiar to me. What about some of these other people standing near

Satan's throne. Can you clean off their faces so we can get a good look at them?"

"Of course I can. It will just take me a few hours. You'll just have to leave and come back later."

More than ever Kevin needed to see that Botticelli at the Hermitage. He just had to figure out a way to do it.

* * *

By the time Mika'il and Lucy's jet arrived in Rome, Mika'il had already made several videos with the production crew on board. Lucy was at the front of the plane and had no idea what Mika'il's message was in the videos. She was too busy mourning the death of her father to care what Mika'il had to say, at least for now. When things settled down in a few days, she would become much more involved in the production of the miracle worker broadcasts, if in fact there were going to be further miracle worker broadcasts. She also needed to get as much vaccine together as possible and send it with a new medical team to China. She still couldn't understand why the Israelis shot down her father's plane. It made absolutely no sense but, then again, what did in this age of miracles and disasters? Lucy needed someone she could talk to and it certainly wasn't Mika'il. She called Kevin and asked him to meet her at the mansion. He was more than happy to do so, hoping to get some needed answers to some puzzling questions.

Gabe and Ahmed arrived with the remainder of the production team a little over an hour after Lucy and Mika'il's plane touched down. Cars were waiting to take them directly to a local television studio owned by Astan where Mika'il was waiting for Gabe to narrate several clips that he wanted on the air immediately. Like usual, Ahmed was kept out of the production room and away from Mika'il by several of his protectors. Even though they had just arrived in Rome, Ahmed seemed to have several people hovering around him just like in Vevey. It was odd, but nobody seemed to question why all these strangers were showing up. It was as if these protectors were invisible to everyone else. Ahmed knew that was an absurd thought, because he did indeed see Mika'il's protectors, and even a few around Gabe, though Gabe never seemed to say anything about them.

Several video clips of Mika'il making a statement had already been broadcast in Russia using a Russian translator instead of Gabe. Now that Gabe was here, Mika'il would go back to using him, since he was a universal translator. Gabe did not question the script he read from for the first few clips. He just did his job like he had been doing in Vevey this past week. When he saw a playback of one of the video clips, he realized he was calling for the people of Russia and the moderate Muslims from all over Europe and the Middle East to march on Jerusalem to protest these terrorist acts. Mika'il was setting himself up to become the leader of this new religious order. A second clip called for the reformist Catholics to all come to Vatican City in three days to show their displeasure with the Pope. They were encouraged to voice their support for the Bishop to lead the Catholic Church.

"What was I thinking when I narrated these?" Gabe said to Ahmed. "Mika'il is attempting to take control of the world."

"It seems that way to me as well," Ahmed replied.

"Well, I for sure won't be narrating any more of his messages," Gabe said, emphatically.

Ahmed contemplated Mika'il's sudden push for power and realized it wasn't sudden at all. Mika'il had been manipulating the miracle workers and Astan since they had all gotten together in Vevey. "Now with Astan out of the way, who would be able to stop Mika'il?"

"I think it best if you not confront Mika'il just quite yet," Ahmed warned Gabe. "Tell them you're getting a sore throat or something."

"Nobody will believe that. Did you forget I'm a miracle worker and immune to any sickness? This is the best I've felt in my entire life. Mika'il would know I was lying, immediately."

"Well, tell him you're homesick and need to go back to California, or maybe you need to comfort Lucy over the loss of her father. Yeah, that's it, Mika'il would believe that," Ahmed said. "At least it would buy you a little time to figure out what to do, a chance to talk to Lucy or Kevin. Maybe even a chance to pray to God for help."

"I think that's exactly what I need to do."

"Really?" Ahmed asked surprised, "you're really going to ask God for his guidance?"

"You know I hadn't really thought about that, but it just might turn out to be my only hope. But first, I plan to talk to Lucy and Kevin to see what they have to say about all of this."

Mika'il had left the studio, so it was not a problem postponing the rest of his scheduled narrations. Gabe and Ahmed had one of the drivers take them to Astan's mansion where they were told Lucy had already arrived.

* * *

Mika'il went to Vatican City to meet with the Bishop. The Bishop, remembering Astan's request to do precisely what the miracle workers told him to do, met with Mika'il in the Doctrinal Office.

"Your time has come. Your desire to reform and oversee the Catholic Church is now upon us," Mika'il said, as he turned on the television, just as one of his clips calling for the Catholic reformers to come to Vatican City in three days to show their support for the Bishop. "Tens of thousands will come. I guarantee it. The Vatican will be yours to run as you see fit."

"Astan had told me to listen to his miracle workers and do as they say, but how did you know that was my secret desire? I did not even tell it to Astan."

"It has always been your destiny for you are the Beast, the Antichrist, and I am here to heal you from the wound Catholicism has caused in your soul. Long ago the dragon gave you his power, his authority, and his throne. It has been yours for quite some time, but you were not prepared to fully accept it," Mika'il told the Bishop.

"This cannot be," the Bishop responded. "And you, are you my prophet? These miracles of yours, have they been done in my name?"

"That is what I shall announce to the world," Mika'il said, boldly. "In three days, tens of thousands of your supporters will arrive here to witness the two of us, as we stand together and announce to the world that we have absolute proof Apostle John purposely left verses out of Revelation 10. Verses that recognize the 'Ascension of Satan' and declare that the new millennium is upon the world. We, as the new king and prophet, will take control of mankind as God's own words command."

"Tens of thousands do not an army make," the Bishop said. "There are too many in this world who will not surrender to our commands."

"Tens of thousands I agree are too few, but at this very moment tens of millions are marching across Russia and Europe on their way to Jerusalem to declare you their Messiah and I your prophet. They come to condemn and destroy the Jews for their malicious acts of terror upon the world. We will be their salvation."

It was exactly how the Beast knew it would always be. It was just a shame Astan Ilves wasn't around to see what he had wrought.

* * *

As he approached, Kevin saw that the crowd at the gate leading to Astan's mansion had grown significantly. There were several more security guards manning the gates, which allowed Kevin to pass quickly through the burgeoning crowd and into the courtyard. Sitting on the ledge of the fountain was Lucy. She smiled when she saw it was Kevin, but he could tell she had been crying. There were over two dozen people standing around the courtyard, but Lucy acted like no one was there.

"Who are all these people?"

"You can see them?" Lucy replied, sounding genuinely surprised.

"What are you talking about? Of course, I can see them."

"Well, I'm surprised. These are my protectors, my angels that have been provided to keep me safe. I didn't know anyone else could see them. They have been arriving for several days, and more keep coming hourly. I'm afraid a battle is coming, a battle of good versus evil."

Kevin stared at Lucy for a moment and then asked her the question he knew must be asked. "And whose side are you on? Did God provide you with those angels or did Satan?"

Lucy was not as offended as he expected her to be. "I hope it is God who has called me to be by His side and who has sent these protectors to me. Yet sometimes, I too wonder."

That was not the answer Kevin was hoping to hear. It wasn't exactly the answer he didn't want to hear, but things had been confusing enough lately, so he didn't need Lucy to make them any worse. "I talked to the officer in charge of investigating the murder of your real parents in Scotland," Kevin said, watching for a reaction. None came.

"He said three bodies were found, a man's body, a woman's body, and a little girl's. All three had their hearts ripped out."

"Astan never told me how they died, nor did he tell me I had a sister," Lucy paused momentarily. "Did I really have a sister?"

"I was hoping you could tell me."

"I was a young child when my parents were murdered. All I know of them is what Astan told me. I just always assumed I was an only child, but then again I never asked."

"Your parents were murdered in the same manner as the two Swiss guards at the Vatican. I believe the same person is responsible for both."

"Are you accusing Astan of those murders?"

"I have said all along that I don't believe a person is capable of such a horrific form of murder. I believe Satan is responsible for those murders."

"Then why am I still alive? Did Satan have a plan for me?" Lucy asked.

"I can't answer that. I do know Satan was either after, or wanted us to find, that Botticelli hidden away in the Vatican vault. You know it's your face on the angel in white on Botticelli's painting, the 'Ascension of Satan'. It matches your face on the painting in the Sistine Chapel."

"I've known about the Sistine Chapel painting since I was a little girl. My father," Lucy paused in distress when she mentioned Astan, "my father pointed that out to me when I was just ten years old. That's why he called it his 'Little Lucy.' I'm not surprised my face is on the other Botticelli, but I'm concerned about the subject of the painting. Am I supporting the ascension or fighting the ascension?"

"Neither, it appears you are just observing. You and Gabe."

"I thought Gabe looked familiar the first time I met him. He's on the Botticelli in the Sistine Chapel too, isn't he? He's the angel in green. Who is the third angel, is it Mika'il?"

"I don't think so, but I can't be sure. I do know for sure it's not Mika'il's face on the third angel in Botticelli's painting in the Sistine Chapel. Mykos is in the process of cleaning the rest of the painting right now. Tonight, I should be able to see the other faces in the crowd and those fighting in the battle scenes. As of now, I've no idea who the third angel is."

"Are you saying I'm really an angel?"

"I would say you're an Archangel, both you and Gabe, and I hope one of God's Archangels and not one of the fallen angels Enoch described in his apocryphal writings. Satan can wrestle control even of God's Archangels if they have fallen. At least that is what I read in Enoch's gospel. That would explain why angels are gathering around you. You will lead them into battle, hopefully, against the evils of Satan."

"And whose face does Satan have in the paintings?" Lucy asked.

"We've been unable to tell. The painting from the catacomb still needs much cleaning to get a clear view. The face on the Sistine Chapel painting is too distorted to make a positive identification."

As they were talking, one of the guards notified Lucy that a car containing Gabe and Ahmed had just arrived. Lucy was expecting them, but not till much later. "Gabe must have finished his narration overdubs at the studio early."

As they entered the room, Gabe went directly to Lucy. "Lucy, have you seen Mika'il's new broadcasts? I feel so bad that I did them without giving any thought to what I was saying," Gabe said glumly. "He has called for a mass march on Jerusalem to demand that they... Damn, I can't remember what he was demanding. He also called on Catholic reformers to march on the Vatican in three days to overthrow the Pope and support the Bishop. What are we going to do?"

"Let's go inside and see if we can find one of his broadcasts," Kevin suggested, "then we can all talk about it."

Inside they saw on CNN that literally millions of Russians, European and middle-eastern Muslims were heading for Jerusalem. The news reporter told how Mika'il had shipped tons of food and supplies to key areas along the route these marchers were taking and had set up a series of sophisticated distribution centers to feed and equip them on their way towards Israel. The news also said several hundred-people had already gathered at Vatican City in anticipation of the announced press conference Mika'il and the Bishop would be holding in three days.

"He's trying to take over the world," Lucy screamed. "He used my father and his media conglomerate to make his case to the world, and Gabe and I helped him do it."

"That's what we came here to tell you," Gabe said, sheepishly. "We were hoping you had some kind of idea as to what we could do about it."

Kevin's cell phone began to vibrate. It was the Pope's personal secretary calling. "Excuse me for a moment, but I have to take this call. It's my boss."

The Pope needed Kevin back at Vatican City as soon as humanly possible to figure out what to do. The Catholic Church was beginning to crack and in three days it would come tumbling down unless Kevin came up with a good idea fast.

"Go to the Hermitage," Gabe said out of the blue.

"What did you say?" Kevin asked.

"Go to the Hermitage. A voice told me that in a dream the day I started having these miraculous powers. It said I would find what I was looking for if I went to the Hermitage. For some reason I think you will too."

Kevin now knew for sure that the Botticelli locked away at the Hermitage in St. Petersburg was the key to stopping Satan's ascension.

"I have to go to St. Petersburg," Kevin declared to the three others. "Gabe, I know that when you narrate, all people hear it in their own language, but is it possible you have the power to not only speak all languages at the same time, but also to say different messages at the same time?"

"I don't understand."

"I do," Lucy said, "Ahmed and I will work with Gabe to see if that is possible. I know where you're going with this idea and I think it just might work. If not, then we'll think of a reason why he needs a break from the narration."

"Maybe we can go help earthquake victims in Turkey or someplace like that," Ahmed suggested.

"Whatever it takes to keep Gabe from helping Mika'il get out his message any more than he has already, that's what's important," Kevin told the group. "You all realize it's not Mika'il whom we are battling, or even the Bishop at the Vatican. It's Satan. Whether Satan has taken over the Bishop or Mika'il's body or has taken over their minds, it makes no difference. It's Satan at work. It's Satan who we must defeat."

They all sat quietly reflecting on Kevin's prophetic word. "Ahmed, I don't know what part you play in this battle, but I'm sure God has placed you here with us for a reason. Gabe, I believe you are one of God's Archangels and He will send you protector angels in preparation for the battle to come."

"He already has," Gabe replied, "they've been coming to my side for days, but I was afraid to tell anyone."

"I expect Mika'il will ask all of you to be at the Vatican in three days when he stands in front of the cameras. For some reason I think we all should be there. Why, I'm not sure, but it may be our best chance to show the world Satan is behind all of this. Until then, do what you can to resist, but don't make it obvious. We want

Mika'il to continue to believe we're going along with his plan. There's one other thing I need you all to do."

"What is that?" Gabe asked.

"Pray! Pray to God like you have never prayed before. Pray for his guidance, pray for his mercy, and pray for mankind. God knows we're in for a great battle." Kevin had always believed in the power of prayer, but now more than ever did the rest of the world need to believe it too.

* * *

The Stranger had chosen well. The Beast from the sea, the Antichrist, had been healed from the terrible malignant tumor of Catholicism that was slowly overcoming the evils of temptation the Stranger had placed in the Beast's mind years before. Now the Beast was strong and powerful. Legions would look to him for enlightenment, but he was no more than a puppet on strings manipulated by the desires of the Stranger. The Prophet, the Beast from the earth, had more than met the Stranger's requests. Together they formed a powerful, unholy trinity that soon would be strong enough to stand up to the Holy Trinity, God the Father, God the Son, and God the Holy Spirit. Their final and ultimate power would come in just three more days. Three more days until the Prophet and the Beast from the sea revealed the true verses of Revelation 10. Then the other two miracle workers, these two other Archangels who had been manipulated so easily, Archangels like he once was, would realize they had been doing Satan's work. Fallen angels just as he had become when he challenged God so long ago. Soon they would belong to him, and with Mika'il (Azazyel), his Archangel Prophet, who fell from heaven long ago and taught the evils of war to mankind, would lead his legions of fallen angels in battle against God. A battle Satan could now win.

CHAPTER THIRTY-SEVEN

Watch out that no one deceives you. For many will come in my name, claiming, 'I am the Christ', and will deceive many. You will hear of wars and rumors of wars, but see to it that you are not alarmed. Such things must happen, but the end is still to come. Nation will rise against nation, and kingdom against kingdom. There will be famines and earthquakes in various places. All these are the beginning of birth pains.

Matthew 24:4-8

CNN news was reporting about the millions of Russians heading towards Jerusalem. Tens of thousands of Russian troops were included in this number despite orders to the contrary from the Russian government. The Russian Orthodox Church had condemned the call for the Russian proletariat to join in the march to Israel. Several other governments and religious groups, especially the Fundamentalist Christians, were decrying the call to come to Rome and Jerusalem. They claimed it was the Antichrist behind Mika'il's message, but these warnings fell on deaf ears. Still, many viewed this as the beginning of the great war of good versus evil.

Mykos was waiting for Kevin just outside the Pope's office as Kevin had requested when he arrived at

Vatican City. Hundreds of supporters of the Bishop, along with several hundred devout Catholics, were gathering in the streets near Vatican City, slowing Kevin's return. These groups were kept separated by an ever-increasing police presence. Soon it would take more than the police to keep these groups calm and separated. Mykos was visibly shaken by all that was occurring.

"The Bishop has ordered me to join him and Mika'il at the broadcast that they've scheduled in St. Peter's Square in three days. What should I do?" Mykos was frantic.

"First you need to calm down. Next, we'll talk to the Pope and decide what you should do about the Bishop's request," Kevin said in a calm voice. "Just don't go fainting on me again. You got it."

"Of course, I got it, there's no need for such a hissy fit."

Kevin had never seen the Pope so visibly worn than he appeared when they entered the room. Then again, he had a right to be. The Catholic Church was about to collapse, millions were marching on Israel, many nations were threatening war, and the Antichrist was about to take over the world. There was very little the Pope could do to stop it.

"I hope you have a good idea about what we can do about all of this Kevin," the Pope said. "Will the letter I gave you help at all? I certainly hope so. The Bishop has informed me that he'll announce to the world about the missing verses from Revelation 10 during their broadcast."

"You should just stop the broadcast and throw the Bishop out," Mykos interrupted.

"That would only make his position appear stronger than it already is. He expects Mykos to verify the verses are real."

"I won't do it, I just won't do it." Mykos said. "He can't make me, and I won't do it."

"Mykos shush," Kevin said. "You'll be there and you'll authenticate the verses just as you should. Do you understand?"

"I do understand," Mykos paused. "No, I don't understand. Why should I help them? Aren't they trying to take over the world or something like that?"

"That's what some of us believe," the Pope said.

"You helping them might be the only way we can stop them," Kevin told Mykos.

"Well, I don't understand it at all, but you're the boss," he said to Kevin. "I mean, you're the boss," he said turning to the Pope. "Oh, I'm so confused."

"Mykos and I need to get a look at that Botticelli in the Hermitage. Not only see it, but bring it back here to Rome. It may be our only hope," Kevin told the Pope. "We need your help in convincing the Russians to give it to us."

"I can call the Russian president, but I don't think that will do much good. He is not a big fan of the Roman Catholics."

"No, he's not," Kevin said in agreement, "but he's a devout member of the Russian Orthodox Church and I'm sure he loves his country dearly. Neither he nor his church can be too happy about the Russian military and proletariat ignoring requests to stop their march to Israel. Russia must be on the verge of open rebellion. Call the Patriarch of the Russian Orthodox Church. He might be able to convince the Russian President to loan us the Botticelli. They must be made to understand that this could be our only chance to stop Satan from taking control of the world."

"Is that truly what we want?" the Pope's secretary asked Kevin. "Doesn't the Book of Revelation speak of these things to come?"

"Yes," Kevin said, "but not in the way Mika'il and the Bishop are about to announce to the world."

The secretary didn't understand what Kevin meant, but then again, he was not aware of the epistle or the altered canon the Pope had given to Kevin.

"If you're sure that's what must be done, then I'll make the calls and do everything in my power to get you the Botticelli," the Pope told Kevin.

"Then Mykos and I will leave immediately for St. Petersburg."

"May God guide you with all of His wisdom," the Pope said to Kevin.

* * *

Lucy and Ahmed worked with Gabe to see if he could alter his narrative as he spoke in all tongues at the same time. They soon realized that even if Gabe could do it, they couldn't tell. They decided it would be better if they got him out of town for a few days. Lucy arranged for Gabe and Ahmed to leave on a medical mission with one of her foundation teams to Cyprus. She reminded them that they must be back for Mika'il's broadcast in three days and that a plane would be there for them in two days. That would give them all a chance to talk over their strategies before they had to attend the broadcast.

Once Gabe and Ahmed were safely on their way, Lucy decided it was time to confront Mika'il. Before she left, one of the producers came looking for Gabe to shoot some narration clips. She told him that Gabe had gone away to help victims of the earthquake.

"It's his way of dealing with my father's death." she told the producer. "He was terribly shaken and wanted time away."

"Mika'il's not going to like this one bit," the producer said.

Mika'il was angry, but not nearly as angry as the producer had expected him to be. Mika'il told him to just keep running the clips that Gabe had already narrated. He said the wheels were already in motion and it was too late to stop them now. The producer didn't know exactly what Mika'il meant by this, but didn't care, just as long as he didn't have to suffer through another of Mika'il's angry tirades. When Lucy tried to reach Mika'il, he was always unavailable. She didn't even know where he was staying while he was in Rome. She had expected him to stay at the mansion, but so far, he was a no-show and had yet to return any of her calls.

Mika'il and the Bishop had ordered one of the video crews to join them on a series of campaign stops along the routes the marchers were taking on their way towards Israel. Each stop was carefully choreographed and included some faith healing and motivational speeches. They would continue this whirlwind pace for the next day and a half. They would return the day before the big broadcast to make sure all the preparations were going just as the unholy trinity had planned them.

Lucy soon realized that Mika'il was gone. Gabe and Ahmed had gone to Cyprus and Kevin was headed to Russia. There was nothing she could do in Rome but wait for everyone to return. Lucy did not wait well. She had never been one to have to wait for anything and wasn't about to start now.

Lucy wanted to mourn the murder of her father, but with all the evil happening in the world, and much of it due directly to her father's deeds and actions, she could not bring herself to mourn him. Lucy was also haunted by the thought that she might have had a sister who was killed along with her parents. She had promised Astan that she would not try to find out about her real family. She never had the desire to want to know about someone who had been so troubled that they had named their daughter after God's fallen Archangel, Lucifer. How could Astan have kept such information from Lucy? It was just inconceivable. Now that Astan was gone, Lucy did want to know, especially after the information Kevin had told her about how they were killed. Lucy decided that she would fly to Scotland and find out just exactly what were the circumstances regarding the murder of her parents. More than anything she needed to know who the little girl was that was found with her heart ripped out lying next to her parents. It was as if she was jealous or very angry, but angry at whom? And jealously was an emotion Lucy had never experienced. So how could it be that? She hoped and prayed she would find the answers that she was searching for in Scotland. Somehow, she knew she would.

CHAPTER THIRTY-EIGHT

And the angels who did not keep their positions of authority but abandoned their own home—these he has kept in darkness, bound with everlasting chains for judgment on the great Day.

Jude 1:6

Slowly the monstrous truck climbed over the tons of shattered stone and masonry, which had made the street impassable for most vehicles. "Remember, when the temple is built, Islam is over," shouted one of the fervent believers from the Temple Institute.

The Institute, like the Dome on the Rock, like most of Jerusalem, had been reduced to huge piles of rubble. The Israeli government was in disarray and little recovery had begun. Most police, military, and emergency personnel were still fervently searching for victims of the devastating quake.

For the past several years, the men from the Temple Institute had loaded their truck with the two six-and-one-half ton cornerstones which they hoped to use to rebuild the temple destroyed by the Romans in 70 AD. Every year the police were on hand to turn them back, defusing a confrontation between the Muslims, who regarded the Dome on the Rock as one of their most sacred sites, and the Jews, who were determined that their temple would someday rise again.

Today there were no police to turn the procession about. The truck ever so slowly followed a large bulldozer that both removed debris and compressed a path for the truck to follow. Behind the truck a mobile crane, capable of lifting the enormous stones, lumbered along. Behind the crane was a procession of hundreds of Jews. Their number grew the closer they came to the Temple Mount. Walking beside the slow-moving procession, trying to stay hidden among the debris, were armed Jewish militants determined not to let the Muslims or even the police stop the men from the Institute from performing their task. God himself had destroyed the Dome on the Rock. It was a sign that the Tribulations were upon the world and soon the Savior would return. Rebuilding the Temple was destined to occur, for it was written.

As the convoy of vehicles and people made their final ascent, shots rang out. A small group of Palestinian Muslims had heard of the procession and were determined to make a stand. The Jews were well prepared and had expected such resistance. They knew it was now their time to reclaim the Temple Mount and would not be deterred. Within seconds, the heavily armed Jewish force killed the small group of Muslim resistors. The bulldozer swept away areas of debris and the stones were carefully lifted into place. The Jews knew that the huge stones were not properly placed, but the move was symbolic and they were determined not to let them be removed. Hundreds came to join the procession and now hundreds set up an armed encampment to protect the beginnings of the new Jewish Temple on the Mount. Hundreds more would join the encampment when they heard of the resurrection of their temple. There was no reason for them not to join the encampment. Their houses had been destroyed in the earthquake and they were forced to campout anyway.

Things continued to go precisely as the Stranger had planned. Little more fuel was needed to fire the hatred of the Jews by the millions who continued to march on Israel. Still, Mika'il and the Bishop made sure the world knew of this brazen move by the Jewish people.

* * *

As they disembarked from the plane in Cyprus, it was as though the country had been foretold of the coming of a miracle worker. Gabe thought people were there because Lucy's foundation was sending in another medical team to assist the thousands injured in the quake. Then he saw several people had carried injured children and loved ones to the tarmac of the airport. They knew a miracle worker was coming. They were calling Gabe's name even before he reached the door to exit the plane.

"I cannot heal all these people," Gabe said to Ahmed, "my powers are not that strong."

"They are not your powers at all," Ahmed reminded Gabe. "You are but the vehicle God uses to share his graces with the world. The only difference between you and Lucy is that she knows how to pray and she knows God will always answer those prayers."

"Will you help me?" Gabe asked Ahmed. "Will you pray with me as I heal these people?"

"Of course, I will. And I will teach you how to pray as well."

"I would appreciate that," Gabe replied.

Together the two men went from one injured child or person to the next, laying their hands upon them while Ahmed prayed for God in all his goodness to heal the injured. They were all God's children and believed in God Almighty and the miracles he could perform. As Gabe learned to pray, he no longer needed Ahmed by his side. Nor did Ahmed need Gabe by his side. It happened gradually and naturally. Nothing was said between the two men acknowledging they both had just moved closer to God. There was no need for words. Their smiles and the smiles of the victims who were now healed said it all. Thankfully, there was not a camera in sight recording these miracles of God.

* * *

The papal jet had just entered Russian airspace when the pilot received orders to land in Moscow. They had no choice but to abide by the request. As the plane rolled to a stop on the tarmac, a car was waiting for Mykos and Kevin. The car drove them about a quarter mile from where the jet had come to a stop to where a military helicopter was waiting for them to board. Once aboard, the helicopter lifted off even before their seatbelts were secured and they were on their way towards the Kremlin.

"Somebody must want to see us pretty badly to go to this much trouble," the white-knuckled Mykos said. He was not a fan of helicopters. In fact, this was the first time he had ever been in one. "They could have at least driven us to the Kremlin."

"I take it you haven't flown into Moscow before. Driving would have taken over an hour for us to get there. They must know we don't have that kind of time."

"It would have been worth it to me," Mykos replied, looking a little green in the face.

Within a few minutes they were landing behind the Kremlin walls where a contingent of uniformed and armed soldiers was waiting to escort them to their host. They were taken to a building with the typical five canonic domes associated with Russian Cathedrals, but the architecture of the entrance was decidedly Italian Renaissance. At least that was how Mykos explained it to Kevin in a nervous running commentary.

"Oh, my goodness," Mykos gasped, "I know what this building is. This is the Archangel's Cathedral. Ivan the

Terrible is even buried in a special shrine in the altar area. I believe it is a museum now."

"You know your Russian history, my friend," a voice said from out of the shadows of the sanctuary. "It is true that this is a museum, but we still hold church services here weekly." The Russian President walked out of the shadows to greet the two men.

"It's an honor to meet you, Mr. President," Kevin said, shaking his hand.

Mykos was vibrating, he was so overcome with excitement, and became tongue-tied, but did stick his hand out to shake the President's hand. "This is my friend, Mykos Zorko. He is the art historian for the Vatican. He is a little overwhelmed meeting you and is at a loss for words which, believe me, is quite unusual," Kevin said laughing.

"You must be Kevin Bridges." Kevin was a little surprised the President knew his name. "Don't be shocked, the Vatican sent us a file on both of you when the Patriarch of our Russian Orthodox Church informed us you were coming."

Just then the doors swung open and a regal-looking, bearded man in a long-flowing, black cassock entered the Archangel Cathedral. There were several other men with him who you could tell were officials in the church by the ornate garb they wore. The Patriarch turned and asked these men to wait outside while he spoke with the Russian President and these two representatives from the Vatican.

"If you would please walk with me," the Patriarch asked of the three men. He led them to the paintings on the western wall of the cathedral. "These paintings are dedicated to the Symbol of Faith. The circle of faith." The Patriarch paused, "they continue the theme of Prince Vladimir's selection of Christianity as the national religion and the triumph of the Russian Church starts there in the loggia." He pointed to the painting in the side hallway. "It demonstrates the idea of the protection of the faith as the principal duty of those in power." He looked directly at the President. "The Symbol of Faith circle represented here is completed with the Judgment Day composition that covers the rest of the western wall." No one else spoke. "Mr. Bridges, do you truly believe the judgment day is upon us?"

Kevin responded. "I know a great evil is trying to take control of the religions and the people of the world. An evil bent on uniting them under the control of one man. A man who is willing to wage war against all nations to achieve his goal. Is this man, this so-called Bishop of the Catholic Church, the Antichrist? Is the miracle worker, Mika'il, his prophet? I cannot be sure. I do know they plan to declare the Book of Revelation, Christ's own words of prophesy as told to the Apostle John, to have been purposely altered. They will claim it was to keep Satan from ascending to the Throne."

"How can they make such claims? What proof do they have?" the President demanded.

"The verses are authentic," Mykos said. "There were several sources confirming what they are about to claim is in fact true. They plan to announce this to the world in three days at a ceremony in St. Peter's Square in Rome."

"God help us," the Patriarch exclaimed.

"It's your help we need to try to stop this. Yours and God's," Kevin told the Patriarch and the President.

"Please explain," the President said.

"I believe the key to stopping them will be found with the Botticelli painting recently confiscated by your government that is now at the Hermitage. A group of monks called the Brotherhood of the Divine has for over two thousand years kept the secret of the missing verses from Satan. I believe they kept an even greater secret, a secret that can stop Satan's ascension, and stop the madness which seems to be tearing the world apart."

"What is this secret?" the President asked but, before Kevin could answer, the Patriarch held up his hand to silence Kevin.

"If indeed a secret of this magnitude exists, the fewer to know, the safer it will remain from Satan's grasp. Even I'd not wish to carry such a great burden as to be privileged with such knowledge."

"At least tell me why you believe this particular painting holds the clues you're searching for," the President asked.

Kevin explained about the murder of the two Swiss guards, the finding of the Botticelli, and the letter from Savonarola describing the painting and telling of a second Botticelli that holds the secret epistle of Apostle John. When Mykos received e-mailed photos from this Jacob who bought the Botticelli in Perm, they knew it had to be the one Savonarola had described in his letter. The President knew that there had to be more Kevin wasn't telling but, as the Patriarch had said, no one needs that kind of burden, especially after Kevin had told him about the bloody talon prints found at the scene.

The Patriarch was convinced that Kevin and Mykos should be given the painting even before he had met with them. He had asked the President to meet with them at the Archangel Cathedral purposely to show him it was his duty to support the Church in every way possible. That included giving away a priceless piece of art if necessary. Being so generous was something the Russian President was not known for, but if it could save Russia from the verge of collapse, which seemed very likely at the moment, he was willing to do just about anything.

"I will arrange for the painting to be waiting for you when your plane arrives in St. Petersburg," the President said. "I pray you are right about the clue to stopping this Antichrist will be found in this painting by Botticelli."

"We all pray for that," the Patriarch added. "I do hope we will have the opportunity to discuss this matter after you succeed in your task."

"We will look forward to that meeting," Kevin said, as all four men walked through the loggia and onto the cathedral's porch and its white-stone portals, into the bright Moscow sunlight. The armed soldiers were waiting to escort Mykos and Kevin back to their waiting helicopter. Within three hours they would be returning to Rome with the Botticelli safely aboard.

* * *

Lucy's first stop was the General Register Office in Edinburgh. Here she would find birth, marriage, and death records for all of Scotland. She went straight to the death records where she found death certificates for both her parents and for a four-year-old girl named Jillian, Jillian Lucy Sexton. "How odd!" Lucy whispered. All three death certificates had the same date and listed murder as the cause of death. A note was attached that said "refer to autopsy report."

"So, I did have a sister," Lucy said to herself as she read the death certificate. "Wait a minute... that doesn't make any sense." Something she read on the certificates confused her.

She hurried to another office and looked for her own birth certificate, but was unable to find it. There were several Sextons, but none with the first name of Lucy or Lucifer, and none born the year of her birth. She did find her sister's and even her father's, but not hers. She would have looked for her mother's birth certificate, but didn't know her mother's maiden name. She went to look at the death certificates again, with plans to visit the doctor in Stirling who signed them. Something was just not right. She left for Stirling which was less than sixty km away. It was a beautiful day and should have been a delightful drive, not necessarily the most scenic since the motorway passed through many of Scotland's largest industrial areas, but Lucy's thoughts were occupied by what she had seen on the death certificates.

"I bet the orphanage would have that information," she said to herself as she drove. Then she remembered Astan had never bothered to tell her the name of the orphanage. "I should have asked more questions." Tears started running down her cheeks. "I can't believe he never told me I had a sister." Lucy's silent tears turned to sobs.

When she arrived in Stirling, Lucy went directly to the police station to see the investigator's report on the murders. Like Kevin had discovered, all such records had been lost in a fire a few years after the murders. And unlike Kevin, she was not lucky enough to find Bob to tell her about his part in the investigation. She was able to track down the doctor at the local surgery who had signed the death certificates and performed the autopsies on the bodies. She learned little more from him than she had learned from Kevin. It seems all of his findings were also lost in the fire at the police station. The doctor told her all three victims had died from having their hearts ripped out.

Something tore open their chests, grabbed their hearts, and ripped them not so very cleanly from the chest cavities and tossed them on the floor nearby. In fact, it was quite a gory extraction. He remembered the woman's body to be even more damaged than the others, almost to the point of being completely disemboweled. The doctor did admit no toxicology tests or in-depth autopsy were performed on any of the three bodies. The cause of death was so horrifically obvious, that only an abbreviated autopsy was performed on the male victim. As Lucy was leaving the surgery, what the locals called any hospital, doctor's office, or veterinarian office, an old frail man approached her.

"You be the lass asking about the Sexton murders?" the man asked politely.

"Why yes, I am," Lucy answered, relieved the man was not there to seek her healing.

"I'm Doc Chirst. I was the Sexton's family doctor," the man replied rather matter-of-fact. "I was a hopin' someone would come about asking questions someday. You know I raised a bit of a ruckus after the murders, but no one seemed to give me no mind. I was out of town on holiday, in Spain I believe it was, when the murders happened. By the time I returned they were all dead and buried. T'was really a shame. They never caught the culprit who was responsible you know. I once..." Lucy finally interrupted.

"What is it I can do for you, Doctor Chirst?" Lucy asked.

"Dr. Ilves, I may be an old man, but I do watch television, and I know all about you. And although it takes me a bit to get to a point, I have not lost many of my faculties and I do know what I'm talking about."

"Forgive me for my impatience," Lucy replied, "today has been rather trying for me. The Sextons were my parents. At least that is what my adoptive father told me. I can't seem to find any record of that anywhere. According to what I've been told, their only daughter, Jillian Lucy Sexton, was murdered along with them. It just doesn't make any sense to me," Lucy said, as tears began to well up in her eyes. "It's like all traces of my birth have just disappeared!"

"They didn't disappear," Doc Chirst replied, "they never existed. No record of your birth was ever recorded. In fact, technically, you were never born."

Now Lucy was sure the old man was crazy, but she had to hear more of his story. "Just what are you trying to say?"

"The same damn thing I told the police when I got back to town. They refused to listen. Mrs. Sexton was eight months pregnant when she was murdered, yet no fetus or baby was found. I saw the murder scene photos and it looked to me like the baby was ripped from the womb. Nobody would listen to me. The bodies had long been buried and the town was livin' in fear of the devil.

Everybody was certain it was the devil who had kilt' the family and wanted it to be forgotten as quickly as possible."

A chill ran down Lucy's spine as she listened to the old doctor's story.

"T'was never much a believer in that devil nonsense, nor have I put much worth in those miracles you and your friends perform on television, but I do believe I know what happened to that baby the night the Sexton's were kilt'," the doctor said, staring at Lucy. "You are the exact image of your mother, lassie."

Lucy was stunned. Of course, that is why the dates on the death certificates made no sense to her. According to what Astan had told her about her birthday, she was born almost a month after her parents were killed. Now she understood why Astan would never allow her to try to discover anything about her real parents. There had never been an orphanage. She was never named Lucifer as Astan had claimed. Lucy could not help but wonder what other lies Astan had told her throughout her life.

"Little Lucy," a voice called.

"What? Who's there?" Lucy said, spinning quickly around.

"Little Lucy,"

She quickly turned the other way. "I said who's there," Lucy cried, her voice getting louder.

"Are you, all right?" Doc Chirst asked.

"Little Lucy. Little Lucy," the voice kept calling as Lucy spun from side to side to try to see who was calling. No one was there. Then the ringing started. That terrible piercing ringing she had heard in the Sistine Chapel. Her head began to spin.

"Little Lucy," it was her father, Astan. At least it was his voice. "You now know the truth, my Little Lucy, the truth about your parents and the truth about your sister. It was her I named you after." Lucy tried to speak, but couldn't. She tried to see where her father was, but she was blinded by a bright white glow. "You are mine, Little Lucy, mine forever. You were born to be one of the fallen angels, or should I say fallen Archangels. Just like I once was, Little Lucy," his voice was taunting. "Your parents knew of the fallen angels. They were experts in eschatology and very devout Christians. That was why they had to be killed. They knew the secrets in the Book of Enoch that James Bruce never allowed to be published, the missing verses. The verses that foretold of the fate that is now upon the world. The verses that give me power over the fallen Archangels. Yes, Little Lucy, my time has come. It is inevitable and irreversible. Soon the ascension of Satan will be upon us and I will rule the world."

"Dr. Ilves, Dr. Ilves, can you hear me, are you, all right?" Doc Chirst was holding Lucy's hand, trying to steady her. "Dr. Ilves, what's wrong?" Suddenly Lucy seemed to snap out of a dream and was as lucid as ever.

"I'm fine, completely fine."

"Well, you seemed to slip away there for a wee bit. I thought you were going to faint. If you would take a little advice from an old country doctor, I think you might be a little overworked and could use a bit of a break. Spend a little time in Stirling and see the local sights. Visit a few of our pubs, it would do you good. Maybe even stop by one of our old churches. You just might find it enlightening."

"Well, thank you for your prognosis and prescription, doctor, but I need to get back to Rome. I found what I was looking for here in Scotland, thanks to you. I greatly appreciate your help," Lucy told the doctor, who was still holding her hand. Looking down at her hand in Doc Chirst's hand, Lucy spoke again. "You know I perform miraculous healings on anyone whom I touch. That means, by holding my hand, you have been healed of any ailments you might have suffered. I am a vessel for God's love."

Doc Chirst slowly allowed Lucy's hand to drop from his own. "It is you who are now healed," the doctor replied, as he headed out the door. Lucy called to him several times, but he never turned around.

Lucy saw no point in chasing after the doctor or even staying in Scotland. As she began to drive out of Stirling and back to Edinburgh, Lucy saw the Church of the Holy Rude near the Stirling castle and decided to take the doctor's advice and stop in for a moment. The organ was blasting a hymn when Lucy entered. The organist stopped as soon as she saw Lucy walking towards the pulpit.

"Welcome to the Holy Rude," the organist said. "You know that this is where the coronation of Mary Queen of Scotts occurred."

It was the standard story which she told to all visitors who stopped by the church. "It was a Catholic Church up until the Reformation. We have several books that tell the history of the church for sale if you are interested."

"Thank you, but I don't believe I'm interested at this time," Lucy replied politely. "Tell me, what does Holy Rude mean?"

"It is a medieval term that means 'cross of Christ's crucifixion.' It is said here is where you come to be reborn in Christ, to acknowledge that he died on the cross, the Holy Rude, for our sins, so that we may live," the organist replied. "Take your time and look around. I need to get back to my hymns. Remember, if you want to buy a book, just come get me."

"To be reborn," Lucy thought to herself. "I was never born into life the first time. How could I have been born to be a fallen angel when I was never even born?" It was an epiphany for Lucy. "Satan does not have power over me," Lucy said out loud and excitedly, but her words were drowned out by the overpowering organ. She ran quickly to the organist.

"Is there a reverend here today?" Lucy asked, sounding out of breath, "I need to speak to a reverend."

"Why yes, of course. Reverend Douglas is here. I'll get him for you," the organist replied, somewhat surprised by the request. A few moments later the organist returned with the Reverend.

"How can I help you, miss?"

"I need to be baptized immediately," Lucy responded, "I see you have a font and basin to perform baptisms right over there. I really must be baptized right now."

"We would be happy to baptize you," the Reverend replied, "but doing so at the spur of the moment like this is rather unusual." The Reverend was trying to be polite, but Lucy could sense he thought she was crazy.

"Don't you recognize me? I'm one of the miracle workers. I'm Dr. Lucy Ilves."

"It is you. I've seen you on television several times," the organist gasped.

"I've seen you perform your healing miracles as well," the Reverend added, "you're a true servant of our Lord."

"Then please, baptize me immediately. I have never been baptized and I need to be so I can be born."

"You mean reborn," the organist said, but Lucy did not reply.

Over the next thirty minutes, Lucy and the Reverend discussed her baptism and he duly baptized Lucy as she had requested. In return, Lucy agreed to heal several of the very ill church members who resided near the church and were able to get there before Lucy had to leave for Edinburgh.

Lucy now knew whose side she was on in this battle of good and evil. She had been born and reborn as a true believer in Jesus Christ, her Lord and Savior. She no longer feared what was about to happen and she couldn't wait to get back together with Kevin, Gabe, and Ahmed to share her good news.

* * *

For the slightest moment, the cool breeze seemed to be interrupted by a gust of warm wind coming from the Northeast. It was just enough to make the Stranger look up from his book as he sat on the deck of the yacht off the coast of Israel. He stared off into the distance as if searching. Something had just occurred, a slight hiccup in his evil plan, but not enough to warrant his attention. He could send one of his fallen angels to see what had occurred, but they were all needed in the battle that was about to begin. He knew it was too late for anything to stop him now. The Ascension of Satan was not to be denied.

CHAPTER THIRTY-NINE

Then he told me, "Do not seal up the words of the prophecy of this book, because the time is near. Let him who does wrong continue to do wrong; let him who is vile continue to be vile; let him who does right continue to do right; and let him who is holy continue to be holy."

Revelation 22:10-11

Just as promised, the Botticelli painting was waiting at the airport in St. Petersburg when the papal jet arrived. As soon as the crate was loaded onto the plane, Kevin had it opened to make sure it was the correct painting. Mykos compared it to the photos Jacob had e-mailed him to confirm it was the same painting. It had a bizarre wooden backing and heavy wooden frame which was not the least bit ornate or similar to any frame Mykos had ever seen on a Renaissance painting. The painting, as expected, was in terrible condition. Someone had tried to clean it recently, but stopped when they noticed they were flaking off some of the paint. Fortunately, it was limited to a minute area of background. Mykos had brought equipment and tools to begin a superficial removal of some of the dust accumulated over the centuries. Removing that would allow them to have a clearer look at the faces of the main subjects in the painting.

“You know, Mykos,” Kevin began to say, “I think the wooden backing was added to the painting to protect something hidden inside. Why else would it have such a heavy backing? It would make it too awkward to hang with that much weight. What do you say we pry off those planks?”

“We can’t just pry them off. We need to do an MRI to see what’s hidden beneath, then slowly and carefully remove them over time.”

“Well, we don’t have that kind of time,” Kevin replied, grabbing a hammer and screwdriver.

Mykos shrieked at the thought of what Kevin was about to do. “No, no, please, please, let me do it. If it must be done, it must be done gently and carefully, not attacked by some brute.”

Kevin smiled and passed the screwdriver and hammer to Mykos. Mykos sat them back on the portable workbench that had been set up in the plane and pulled a razor knife from his tool chest. “It must be done ever so gingerly,” Mykos said, as he slowly ran the razor along where the boards were joined together. Kevin sat back and smiled. He knew that if Mykos didn’t have those wooden planks off the back by the time they reached Rome, he would finish the job with his trusty hammer.

Mykos had the exact tools necessary to remove the wooden backing without even leaving the slightest indentation from the prying. Each one was carefully labeled and photographed as it was removed. Mykos knew after the first plank had been removed that there was an inner-structure secured between a separate wood backing. Mykos decided not to tell Kevin until he was ready to begin removing this concealed structure. He knew Kevin would be too impatient and try to rush him.

"I think this may be what we are looking for," Mykos said to Kevin, motioning him to come have a look. "It's a wooden box that has been padded in order to protect it from being jarred and damaged. That must mean there is something breakable inside."

Kevin watched as Mykos carefully removed the wooden box while one of the assistants continued to snap pictures. Mykos placed the box on the table in front of them. He pulled out his razor knife and began the painstakingly slow procedure of opening this box without leaving any traces of it being forced.

"I feel like a kid on Christmas morning," Mykos said, laughing. "I've freed the lid, are you ready for the big surprise?"

Ever so slowly Mykos removed the wooden lid to reveal the four glass plates inside. "There are papers between the glass plates," Mykos said, excitedly. "The glass is meant to preserve the documents. It was often done in the Renaissance to protect and display ancient documents."

"Can you read them?"

"This one is in Greek, but is not written by the same person who wrote the Greek canon copy we found,"

Mykos explained, then got quiet as he continued to read. "Oh...my...goodness!" Mykos exclaimed, as his hand covered his mouth in shock. "This is the original that the scribe had copied from when he copied the epistle you told me to tell no one about. This one explains sections were purposely left out of the copies, just in case they were discovered. This is the original epistle written by Apostle John. My God! This is one of the greatest discoveries known to man."

"Greatest discoveries unknown to man, and it needs to stay that way for a least two more days," Kevin said sternly. "What is the other letter?"

Mykos began to read. "It is written in Italian by Savonarola. The same coded numbers are written in the corner of this letter as are written in the one we found at the Vatican vault. He did that purposely to make sure there would be no question as to authenticity."

"Well, what does his letter say?" Kevin asked

"It's about a group called the Brotherhood of the Divine, who have protected this secret epistle written by Apostle John. It says a lot of the things that we have already learned from the copy of the epistle. It does explain the Botticelli paintings and how God told him what to do. This is just incredible. Savonarola was one of these Brothers who had protected the epistles and canons."

"Is this enough proof to authenticate what is written in the epistle we found?" Kevin asked.

"Since the same scribe wrote both the epistle and both copies of the Greek canon now in our possession, plus the fact we now have Savonarola's letter and Apostle John's original epistle explaining everything, I can absolutely swear to the authenticity of the epistle."

"That's all I needed to hear. Tell no one, and I mean no one, what we have discovered. As a matter of fact, neither you nor your assistant is to leave my sight for the next two days. Do you both understand?"

They both agreed to Kevin's demand, although rather unhappily, until he told them they would be staying in the late Astan Ilves mansion. That seemed to cheer them up. Kevin arranged for the necessary cleaning, restoration materials and tools to be sent to the mansion so a workshop could be set up and waiting when the three of them arrived.

Kevin was not surprised, but was a little disappointed, to hear Ahmed took Gabe to Cyprus to work with earthquake victims. That meant that they were not successful in altering Gabe's televised narratives. He was surprised to learn from the mansion staff that Lucy had left for Scotland soon after Kevin and the other two miracle workers had departed the previous day.

"I bet I know what she's doing there," Kevin said.

"You talking to me?" Mykos responded, in his best imitation of Robert Di Nero from the famous taxi driver scene. "I said, are you talking to me?"

Kevin couldn't help but laugh at the effeminate Mykos with his Greek accent trying to sound like a New York cab driver.

The Botticelli found in the catacombs was also brought to the mansion so the two paintings could be compared side by side. It was remarkable seeing the paintings sitting next to each other. The subject matter of the two Botticelli paintings could not have been more different, but their structure, perspective, balance, and symmetry could not have been more exact. In the foreground of "Ascension of Satan," you see Satan sitting on a throne with three fallen Archangels with black wings gathered around him. A man dressed in liturgical garb is placing a golden crown upon his head. In the background are vignettes of violent slayings, tortures, and massacres as the legions of Satan's fallen angels and unworldly beasts punish the believers of Christ. In the "Condemnation of Satan," an Archangel drapes a black jagged chain across Satan's shoulders as an Abyss begins to open beneath Satan's talon feet. Just as in the "Ascension" painting, three Archangels watch over the proceedings, but these are not the fallen Archangels. Two are dressed the same, but one is completely different than the third one who had the talon feet in the "Ascension" painting. They also did not have the black wings as did the fallen Archangels.

The man in the liturgical robes, along with the fallen Archangel with the talons, are present in the "Condemnation" painting, but in a completely different location. In the “Ascension” painting, a vignette that is the second point of focus shows the flaying of what appears to be two monks by several fallen angels. In the “Condemnation” painting, the vignette features the fallen Archangel with the talon feet and the man in liturgical robes who had been crowning Satan being cast into a burning lake. In the background of this painting are several more vignettes of violence, but these all show good triumphing over evil.

As Mykos and Kevin stared at the two paintings, Lucy rushed into the room. She seemed to radiate happiness as she gave Kevin a kiss on the cheek, almost sending Kevin into shock. A feeling of contentment and peace flowed through his body.

“Wow! It’s good to see you, too. I guess you had a good visit to Scotland.”

“I had a fabulous trip to Scotland. I learned so much and for the first time in my life I feel truly at peace with myself.”

“Well, it shows.”

“Am I right in assuming this is the reason you went to the Hermitage? This painting must be the one from the Vatican vaults you told me about.” Lucy looked closely at the faces of the Archangels. “You’re right. That is my face on the Archangel in white, and the Archangel in green is definitely Gabe. Those black wings send a shiver down my back, but I know now for sure they’re really not black.”

“You know for sure?” Kevin asked.

"I know for sure." Lucy smiled at Kevin.

Kevin felt a wave of relief wash over his body; however, he still was not going to tell Lucy about the epistle or letter from Savonarola.

"The third Archangel in this painting does look a little like Mika'il." Lucy turned her attention to the Botticelli Kevin and Mykos obtained from the Hermitage. "That's more like it. That's me as the white Archangel in this painting, too. See, my wings are definitely not black," She stressed the word "not" so Kevin would be sure to get the point. Kevin came over to have a look.

"That does look like you, and the Archangel in green looks like Gabe. The third Archangel in this picture is totally different than the one in this painting," Kevin said to Lucy.

"That's the same as the third Archangel in the Sistine Chapel painting. The face looks really familiar to me, but I just can't place it," Lucy explained.

Kevin came over to have a closer look the faces. "I don't recognize it, but it's still a little too dirty and cloudy-looking for me to be sure."

"Well, it wouldn't be if you two would get out of my way and let me do my job," Mykos said.

"Okay, we'll get out of your way." Kevin opened the door leading out of the library and asked one of the Swiss Guards he had accompany the Botticelli painting from the Vatican to come in and keep an eye on Mykos and his assistant.

Kevin and Lucy went into the game room and asked the staff to prepare them something to eat. Both were starving and exhaustion was setting in. Neither had slept for almost thirty-six hours. Kevin was too absorbed in discovering the secrets of the painting to sleep on his flight and Lucy had been too excited about her trip to Scotland. Now their lack of sleep was catching up with them.

"It appears you had a productive visit to Scotland," Kevin said. "I wasn't surprised to find you had gone there."

"After our talk, I had no choice. There were a lot of questions I needed answered. Astan had convinced me that I should never seek out what happened. You changed my mind."

"Did you discover what you were hoping to find?"

"I learned more than I ever could have imagined."

Kevin waited for her to tell him what that more consisted of, but Lucy remained silent on the subject.

"Did your trip to the Hermitage supply you with the information you were hoping for?"

"I pray to God that it will. Now it is up to Mykos and his expertise. I am sure God will help us in our hour of need."

"Will you be present at Mika'il and the Bishop's live televised broadcast?"

"I wouldn't miss it for the world," Kevin replied. "In fact, I will be there with Mykos. I have been told the Pope and the Patriarch of the Russian Orthodox Church will be in attendance. I tried to discourage them from coming, but to no avail."

"If it is going to be as world shaking as Mika'il has been claiming, I cannot blame them for wanting to be present to witness the birth of the new world religion, as Mika'il is calling it. Have you heard anything about all the armies and people who are marching towards Jerusalem?"

"Only that their numbers continue to grow. They are expected to reach Jerusalem about the same time as the scheduled broadcast from here in Rome. Mika'il ordered one of the production crews to Jerusalem to record the arrival of the armies," Kevin explained.

"Will the Israelis put up a fight?" Lucy asked.

"I don't think there is much of a government left to put up a fight after that earthquake. What government there is, is still reeling from the negative world publicity.

"What about the Jews who had camped there to protect their shrine?" Lucy asked.

"Most fled when they heard of the millions of people and troops about to reach them. Those troops are going to walk straight to the Temple Mount practically unopposed. Who knows what will happen when they get there? Whatever happens, you can be assured Satan will be behind it."

"I would agree with you on that," Lucy replied.

Two servants entered with food and an exorbitantly expensive bottle of wine.

"It's my turn to supply the wine," Lucy said smiling. Kevin looked at the label.

"I don't want to ask, but I would guess from the label that a bottle like that would cost me a month's salary."

"More likely a year's salary." Lucy replied, "but it's made for drinking, so enjoy. Cheers." The wine steward poured them two big glasses of the cabernet. "Leave the bottle," Lucy said with a twinkle in her eye.

* * *

Kevin awoke around noon the next day. When he went downstairs to check on Mykos and the assistant, he found them both asleep on couches in the library. A different Swiss Guard remained awake and vigilant in watching over them. Kevin was tempted to see what progress had been made on the paintings, but they were both covered and Kevin was not willing to suffer through the wrath of Mykos by taking a peek. Kevin went to have some breakfast and to see where Lucy was. He was told that she had awoken early when Gabe and Ahmed returned from Cyprus. The three of them had gone down to the television production studio so Gabe could re-narrate some of the spots he had recorded for Mika'il. The servant also told Kevin the Pope's secretary had called from Vatican City and wanted him back at the Vatican as soon as possible. The Pope needed a progress report and wanted to discuss security for the Russian Patriarch during the broadcast. He also said Mika'il had requested a meeting that evening with the Pope and had specifically asked for Kevin and Mykos to be present at that meeting. Kevin had hoped to talk to Lucy and Gabe before he returned to the Vatican, but that was not going to be possible. He finished his breakfast and asked the servants to send some breakfast to the library for Mykos and the assistant.

* * *

Gabe insisted on redoing the narratives he had previously recorded for Mika'il. He told the producers it was Mika'il's idea, but in actuality God had spoken to Gabe and told him what to do. This was the first time God had spoken directly to Gabe. Gabe was relieved to finally be given guidance as to the purpose of his miraculous gifts. Ahmed and Lucy accompanied him to the station and listened as he did the narratives. Gabe even did voice-overs for the videos he previously had not narrated. The production team did as they were told and sent the newly recorded spots to replace all of those being aired throughout the world. After several hours Gabe was happy with his accomplishment and the three friends returned to the mansion.

"I've been a little afraid to mention this," Gabe finally admitted, "but does anyone else see these thousands of people who are constantly hanging around us where ever we go?"

"They are our protector angels," Lucy replied. "They are here to protect us and fight in the great battle of good versus evil which is almost upon us."

"I'm just glad someone else sees them. I thought I was going crazy."

Ahmed didn't respond to Gabe's question. He too had seen these so-called protectors hanging around Gabe and Lucy. He had also seen many surrounding Mika'il, which looked no different than Lucy or Gabe's. Ahmed considered both Lucy and Gabe to be his friend, but Mika'il had also been Ahmed's friend. Kevin was convinced Mika'il was one of Satan's Archangels. Ahmed had to agree with him, especially considering what Mika'il was saying and how he was acting right now. Ahmed got the feeling Kevin was not always sure about whose side Lucy and Gabe were on. At times, Ahmed wasn't so sure either.

When Ahmed and the two miracle workers arrived back at the mansion, a message from Mika'il was awaiting them. The message said the destiny of the miracle workers was now at hand and they were to be present at the broadcast. It was time to take their rightful places as the new millennium began. Ahmed didn't like the sound of that. Mika'il specifically mentioned in the message that he desired Ahmed to be present to witness the "Ascension". Gabe and Lucy both went directly to their rooms to get some needed rest. They would have to leave the mansion very early in the morning. Ahmed was too troubled by the message to sleep and went wandering about the mansion, contemplating what to do. That was when he walked into the library startling the Swiss Guard on duty who almost dropped his weapon.

"It's okay," the assistant said to the guard, "this is Ahmed. He has been with the miracle workers from the beginning."

"So, these are the two Botticellis I've heard everyone talking about," Ahmed said, as he walked up to get a closer look at the paintings the assistant had been cleaning. Suddenly his jaw dropped when he looked at the Archangels. "It can't be, it just can't be."

* * *

Mykos had left his assistant at the mansion to continue cleaning the two Botticelli paintings when he and Kevin went back to Vatican City to meet with the Pope. They took the two letters sealed inbetween the glass sheets back to the Vatican with them. Kevin left Mykos in the foyer under the watchful eye of the Pope's secretary. It really wasn't that Kevin didn't trust Mykos, it was just that Mykos, in his excitement and vast exuberance, often let comments slip that were supposed to remain untold. Kevin could not afford that to happen in this case.

Kevin told the Pope what was discovered hidden in the frame of the Botticelli from the Hermitage. He also shared the subject matter of the painting with the Pope. The Pope's demeanor improved as Kevin described the painting and the ramifications of what they had discovered inside the painting. Kevin advised the Pope to go along with any request Mika'il or the Bishop made regarding tomorrow's live broadcast. The Pope was more comfortable with agreeing to Kevin's request now that he had heard Kevin's plan. Kevin still didn't care for the idea that the Russian Patriarch planned to attend, but such a request could not be denied after all the Patriarch had done for Kevin. Kevin sent Mykos back to the mansion with two Swiss Guards providing security and babysitting services to insure Mykos behaved properly. For the next hour Kevin explained details of his plan to the Pope.

Mika'il and the Bishop arrived at Vatican City under heavy security. Kevin looked out from the Pope's window overlooking the piazza and saw hundreds of protector angels surrounding Mika'il, the Bishop, and their human security team.

"They look just like the ones I saw at the mansion protecting Lucy."

"I beg your pardon," the Pope said, "I didn't hear you."

"I was just talking to myself like always." A few moments later, the two antagonists entered the Pope's chambers escorted by several armed security guards. Kevin had prepared for such an intimidating move and had requested several armed Swiss Guards to be present as a counter deterrent to any ideas Mika'il and the Bishop might have planned. Mika'il was the first to speak.

"By now you know the reign of the Catholic Church is over," Mika'il said bluntly to the Pope. "Tomorrow a new religion will rise and there is nothing you can do to stop it. In fact, you will not even try to stop it, for your own God has written that it shall be. Though I must admit this Brotherhood of the Divine has done a superb job of keeping God's true words secret for the past two thousand years. You cannot deny the words of your own God. Ironic isn't it. Ironic that your own God told Apostle John of the ascension of Satan, and as believers in the word of God, you must accept it."

The Pope began to speak. "You cannot come in here..."

"Please I did not come here to debate or to listen," Mika'il interrupted the Pope. "I came here to tell you how it will be in the morning and what I expect from you. Tell your guest the Patriarch what I expect as well. I was informed that he is on his way to Rome to stand with you during the broadcast. A noble, but futile, gesture."

"And just what is it you expect of the Pope?" Kevin asked, defiantly stepping from behind the Pope.

"Mr. Bridges," the Bishop spoke up, "I was wondering when we were going to hear from you."

"We will expect the Pope to do exactly as we say during the broadcast," Mika'il angrily told Kevin.

"We also expect you and your friend Mykos to stand near us on the stage as well, Mr. Bridges," the Bishop said. "We want Mr. Zorko to confirm my announcement of the authenticity of the missing verses to Revelation 10."

"That will never..." Kevin was interrupted by the Pope.

"I will see to it Mykos Zorko is present and on the stage."

"Then we have nothing further to discuss," Mika'il said. "A new millennium is upon us just as your Christ said in Revelation 10. It is real, and you cannot deny it. Christ's own words state, 'you will lose your share of the tree of life and your place in the Holy City'." Mika'il let out a bellow of laughter as he quoted the verse from Revelation 22. "You see, even Jesus Christ says you must allow the 'Ascension of Satan', or you doom yourself."

As quickly as Mika'il and the Bishop's entourage had entered the Pope's office, they were gone. Now there was nothing more to do, but wait for the morning to come and trust in the Word of God.

* * *

The Stranger's yacht moved closer towards the shore of the Israeli coast. In just a few short hours the Beast and the Prophet would tell the world of his Ascension to the Throne. Then moments later, atop the

Temple Mount, he would reveal himself as the new world leader. He would be surrounded by his armies who were already at the outskirts of the city of Jerusalem. An army estimated to be close to two hundred million from Russia, Asia, and the Middle East. All of them would be at his command, ready to conquer and kill all those who refused to accept Satan's mark and declare Satan as their God and Savior. "Precisely," the Stranger said.

CHAPTER FORTY

I warn everyone who hears the words of the prophecy of this book: If anyone adds anything to them, God will add to him the plagues described in this book. And if anyone takes words away from this book of prophecy, God will take away from him his share in the tree of life and in the holy city, which are described in this book.
He who testifies to these things says, "Yes, I am coming soon."
Amen. Come, Lord Jesus.
The grace of the Lord Jesus be with God's people. Amen.

Revelation 22:18-21

It was still over four hours until the broadcast. All was ready and more than sixty thousand people had gathered on the streets in front of St. Peter's Piazza. Police had blocked off the square and exedra to anyone entering from the streets. An hour before the broadcast, they planned to open most of the square so the crowd could gather close to the stage. The producers said it would make a much more dynamic presentation showing the cheering crowds pressing in. Hundreds of police would remain hidden from the television audience view in the exedra in case the situation got out of hand.

Mika'il and the Bishop had spent the night in the two Presidential Suites at the Hotel Hassler atop the Spanish Steps. The suites offered an exquisite view of Vatican City and the crowds that continued to gather on the surrounding streets. Mika'il had joined the Bishop for an early breakfast on the veranda overlooking The Holy See.

"It is the dawn of a new age," Mika'il told the Beast, "an age in which we will rule as Satan's honored servants."

"Tonight, the Eternal City shall be ours," the Bishop said, "it and all the treasures it holds."

"Power will be our treasure," Mika'il replied, "power no man can ever take from us. Power promised by Christ himself in the missing verses. The true word of Jesus as he prophesized will be added to every Bible in every language. The foolish lies of Apostle John will finally be exposed."

"And as we declare the ascension of Satan to the world, he shall assume command and lead the armies who will have gathered at the Temple Mount, crushing the Jews and any others who dare to oppose his rule."

The Prophet and the Beast finished their breakfast, then left in a limousine for their appointment with destiny.

Mika'il had sent a car to Astan's mansion to retrieve Lucy and Gabe. As fallen Archangels, they each had important parts to play in Satan's Ascension and in the battles that were sure to follow. Gabe would narrate the event in order that the peoples of the world would all hear at once of Satan's glorious ascension. Lucy would be there as a familiar face known to the world for her foundation and her healing. She would help legitimize the new regime. Ahmed was allowed to travel to Vatican City with the two miracle workers, but was separated from them upon arrival. Kevin was informed of his arrival by one of the Swiss Guards and invited Ahmed to join him and Mykos at the broadcast.

Kevin had spent the night in his office. What was different was that this night he had actually slept soundly. He was awakened by a call from Mykos who had spent the night in his office under the watchful eye of the Swiss Guard. Mykos was called by one of Mika'il's assistants and told to bring the Botticelli painting of the "Ascension of Satan" with him to the stage. Mykos called Kevin who in turn called the mansion and ordered the assistant who was still cleaning the two paintings to bring them both to him at his office.

"Two people can play that game," Kevin said to himself. "I can bring visuals for the auditory challenged viewers just the same as you can."

When Ahmed walked into Kevin's office, Kevin almost fell over with surprise.

"Your beard, what happened to that big bushy beard of yours?" Kevin asked.

"I just thought it was time for a new look. Do you have anything to eat? I'm starving," Ahmed said, trying to change the subject.

"I was just about to have breakfast sent up. What would you like?"

The two friends decided on breakfast and enjoyed each other's company. They leisurely ate awaiting the delivery of the two Botticelli paintings. Mykos joined them with the script that Mika'il had sent to him of the upcoming broadcast. It was apparent that they did not intend to beat around the bush and were going to get straight to the point announcing Christ's true Revelation. They would introduce Mykos Zorko, the Vatican's expert historian. Mykos was to step forward to confirm the authenticity of the missing verses and how he arrived at his conclusion. He was then to show the Botticelli that depicted the missing verses. He was to tell how the painting along with the canon were hidden away and just recently discovered in an old forgotten vault. Of course, he was to leave out the part about the two murdered Swiss Guards. Kevin spent the next half an hour carefully explaining what Mykos needed to do when he made his presentation. He told him to make sure to bring all the documents, including the letters found in the Russian Botticelli, Haile Selassie's copy of the epistle, and Savonarola's letter found with the Vatican Botticelli. Of course, he was to bring the Russian Botticelli on stage as well, but keep it hidden until the proper moment. That is, if the assistant ever made it with the two paintings through the mass of spectators who now crowded the streets of Rome.

There were three levels to the stage that had been set on the steps in front of the basilica. Mika'il and the Bishop would be up front on the center and tallest part. Behind them on the center section would be Lucy and Gabe. Gabe would be standing to their right and slightly behind them narrating the event so the world could all hear the broadcast in their native language as it was happening. Lucy would be standing to their left and slightly behind them. To their right on a lower section would be Mykos and his assistants with the Botticelli painting, the canon and other documents. Ahmed would join Mykos on this stage along with several Swiss Guards to protect Mykos and the treasures. To the right of the main stage, also at a lower level were the Pope and Patriarch. They were instructed to listen and do as Mika'il and the Bishop commanded. Kevin had decided he would join them on their stage with several Swiss Guards to provide protection for the two holy men. Behind the stage and at several locations around the piazza and the streets around Vatican City, were large screens set up to show not only the Vatican broadcast, but also the Temple Mount in Jerusalem where the armies of the world were gathering. At the Temple Mount other large screens had been erected that showed the broadcast at Vatican City.

* * *

At first the impact seemed negligible. As the short television spots designed to energize the armies and the proletariat marchers on their crusade towards Jerusalem continued to air with Gabe's re-recorded narrative, hundreds, then thousands, then tens of thousands, then hundreds of thousands began to peel off from the millions who had gathered. By this time all news coverage of the crusade had shifted to Jerusalem and to Vatican City where the broadcasts were soon to begin, so no one was there to report the millions who were ending their march and returning home. Gabe's new narrative explained that the march was in support of Satan and his war against God. Those who supported Satan did not hear the same words the godly people heard. The message heard depended on to whom your soul really belonged, either with God, or with the evils of Satan.

The Stranger relaxed on the deck of his yacht, waiting for the proper moment when he would unfurl his wings and make his grand entrance soaring from above onto the cornerstone blocks set on the Temple Mount. They had unwittingly prepared his stage and now they had all been killed by some of the thousands of his devoted followers who had already arrived and taken up position in preparation of the genocide of the remaining Jews. It had been almost two thousand years since Apostle John had written Christ's prophesies in the Book of Revelation. At least the prophesies that denied Satan of his rightful rewards. Of course, Apostle John had to remove those verses or Christianity itself would not have succeeded more than a few years. Who would want to serve a God who admitted in his own prophesies that Satan would someday reign over the world as the real savior? The time was ever so near.

* * *

Kevin looked out of his office window at the gathering crowds.

"I thought they were still keeping the piazza clear of people," he said to one of the Swiss Guards.

"They are, sir." the guard responded as he looked out the window. "I see no one inside the perimeter except security personnel and the production crew."

Kevin looked back out the window and saw literally thousands gathered in the square. He started to scold the guard, but then realized it was protectors, not people, who were gathering by the thousands. "But whose protectors?" Kevin wondered. Kevin reviewed his plan with the nervous Mykos. It was a lot to ask of Mykos, but his role was essential if Kevin's plan was to succeed. Kevin was counting on Ahmed to keep Mykos calm and focused.

Lucy wished she could see Kevin before the broadcast. She knew he still had doubts about whose side she was on. She wanted to prove she was an Archangel of

God and not a fallen Archangel of Satan's as the Prophet and Bishop claimed. She wanted to help Kevin any way she could, but by not knowing his plans she feared being a hindrance more than a help if she acted on her own. She would just have to appear on stage as Mika'il insisted and pray God would guide her.

It was Gabe that Kevin most wished he could talk with before the broadcast. Kevin knew Gabe would narrate the proceedings, repeating exactly what Mika'il and the Bishop said for all to hear and understand. For his plan to work, Gabe would have to repeat Mika'il's and the Bishop's words precisely. At least up to a point. Where that point was, Kevin had absolutely no idea. He prayed that when the time came, Gabe, through God's grace, would know what to do and say. The miracle of the Pentecost was an incredible gift given to Gabe, but the true miracle was in the hearing and the spreading of the Gospel. Kevin prayed it would be God's and not Satan's Gospel that was ultimately spread throughout the world.

The two Botticelli paintings did not arrive at Kevin's office until after he left to join the Pope and the Patriarch. Mykos' assistant brought both paintings into Kevin's office and placed them on easels side by side. The assistant did a good job, an adequate job according to Mykos, in cleaning away much of the dirt and grime from the primary faces on both the paintings.

"Botticelli was truly God's own hands when he painted these paintings. They are absolutely phenomenal.

Who else but God would have known what the angels looked like? There is absolutely no doubt the Archangel in white is Lucy and the green one is Gabe." Suddenly Mykos did a double-take as he looked at the two paintings and then at Ahmed. "Oh, my dear God," Mykos could not speak.

"Look at the man placing the crown on Satan," Ahmed said, hoping to distract Mykos, "that is the Bishop. I am sure of it, and look at that Archangel dressed in blue in the Ascension painting, I am sure it is Mika'il," Ahmed insisted.

"I would have to agree," Mykos replied, "and look at the face of Satan in the Condemnation painting. Do you have any doubt as whom that face belongs to?"

"None whatsoever," Ahmed replied. Suddenly, what was about to become an awkward discussion was abruptly diverted when there was a loud knocking at the door. Two security guards had arrived to tell Mykos it was time to move to the stage. With the help of three of the Swiss Guards, Ahmed, Mykos, and his assistant moved all the documents, letters, and the two paintings to their section of the stage. They made sure the Russian Botticelli remained covered and out of sight.

The security guards in the piazza had removed the first line of barricades allowing the multitude of peoples gathered to rush forward to the secondary barrier. It followed the line of the ellipse formed by the exedra cutting across St. Peter's Piazza. The remaining distance between the stage and these barriers was filled with television cameras, still photographers, and journalists, all invited by Mika'il and the Bishop to witness the coming of the new age. The age of Satan, as these journalists would soon learn.

Just as Mika'il had scripted, Mykos and his assistants were in place ten minutes before the scheduled broadcast. Though Mika'il didn't include him, Ahmed entered with Mykos. The Pope and Patriarch, joined by Kevin and several Swiss Guards, were asked to be in place five minutes before the live broadcast was to start. The broadcast would begin with the triumphant entrance of the Bishop and Mika'il being led in by the two Archangels, Gabe and Lucy. Once in place they would get right to the point, for at fifteen minutes after the start of the broadcast, the screen behind them, along with the dozens of other screens placed throughout the piazza and city, would switch from showing an enlarged view of the proceedings at Vatican City to the view of the Temple Mount featuring Satan's grandiose entrance.

All parties were in place when a haunting fanfare echoed through the speakers and Gabe and Lucy came into view leading the way for Mika'il and the Bishop. A roar arose from the gathered crowd, for most of those allowed into the piazza had the mark identifying them as followers of the Bishop. As they made their way to the stage, loyal supporters began passing out copies of the new Book of Revelation, the version Mika'il and the Bishop were about to proclaim as the true word of God. When they reached the stage, Gabe was handed the transcript from which he was to narrate. The Bishop would be first to speak, then Gabe would repeat it using his unique gift from the Holy Spirit.

On cue, the Bishop rose to speak. "I'm here today to declare the beginning of a new age. An age that Jesus prophesized when he spoke to the Apostle John in Patmos almost two thousand years ago. Jesus directed Apostle John to write these prophesies in the Book of Revelation, but Apostle John deliberately ignored and left out several of the verses which speak of this very day. A day when a new world religion will unite the world in peace." A cheer arose from the crowd. The Bishop raised his arms to restore quiet. Then he continued. "A peace provided by the true savior as acknowledged by Jesus in these verses. I and my prophet, Archangel Mika'il, will lead the way. As his name was mentioned, Mika'il unfurled his huge black Archangel wings, bringing a gasping awe, followed by a cheer from the gathered crowd. "We've been commanded by our new savior to serve him by leading the people of the world into our savior's new religion." Mika'il was upset, for as soon as he unfurled his wings, Gabe and Lucy had been instructed to do the same, but neither one did so.

The Bishop continued. "We ask the people of the world to surrender their souls to our savior and now ask our invited guests, the Pope and the Patriarch of the

Russian Orthodox Church, to relinquish their roles as leaders of their respective Churches and bow down before our new savior." Neither the Pope nor the Patriarch changed their expressions or even acknowledged the Bishop's request. "For those who question the authenticity of these verses, as our two guests seem to be doing, I have asked Mykos Zorko, the Vatican's own world-renowned expert, to verify the validity of our claim." The cameras all turned towards Mykos, who slowly rose from his seat.

"What the Bishop claims is true. These verses were given by Jesus to Apostle John, but were not included in the Book of Revelation. Specifically omitted in Revelation 10, where Apostle John writes, 'a voice from heaven said seal up what the seven thunders have said and do not write them down.' These are those verses. The verses entitled the 'Ascension of Satan' as pictured in this fifteenth century painting by Botticelli." The camera zoomed in on the painting. "However, the evidence that does indeed authenticate these verses also authenticates this epistle from Apostle John which explains why these verses were not included in the Book of Revelation. Evidence discovered in this second Botticelli painting from the Hermitage entitled the 'Condemnation of Satan.'"

Mika'il leaped from his seat, screaming. "What kind of trickery is this? I knew of no such second painting by Botticelli."

"Nor did you know of the confirming copy of the epistle given to Pope Paul VI by Emperor Haile Selassie during his reign. Or even the letter written by Girolamo Savonarola, a fifteenth century monk and member of the Brotherhood of the Divine, who were charged with keeping these verses and this epistle secret for so many centuries." The camera zoomed in on the Russian Botticelli as Mykos' assistant sat it on a second easel for the world to see.

"Enough of this," Mika'il yelled in rage and raised his hand, sending tongues of fire and lightening shooting towards each individual standing on stage with Mykos. Flashes of gold, silver, and purple sparkles instantly appeared in front of the platform, as golden wings sprung from his back, revealing Ahmed to be the golden Archangel Azrael. Azrael's golden wings served to protect Mykos and all the others on the stage. He turned the fire and lightning to brittle strands of ice that dropped harmlessly to the ground. Before Mika'il could react, golden Archangel wings sprung from Lucy and Gabe leaving absolutely no doubt as to what God these three Archangels served. Mika'il shrank back to his chair as did the Bishop, hoping their savior would somehow come to their aid. Unfortunately, their savior, Satan, was high above the Temple Mount waiting for the exact moment to make his entrance, totally unaware of what was transpiring at Vatican City, although he was troubled by what appeared to be a much smaller army than he had expected surrounding the Temple Mount.

Kevin and his Swiss Guards took a defensive position to protect the Pope and the Patriarch. The Pope told them to put their weapons down. "There is no need for further concern. There will be no fight, for Jesus already guaranteed victory when he died on the cross for our sins and rose from the dead."

Kevin wished he could be so sure.

Ahmed stood with his golden wings outstretched, protecting Mykos from any further danger. He turned and told Mykos to continue his presentation.

"The epistle from Apostle John explains that these missing verses were part of God's perfect plan from the very beginning to fool Satan, the Beast, and the prophet into believing they could actually ascend to power. It was always meant as God's way to call them into battle when the days of judgment were upon the world. God knew Satan could be deceived by this fake revelation and would waste much of his time seeking out the verses from the clues God provided throughout the centuries. Wasted time which Satan would otherwise had spent performing more of his evil deeds."

Gabe had been repeating and thus translating through the Holy Spirit all that occurred on stage for the world to hear. Now he began speaking on his own and the entire world listened. "It was all part of God's perfect plan from the very beginning. *Then I saw the beast and the kings of the earth and their armies gathered together to make war against the rider on the horse and his army. But the beast was captured, and with him the false prophet who had performed the miraculous signs on his behalf. With these signs he had deluded those who had received the mark of the beast and worshiped his image. The two of them were thrown alive into the fiery lake of burning sulfur. The rest of them were killed with the sword that came out of the mouth of the rider on the horse, and all the birds gorged themselves on their flesh."* No sooner had Gabe finished reciting Revelation 19:19-21, did the protector angels suddenly materialize for all to see and swoop down upon all those in the crowd who bore the mark of the beast along with the protector angels who had surrounded Mika'il. As the cameras continued to record the carnage taking place, the seventh angel sounded its trumpet from heaven above announcing the mystery of God was about to be accomplished. Then, directly in front of the stage, a fiery lake of burning sulfur appeared.

Gabe, with his golden wings outstretched, rose from the stage grabbing the Bishop in his arms. Lucy, on the other side of the main stage, unfurled her wings of gold and she too lifted her angelic body from the stage, grasping the false prophet Mika'il in her hands. Neither Mika'il nor the Bishop struggled as they were lifted above the area in front of the main stage by God's two Archangels, Gabriel and Raphaela. They knew they had condemned themselves to this fate when they declared the missing verses as part of Revelation. That too had been part of God's perfect plan when Jesus Christ breathed the words of Revelation 22 to Apostle John's heart and mind. For a brief moment, the two Archangels hovered in the sky, just long enough for the cameras to record the agonized faces of the two beasts. The same faces Botticelli had painted on the "Condemnation of Satan". The two were dropped into the fiery lake of burning sulfur, which quickly swallowed the beast from the land and the beast from the sea. The lake of fire disappeared just as quickly as it had formed.

At that moment, exactly on cue as previously arranged, the giant screen behind the stage and the screens throughout the city came alive with an ear-piercing screech, as the cameras at the Temple Mount captured Satan's entrance. He swooped over the crowd and landed on one of the cornerstones. The cheers Satan expected did not come, only a stunned silence. The armies gathered had witnessed God's army of angels destroy those with the mark of the beast at Vatican City and realized they too had been deluded into worshipping Satan, the dragon. They knew that very soon God's sword would fall upon them.

A gasp was heard from those believers without the beast's mark who remained in St. Peter's Square when they saw the face of Satan. Ahmed and Mykos already knew, for they both had recognized the face of Satan on Botticelli's painting. Lucy (Raphaela), knew as well, for it was Satan who had stolen her from her parents before she was even born and raised her as his own. Even Kevin was not surprised when he saw Astan standing upon the giant stone with his talon feet and his black wings, the same talon feet used to rip the hearts from the Swiss Guards and Lucy's parents and sister. Astan (Satan) had of course survived the assassination attempt by the Israelis. He had made the anonymous call to the Israeli government telling them of Mika'il's fictitious terrorist plot. It had all been part of his plan.

Astan saw what occurred at Vatican City as he hovered above the Temple Mount, watching the huge video screen he had ordered to be erected. He had been thoroughly fooled by God's divine perfection. So much time had been wasted chasing down these secrets that the Brotherhood of the Divine had protected. God's perfect plan. A perfect plan meant to deceive Satan from the very beginning. God's plan to manipulate Satan into committing his followers into the battle they could not win. So perfect, even Astan (Satan) was fooled into helping to heal so many sick and injured people with the television shows. God had foreseen it all, and Astan fell for it completely, just as God knew he would. There was no need to try to run.

Gabe began to speak quoting further from Revelation for the world to hear. *"And I saw an angel coming down out of heaven, having the key to the Abyss and holding in his hand a great chain. He seized the dragon, that ancient serpent, who is the devil, or Satan, and bound him for a thousand years. He threw him into the*

Abyss, and locked and sealed it over him, to keep him from deceiving the nations anymore until the thousand years were ended." As he spoke, the cameras focused on another Archangel with golden wings who came floating down from the sky above the Temple Mount. In its arms it held a great chain. As it came closer to Astan, the earth beneath the granite pillar began to split apart. The chain seemed to float from the Archangel's hands and then wrapped around Satan, binding him securely. Astan let out a piercing scream, causing many of the soldiers present to turn and run in fear. This Archangel, Uriel, then landed beside the chained, fallen Archangel Satan, and pushed him into the Abyss that had opened before them. With a wave of the hand, Archangel Uriel locked and sealed the Abyss for a thousand years. "This is not Satan's punishment," Gabe explained to the world, "that shall come later when he joins the Beast and the false Prophet in the lake of burning sulfur. *I saw heaven standing open and there before me was a white horse, whose rider is called Faithful and True. With justice he judges and makes war. His eyes are like blazing fire, and on his head are many crowns. He has a name written on him that no one knows but he himself. He is dressed in a robe dipped in blood, and his name is the Word of God. The armies of heaven were following him, riding on white horses and dressed in fine linen, white and clean. Out of his mouth comes a sharp sword with which to strike down the nations. 'He will rule them with an iron scepter.' He treads*

the winepress of the fury of the wrath of God Almighty. On his robe and on his thigh he has this name written:
KING OF KINGS AND LORD OF LORDS."

And as the world watched, Archangel Michael and the angels of God, led by the Word, struck down the armies of Satan who had gathered at the Temple Mount to destroy the Jewish State.

CHAPTER FORTY-ONE

When the son of man shall come in his glory, and all the holy angels with him, then shall he sit upon the throne of his glory: And before him shall be gathered all nations: And he shall separate them from one another, as a shepherd divideth his sheep from the goats: And he shall set the sheep on his right hand, but the goats on the left. Then shall the King say unto them on his right hand, Come, ye blessed of my Father, inherit the kingdom prepared for you from the foundation of the world...Then shall he say also unto them on the left hand, Depart from me, ye cursed, into everlasting fire, prepared for the devil and his angels...And these shall go away into everlasting punishment but the righteous into life eternal.

Matthew 25:21-34, 41, 46

No one was probably more relieved than Kevin to see both Lucy and Gabe unfurl their golden wings. Even though he had seen both their faces on Botticelli's "Condemnation of Satan" painting, he still harbored some doubt as to whom they truly served. Kevin was probably the person most surprised when Ahmed saved Mykos by unfurling his golden wings and showing that he, too, was one of God's Archangels. It was Mykos who was the first to recognize Ahmed's face as the third Archangel on the Botticelli, and then only after Ahmed had shaved his beard. Ahmed knew longer than any of the others that he had been chosen to perform a very special service. It wasn't by chance that he had been Mika'il's bodyguard for all those years. He was there not only to protect Mika'il, but to guard the world from Mika'il, who God knew was the fallen angel Azazyel. God had known all along that Mika'il would one day be the false prophet and had sent His Archangel Azrael to be his constant companion. It was only in the past week that Ahmed had come to realize that it was God and not Muhammad who had chosen him and that he too was an Archangel capable of performing miracles. Ahmed led Gabe across that line to Christianity and, as Gabe accepted Christ as his Lord and Savior, God revealed to both Gabe and Ahmed that they were in truth His Archangels Gabriel and Azrael.

Just as the first chapters of Revelation address problems in the seven churches of Asia, God knew all would not be right with the churches today. Reuniting the Catholic Church with the Russian Orthodox Church had always been part of God's plan. Now both the Pope and the Patriarch understood it was always meant to be, for Christ so dearly loved and had compassion for the Church and would not long tolerate strife or sin. It would not be an immediate reunion, but the seeds had been planted and God knew that, in the end, His Word would unite the churches of the world, for it was now the age of the Church. Whether Christ would reign in the hearts of man, or reign upon the throne until the time of Satan's final defeat, was yet to be seen. Regardless of what God had decided, Jesus Christ would unite all believers as they prepared for the final Day of Judgment.

The "Condemnation of Satan" painting by Botticelli would return with the Patriarch back to Russia to be displayed at the Hermitage. The Pope agreed to send the other Botticelli to be displayed alongside the Russian Botticelli, but only after Mykos was allowed to thoroughly restore the painting. In return, the Vatican would be allowed to keep the original epistle written by Apostle John and the second Savonarola letter that were discovered inside the Russian Botticelli frame.

In the chaos that ensued following the broadcast at St. Peter's Piazza, Kevin lost sight of Lucy. Gabe and Ahmed were both floating ethereally above the piazza on either side of St. Peter's Basilica, creating quite a surreal tableau for the believers that now poured into the piazza and for those viewing the continued coverage on television around the world. Millions were waiting for either Gabe or Jesus, whom they had seen with the Archangel Michael, destroy the armies of Satan in Israel, to speak to the world. That was not to be. For those who truly believed, God had already spoken to their hearts and no more needed to be said.

As Kevin searched the crowd for any sign of Lucy, he felt a warmth embrace his body and with it came the knowledge as to where he would find Lucy. Less than a week ago, Kevin would have considered it to be an intuitive leap of understanding that told him where he would find her. Now he knew it was a divine message from God that guided him and had always guided him.

Kevin crossed in front of the entrance to the basilica and headed for the Sistine Chapel. He knew that was where he would find Lucy. When he entered, Lucy stood standing in front of the altar staring not at Botticelli's "Temptations of Christ" on her right, but at Michelangelo's painting of the "Last Judgment".

"I thought it was the Botticelli that fascinated you?" Kevin said, as he walked up to Lucy.

She turned and smiled, then looked up at Botticelli's work. "This painting once brought me so much joy, and now brings me great sorrow. Botticelli clearly was the hands of God. God knew from the beginning the faces of the Archangels, as well as the face of Satan. I should have recognized him for what he was long ago." Kevin could see tears beginning to run down her cheeks.

"Please don't be sad," Kevin said, "it pains me to see you cry."

"These are not tears of sadness, but tears of joy. Satan has been defeated and the Beast and the false prophet have been cast into the lake of burning sulfur. Christ's prophesies as told by Apostle John are being fulfilled. There's much to be joyful about."

"Still, I sense not all of those tears are joyful ones," Kevin said.

"That's true. I've come to have one final look at the chapel and the magnificent artwork that cover its walls and ceiling. This was my favorite place in the world to visit."

"Are you telling me you must leave?"

"God has called for his Archangels to return to heaven. For now, our tasks have been completed on earth."

"Will you be back; will I ever see you again?"

"If it's part of God's perfect plan for us to someday return, I cannot say. Only God knows the answer. I do know we will one day meet again. That's why I was looking at Michelangelo's work above the altar. He too was the voice and hands of God when he painted. I was looking for clues in his painting that would help me answer that very question. For I too hope I'll see you before the Final Day of Judgment depicted here. But if it's not to be, I know I'll see you in heaven at the side of our Lord and Savior, for you are truly a member of the Brotherhood of the Divine."

There was so much more Kevin wanted to say to Lucy, but the time had come for her to leave the earth. She glided to where he stood in the chapel and slowly kissed his forehead, causing him to close his eyes. Instantly all fear and sadness left his body and for the second time that week, he was at peace with himself and with God. When he opened his eyes, Lucy was gone, and Kevin knew his friends Gabe and Ahmed had returned to heaven to stand by the side of God along with Lucy.

Soon, many people of the world would forget what they had witnessed that day at Vatican City and at the Temple Mount. Perhaps that was why God planned to release Satan in a thousand years, to discover just who still had forsaken him, and those who were truly faithful and had taken God into their heart. Kevin knew he would stand among the righteous and looked forward to the day of General Judgment when he too would pass into eternal life with God.

www.ingramcontent.com/pod-product-compliance
Lightning Source LLC
Chambersburg PA
CBHW030105100526
44591CB00009B/282